Why Can't
I Get What
I Want?

Why Can't I Get What I Want?

How to Stop Making the Same Old Mistakes
and Start Living a Life You Can Love

Charles H. Elliott, Ph.D.

Maureen Kirby Lassen, Ph.D.

foreword by Aaron T. Beck, M.D.

Davies-Black Publishing, Palo Alto, California

Published by Davies-Black Publishing, an imprint of Consulting Psychologists Press, Inc., 3803 East Bayshore Road, Palo Alto, CA 94303; 1-800-624-1765.

Special discounts on bulk quantities of Davies-Black books are available to corporations, professional associations, and other organizations. For details, contact the Director of Book Sales at Davies-Black Publishing, an imprint of Consulting Psychologists Press, Inc., 3803 East Bayshore Road, Palo Alto, CA 94303; 650-691-9123; Fax 650-988-0673.

Cover image © Chris Ferebee/Photonica

02 01 00 99   10 9 8 7 6 5 4 3 2
Printed in the United States of America

Library of Congress Cataloging-in-Publication Data
Elliott, Charles H., 1948–
Why can't I get what I want? : how to stop making the same old mistakes and start living a life you can love / Charles H. Elliott, Maureen Kirby Lassen ; foreword by Aaron T. Beck.
p. cm.
Includes bibliographical references and index.
ISBN 0-89106-112-6
1. Schemas (Psychology) 2. Cognitive psychology. 3. Change (Psychology)
I. Lassen, Maureen Kirby, 1947– . II. Title.
BF313.E45' 1998
158—dc21   97-36599 CIP

FIRST EDITION
First Printing, 1998

To Brian
CHE

....

To Gary L. Lassen,
my husband and best friend
MKL

CONTENTS

FOREWORD

Several decades ago, I observed that depressed patients had a consistent negative bias toward themselves, their future, and their past. Specifically, they had a very poor self-image, interpreted most events as reflecting badly on themselves, saw the future as dismal, and viewed the past as full of failures. I found, to my surprise, that it was not always necessary to trace this kind of thinking to childhood origins. We could simply concentrate on evaluating the validity of their thinking and try to adjust the conclusions and predictions to a more realistic level. After having established the presence of a thinking disorder in depression, I proceeded to examine various other disorders, such as anxiety, panic, obsessive compulsive neurosis, and hysteria. I found that each of these disorders had its own pattern of unrealistic thinking that could be reversed with a variety of psychological strategies.

Because the patients' problems seemed to relate to their thinking—their cognition—I labeled my therapeutic approach *cognitive therapy*. Since that time, many of my former students and colleagues have expanded the use of cognitive therapy to a wide variety of disorders, including chronic fatigue syndrome, hypochondriasis, and schizophrenia. As many investigators in the field, including those in my own research group, delved deeper into the psychological makeup of our patients, we realized that negative thinking derived from certain unrealistic beliefs, or what are more technically known as *schemas*. In the course of therapy, we found that when these beliefs were evaluated and modified to a more adaptive level, the patients were much less likely to relapse when they confronted the type of stressors that made them ill in the first place.

I am delighted that Drs. Elliott and Lassen have now provided the general public with a book that discusses the basis of cognitive therapy. I have been aware of Dr. Elliott's cognitive therapy skills since the early 1980s, when he served as a therapist in a major study of the efficacy of cognitive therapy for depression. Both authors are highly qualified to share their knowledge and wisdom with everybody who has or is interested in psychological problems.

Their book focuses on the schemas that function as information-processing programs in the mind. Schemas generally lie behind repetitive problems that chronically haunt people while remaining outside of their awareness. Schemas often block progress in therapy. Although people desire change, changing schemas evokes tremendous amounts of anxiety because their schemas, no matter how troublesome, feel like a fundamental part of themselves.

The authors emphasize the role of schemas across a wide range of problems in what they call the three life zones—self-worth, empowerment, and relationships. They demonstrate the value of considering schemas as existing along a continuum and incorporate a few ideas from the physics theory of chaos. Although the underlying concepts are somewhat complex, they present these ideas in an easy-to-understand format with clear applications to everyday life. They guide readers through an assessment of the schemas that may be preventing them from getting what they want out of life. The authors also present numerous clinical examples, along with specific exercises for implementing desired changes. The exercises are both practical and interesting.

The authors show considerable insight, compassion, and empathy. And they demonstrate a keen awareness of the difficulty involved in trying to change one's life. This book has great value in guiding people's self-help endeavors and in serving as an adjunct to therapy.

Aaron T. Beck, M.D.

PREFACE

"Revolutionary. Breakthrough. Quantum Leap." These words splatter the covers of self-help books. And readers (including us) often find themselves disappointed at the end. Perhaps in time, research will justify such lofty claims for our new model of self-understanding. Meanwhile, we doubt you will be disappointed with this book if your goal is to gain a better understanding of yourself, other people, your relationships, and ways of changing. We think you will find a truly new perspective on these issues within the first two chapters of this book. For now, let us present a little history behind our efforts.

For several decades, cognitive therapy (and its cousin, cognitive-behavior therapy) has reigned as the most widely accepted model for improving self-understanding and producing change. Dr. Aaron T. Beck pioneered many of the early developments in cognitive therapy and was soon accompanied by others in this and related areas. A partial list of the pioneers of the various cognitive therapies includes Drs. Albert Bandura, Albert Ellis, Michael Mahoney, Donald Meichenbaum, Brian Shaw, Steven Hollon, Keith Dobson, Arthur Freeman, David Burns, and Jeffrey Young. The cognitive therapy approach is largely based on the idea that the way we interpret events affects our feelings and reactions. People often distort events to such a degree that severe emotional reactions result. Cognitive therapy assumes that changing distorted thinking can improve the way people feel. Originally this model focused on depression. Gradually its focus widened to include an impressive array of areas, such as anxiety disorders, assertiveness, social skills, anger management, sexual problems, unwanted habits, and problem-solving skills.

Cognitive therapy has received substantial research support. For many problems it has proven as effective as psychotropic drugs, but without the side effects. A number of studies have indicated that the approach is *more* effective for some problems than medications over the long term. That's why we have practiced cognitive therapy for more than twenty years. In the 1980s, Dr. Elliott served as a therapist in one of the largest studies on the efficacy of cognitive therapy ever conducted.

In 1981, Dr. David Burns first presented cognitive therapy to the public with his book *Feeling Good.* This presentation focused on depression and received an overwhelming response. Dr. Burns published *The Feeling Good Handbook* in 1989, which addressed a wider range of problems such as anxiety, communication difficulties, and a lack of assertiveness. This book also attracted considerable interest.

Today, books based on cognitive therapy principles occupy a considerable portion of shelf space in the self-help category. They generally focus on specific problems as opposed to an overall model for self-understanding. However, many chronic problems (such as those involving intimacy and relationships, self-concept, a pervasive sense of vulnerability, maladaptive emotional expressiveness, and so on) are not quite that specific. These problems have been somewhat difficult to understand with the standard cognitive therapy approach.

For several decades, cognitive scientists have researched a different kind of cognition or thought process that might help clarify our understanding of such broader, chronic problems. Specifically, this type of thought process is known as a *schema.* Schemas essentially represent information-processing programs in our minds that interpret and organize life experiences, much as a computer's software organizes incoming information. Without schemas, all information would have to be treated as novel with each exposure. The world would seem chaotic and unpredictable and no one could navigate it successfully. Unfortunately, schemas we develop about ourselves and our environment sometimes create enormous emotional havoc. Research on how schemas work and clinical applications of these findings have aroused more interest from practicing psychologists than any phenomena we have seen in a long time.

In addition, since the mid-1970s, chaos theory and its underlying principles of nonlinearity have yielded important discoveries in an amazing array of phenomena. Weather patterns, electrical regulation of the heart and brain, cloud shapes, and traffic flow on a crowded freeway are now more completely understood through the principles of nonlinearity. Chaos theory helps explain actions and behaviors within almost any medium (e.g., water, air, oil, smoke, electricity, economics, and so on). It probably took so long to make this set of discoveries because most of us find it easier to think in linear terms. For example, linear logic dictates that one should simply double an oven's temperature in order to bake a cake twice as fast. But as you know, it does not work that way.

Four years ago, we discovered that chaos theory and its principles of nonlinearity can enhance our understanding of how schemas work. Thus, we developed a model of self-understanding based on these principles—the Schema Polarity Model. We will show how this model enables you to understand yourself, relationships, and repetitive problems in a more complete way than ever before. We will demonstrate how to combine techniques from cognitive therapy, strategies borrowed from other therapeutic approaches, and ideas from our Schema Polarity Model to mount a formidable attack on the problems you experience in life. Our model is optimistic. We believe people can mobilize their current strengths to engineer new, better ways of being.

As this book unfolds, you will discover that the process of change involves five phases. *Awareness* comes first, and you begin that phase in Chapter 1 by learning about the role schemas may play in your life. This phase will continue through Chapter 2, where you will learn more about the way schemas work. The three chapters after that will help you gain more *awareness* (the first phase of change) through a discovery of the specific self-schemas that may spoil your life. The second phase of change shows up in Chapter 6, which helps you learn about the *origins* of your schemas. *Preparation for change* represents the third phase and can be found in Chapter 7. Phase four covers the topic of *developing adaptive schemas* (Chapters 8, 9, and 10), followed by the final phase, *attacking your problematic maladaptive schemas* (Chapters 11 and 12). By the end of this journey, we believe you will likely discover a new, more satisfying life. That's a bold claim, but we feel it is achievable if you put some effort into the process.

We have collaborated equally in the development of this book. In the process, we learned much from each other and about this model. Nothing we have presented to students and colleagues has ever received such a positive response. As one student put it, "Your model captures people's essence, the core of who they are and what they are about. My understanding of myself and my clients has been brought into a sharper focus." Our clients have shown equal enthusiasm about this model. A number of them have reported using the Schema Polarity Model spontaneously to gain a better understanding of their friends, co-workers, and those who work for them. Clearly, they have found something useful and new that goes beyond previous therapy approaches we have tried. We hope you will find these ideas equally exciting.

ACKNOWLEDGMENTS

We are grateful to all those who have helped to develop the material in this manuscript. The therapeutic interventions described in this book are consistent with the principles of cognitive therapy. We, and the entire field of mental health, are indebted to Dr. Aaron Beck, who founded cognitive therapy more than thirty years ago and who has continued to expand its applicability to alleviate human suffering. We particularly want to recognize our agent, Rafe Sagalyn, whose contributions far exceeded the role of an agent and to whom we are especially appreciative. We also have benefited from the helpful assistance and enthusiastic support of our Davies-Black editorial team—Lee Langhammer-Law and Melinda Adams Merino—and from the editing services of Rachel Anderson. We thank the Fielding Institute's clinical psychology graduate students in the Cognitive Behavior Therapy Training Track, who encouraged our efforts and provided helpful feedback on various aspects of our model. We are grateful for the thoughtful suggestions provided by Vista Berger, Joyce Laux, JoAnn Tilque, Luanne Davis, Rita Kemp, Ronda Kunau, Charlotte Deets, and their Mary Kay colleagues on the schema-assessment and schema-change procedures. We also thank Carole Mazurowski, who offered guidance on how to make the text more reader friendly. We have appreciated the careful review of this manuscript by Tom Bien, Ph.D.; Beverly Bien, M. Ed.; Moss Aubrey, Ph.D.; Lauren Aubrey, M.S.; and Ella Nye, M.S.

We are most indebted to two people: Gary Lassen, who encouraged our ideas and supported us from the very beginning of our work, and Amy Duda, who tirelessly critiqued and edited our material. We are deeply grateful for Gary's and Amy's invaluable contributions and patience since we began this journey in 1993. We also want to express our appreciation to our patients; for more than two decades, they have allowed us to participate in the brave explorations of their own disappointments and desires in the pursuit of a more satisfying existence. Their courage and commitment to change continue to inspire us to become more knowledgeable psychologists and more effective psychotherapists.

Do you feel you don't have much impact in life?

Do you feel you can almost always make situations turn out your way?

Do you worry a lot?

Does danger excite you?

RELATIONSHIPS

Do you keep ending up with the same kind of dysfunctional relationship?

Do you always try to keep the people around you happy?

Do you never worry about what others think?

Does one of your worst fears involve ending up alone in life?

Do you avoid emotional commitments?

Do your values and interests depend on who you are with?

Do others usually want to be like you?

Do you feel that almost everyone is out for themselves?

Do you rarely question other people's motives?

GENERAL

Do you procrastinate more than you would like?

Do you often feel confused?

Are you often described as "out of touch with your feelings"?

Do you sometimes think that making changes in your life is a hopeless idea?

Have you ever thought about suicide?

Do you have more headaches, pains, and other physical problems than most people?

If you answered yes to any of the preceding questions, you have highlighted problem areas for which you might find this book useful. Now, wait a second, you might object. Do affirmative answers to all of the questions listed represent problems? Yes, although you'll have to read further to understand why even some of the seemingly positive questions also cause life disruption. Obviously, only one or two affirmative responses to the entire list of questions would suggest that your need to read this book is less urgent than it is for most people. Giving no affirmative responses suggests that you are possibly one of the most well-adjusted human beings on this planet. But if you feel that more than a few of these questions apply to you, the material in this book may help and even surprise you. It might change your view of reality, yourself, and the world.

We organized our questions under the topics of self-worth, empowerment, and relationships or what we call the three Life Zones. As clinical psychologists, we have found more concern and distress associated with these areas than with anything else by a factor of ten. People who experience significant difficulty in one of life's zones usually run into trouble in one or both of the others. And we find that most people—yes, even normal, well-functioning, successful people—experience problems in one or more of these zones, sometimes repeatedly, without understanding why. So if you are stupefied by continual struggles with your relationships, your self-worth, or your sense of empowerment and mastery over life, we have guidelines to help you change these recurrent problems for the better. We also included questions under a "general" category. As you read this book, you'll understand why we have included that category and what it's all about. If you feel that three or more of the questions under any of the four headings above apply to you, you have identified a definite problem area.

This book presents a new perspective and offers solutions for some age-old problems. Some of these ideas have ancient roots that may intrigue you. People and their sometimes incomprehensible actions will become clearer. And you will likely find yourself better able to make changes that will lead you to a more satisfying path in life.

In the past few years, our clients have endorsed the value of this new approach with more zeal than they felt about anything we had previously presented to them. We sincerely believe and hope that you will benefit from what we have to tell you. One caveat, however: The more attention you give this book, the more you will get out of it. The various writing assignments and tasks we've included should help you translate our ideas into action plans for change. No one ever learned to ride a bike, drive a car, or play baseball simply by reading a book. And few people make meaningful changes in their lives without taking action. This book lays out the plan; you must implement it.

1

Why You Do What You Do: Schemas as the Key to Self-Understanding

> *Man looks at his world through transparent patterns or templates*
> *which he creates and then attempts to fit over the realities of which*
> *the world is composed. The fit is not always very good.*
> *Even a poor fit is more helpful to him than nothing at all.*
> —*George Kelly*, The Psychology of Personal Constructs:
> The Theory of Personality *(Vol. 1)*

▷ **Why do you never seem to get what you want?**

▷ **Have you been getting involved in the same kind of dys-functional relationship over and over?**

▷ **Why does your spouse make unreasonable demands?**

▷ **Why do you lose your temper even though you don't want to do so?**

▷ **Do you have the admiration of others, yet suffer from poor self-esteem?**

▷ **Do you ever sense that your actions are self-defeating but not know what to do to break the cycle?**

▷ **Why can't you accept a compliment?**

▷ **Why do you put off important tasks until the last second?**

Perhaps vexing questions such as these trouble you from time to time. . . . You and about twenty zillion other normal people. We don't know anyone who sails through life without occasionally encountering choppy waters. And it often seems impossible to find the way out. No matter which way you go, the storm seems to follow.

As psychologists, we have found that most problems fall into one of three major life zones. The first zone, Self-Worth, involves a variety of concerns about how you value yourself. The second zone, Empowerment, covers issues regarding your sense of competence and mastery of life's tasks. Relationships constitute the third zone, which often befuddles us more than a Rubik's Cube. If you sometimes find yourself bogged down in the marshlands of one or more of these zones, this book is designed for you.

In just the past few years, we have found exciting solutions for problems in these areas. These solutions come from a new way of thinking about what makes people tick. Unlike most previous ideas about people, our approach is not based on a model of mental illness or disease. Rather, our model focuses on the ways that *all* people process information. Because we believe that all people experience problems, it makes sense to use a model that applies to everyone.

SCHEMAS: THE COGNITIVE THERAPY BREAKTHROUGH

Many problems can be vague, subtle, and puzzling. Along with all cognitive therapists, we have had our share of enigmatic cases in which we could not fully grasp the nature of a client's problems. Such individuals often made solid gains, but still suffered from irksome impasses outside the range of our clinical "line of fire." Until recently, nothing in our twenty years of practice provided any better understanding of such cases, so we weren't especially optimistic that the situation would change. But it has.

During the last couple of years, we became intrigued by schemas—a different level and type of cognition or thought that psychologists have known about for decades. Psychologist Sir Frederick Bartlett first used this term in the 1930s, but no one took much notice; in fact, clinical psychologists only recently began exploring schemas and are rapidly uncovering exciting therapeutic value. So far it looks like a treasure trove. Experimental-cognitive psychologists spawned much of this interest when they discovered that schemas influence perception, expectations, and memory more powerfully than anyone heretofore suspected. For example, they have found that schemas often cause gross inaccuracies in eyewitness testimony, even when witnesses state absolute certainty in their rendition of the facts. Subsequent investigations often reveal that witnesses must have erred because of the influence of schemas on their memories and expectations.

But what exactly are schemas and how do they work? *Schemas* are information-processing programs in our minds that interpret and organize our life experiences, much as a computer's software organizes incoming information. They also create our expectations, so we often see what we think we'll see. Therein lies the cause of inaccurate eyewitness reports. Schemas develop automatically. From infancy our brains try to make sense of our world by organizing information on different topics into clusters, or schemas. These schemas not only organize our experiences but also cause us to interpret and react to events in consistent, predictable ways. In another sense, they act as templates or lenses through which we view the world.

We immersed ourselves in books, articles, and workshops about this phenomenon. Soon, all the reading and puzzling clinical cases, along with our own life experiences and observations, cascaded into a fuller, richer understanding of people and their predicaments. We suddenly realized why some people remain bogged down in their problems and often fail to get what they want. It all has to do with this different level of thinking. Clients' issues that previously had seemed blurry finally came into focus.

We weren't the only ones to feel excited about schemas. Recently, psychologists have been flocking to crowded workshops on schema-oriented therapy. In one recent meeting of the Association for the Advancement of Behavior Therapy in New York City, organizers packed chairs more closely than the fire code could possibly permit but still had to turn away many psychologists. Upon exiting, the attendees looked like archaeologists who had just stumbled onto evidence of a heretofore unknown civilization. They had found a powerful tool for understanding their clients and even themselves. We think you will find these tools equally useful and exciting.

TYPES OF SCHEMAS

We have schemas about other people (*role* and *person* schemas), about different life situations (*script* schemas), and about ourselves (*self*-schemas). We have schemas about everything. They organize sublime, horrific, and mundane phenomena. *Everything.*

Role schemas provide you with expectations and information about social roles and how people behave in them. You have role schemas for men and women, mothers and fathers, grandparents, victims, patients, doctors, and criminals. You can thank role schemas for the fact that you automatically know to call the police or reach for mace if a stranger suggests that you remove your clothes, whereas you readily accept the same request from your physician.

Your schemas about other individuals are called *person schemas.* The better you know someone, the more—and more elaborate—schemas you will have about

7

that person. You will have more person schemas about your sister than about a clerk at your bank. Your schemas about your sister may be that she is self-centered, powerful, and domineering. Schemas about other people are a compilation of your memories and current impressions. Like all schemas, person schemas include both generalizations and specific details.

Script schemas organize information about a sequence of events. For example, in much of the Western world, a wedding schema would tell us that a bride, a groom, and an official to marry them are present. Without script schemas, your grocery bagger would have to ponder each item before deciding not to pack grapes and bread beneath cans.

Culture contributes to the generalizations schemas make. The schemas for males and females, mothers and fathers, husbands and wives, different occupations, weddings, and so on will vary with different cultures. Diplomats know that they must master the script and role schemas of their host countries. Otherwise, they may commit disastrous gaffes simply by making the wrong kind of eye contact or using a misleading gesture.

Your most elaborate schemas are about yourself and are called *self-schemas*. These are the schemas you really need to understand. Self-schemas serve as an organized repository of abundant information about your characteristics, strengths, weaknesses, behavior, and preferences, and about the way you relate to others. Consider the examples of Sylvia, Steven, and Lynn.

Sylvia

From childhood, thirty-five-year-old Sylvia has been self-conscious about her body. She describes herself as "5 feet 3 inches of roundness. I have a round body, round legs, and round arms. I feel like a ball. In fact, I have an image of myself as this huge beach ball rolling through life. I'm built just like my dad and his family. We're all beach balls. My doctor says I'm in great health. He says I am in the normal range for my weight but at the upper limit. Those medical charts overestimate how much you can weigh and look good. Jack, my husband, has always said he thinks I am pretty. But I have never felt pretty. I have always wanted to be tall and thin like my mother and older sister. By high school I knew that was not going to happen. I never feel pretty or sexy. I'm here because Jack doesn't want to hear me complain about myself anymore. He wants me to be happy. But I don't think that's possible unless you do body transplants." Sylvia has a delightful sense of humor, but unfortunately she often uses that humor to deprecate her own appearance.

Steven

At Steven's first psychotherapy session, he remarks, "I have avoided therapy for a long time. I thought my success would change the way I feel about myself, but it hasn't." At age forty-two, Steven is a successful physician with a solid practice and is well respected in the medical community. Despite his achievements, Steven has a persistent sense of inferiority when he compares himself with others.

Steven's feelings of low self-worth go back as far as he can remember. His father was a severe alcoholic who never held a job for more than a few months. His mom worked at menial jobs to earn additional money for the family, but there was hardly enough to pay their rent, much less to buy decent clothes. Steven lived in lower-class neighbor-hoods and dressed more shabbily than almost anyone else at his school. He had a few friends, but he was so ashamed of his family life that he kept most kids at a distance. He has never really had a best friend. His wife is the only person whom he has ever allowed to get close to him, yet he keeps part of himself closed off even from her.

His wife often complains that they have no close friends because Steven hates to socialize. He explains, "Really, it's not that I don't like other people. But I always get nervous in social situations. Somehow, I still feel inferior—like other people are better than me and they know it—or they will know it as soon as they ask me any-thing about my past. The only time I feel safe is when I am in my role as a doctor. Then people respect me. I feel safe in that white coat. But take me out of it and I'm still that poor kid from Missouri whose dad was the town drunk."

Lynn

Lynn is a thirty-two-year-old marketing analyst for a national company. Her physician referred her for therapy after she had sought medication for a variety of physical symptoms: difficulty sleeping, frequent headaches, chest tightness, indiges-tion, and alternating bouts of diarrhea and constipation. After several lab tests, her doctor said her symptoms are the result of chronic tension. He did not want to pre-scribe any medication until she tried psychotherapy. In the first session Lynn is reserved and somewhat evasive, admitting she is skeptical that therapy will help. Lynn says she is an action-oriented person and therapy has never impressed her as very action oriented. But she agrees to try four sessions and then decide.

Although anxiety has been Lynn's constant companion since childhood, she describes with pride how her colleagues view her as controlled and not easily panicked.

She entered the marketing field after earning a master's degree and has received several promotions in her company. The increase in her responsibilities has also increased her tension, but she is determined to become vice president of her division.

Lynn's personal life has been much less successful. She has been involved in several long-term relationships, but all have ended unhappily. Lynn has developed a relationship pattern: Initially, she is enthralled with these men, but eventually the thrill turns to disenchantment with how self-centered they are. They become inattentive to her needs and unresponsive to her requests. When Lynn confronts them, they promise to change but seldom do. Some of them begin to go out on her, though they deny it. At first she becomes angry with them, but then she begs them to come back and try again. Some simply refuse, whereas others tell her that they cannot meet her demands. Lynn admits that she is consumed with jealousy and rage when she does not receive the attention she craves.

What most baffles Lynn is that few of these men have been as successful as she. Often, they end up living off her, but they still don't feel obligated to meet her needs. Eventually, they leave her. If they don't, Lynn finally asks them to leave—after she has met someone else. This repeated experience leaves Lynn feeling empty, angry, and overwhelmed by anxiety. She desperately wants a permanent relationship and longs for someone to take care of her. Lynn has an unrelenting fear of abandonment.

Sylvia has a self-schema that she is *Undesirable.* Steven has a self-schema that he is *Unworthy.* Lynn has a self-schema about *Abandonment.* These interesting people also have other self-schemas that you will learn about later.

Schemas certainly have wreaked havoc on Sylvia, Steven, and Lynn. Unfortunately, they cannot see their schemas, so they remain unaware of their very existence. Yet all three of them are ordinary people. They are not sick, mentally ill, or bizarre. They feel satisfied with their lives much of the time, but occasionally feel awful, swallowed up in fear, anger, or sadness. They fight to make those painful feelings go away, but they always come back. The same miserable feelings. The same dreadful thoughts. Again and again.

Are schemas always evil influences, cruelly inflicting themselves on our emotional lives? It might be starting to look that way, but such is not the case.

THE UPSIDE OF SCHEMAS

If we didn't develop schemas, we would treat all information as novel with each exposure. Schemas help us process and organize all incoming information. They guide our recognition and comprehension of new experiences by providing expectations. In other words, they help us *understand* and *predict*. Without schemas, we would have to figure out a football game or a wedding or our spouses with each encounter. It would be like trying to use a computer without software, programming it for each new piece of data. We would not learn from our past. We would not survive very long as a species or as couples or as individuals. *We absolutely could not get through a single day without schemas.*

This organizing function of schemas is essential. Read the following paragraph to see what would happen without the frame of reference that schemas provide:

> *It's actually very simple. First, you must arrange the various types of things into specific groups, depending on how you decide to deal with them. Conceivably, one pile could suffice, but that depends upon quantity and your decision as to how to approach the task. If you must, seek out an alternative setting, but only if you don't have sufficient facilities yourself. You do not want to overdo any part of this task. Thus, it is preferable to do too little than too much at once. At first, this could appear inconsequential, but complications could quickly develop from attempting too much at once. Mistakes could cost you dearly as well. Dwelling on the specifics concerning the manipulation of various mechanisms does not seem necessary, as you should discover that aspect of the task to be largely self-evident. If this is a first experience for you, it could actually appear complicated. It should not take long, however, before you see it as just another part of life. It is quite doubtful that an end to this task will emerge, but we suppose that would be a remote possibility.*

OK, now close the book and recall as much of the above paragraph as you can. Then come back and reread it. How much did you remember? Would your memory have improved if you had known it was about doing laundry? Psychologists found that people who received similar information before reading recalled 73 percent more material than those who did not know the topic beforehand. This demonstrates how a script schema improves understanding and performance. Like all schemas, script schemas provide predictability about events, people, and ourselves. There is a downside to schemas, however.

THE DOWNSIDE OF SCHEMAS

Unfortunately, expectations based on schemas can deviously mislead by influencing what we perceive. Tragic consequences can even occur when expectations influence perception, as seen in the following example.

11

A group of five men went deer hunting one hazy afternoon. They drove through a muddy, snow-covered field. Their vehicle bogged down. As they attempted to extricate themselves, the transmission broke, leaving them stranded. Two of the men offered to look for help at a farmhouse they had passed. One of the volunteers decided that both of them weren't required for the task, so he decided to go hunt for deer. The men remaining near the car had no idea that their friend had gone on an excursion that took him in a circle down a hill in front of the car. One of them thought he saw movement and remarked to his friend, "Isn't that a deer?" The friend confirmed his impression, so he took a shot. The deer cried out in pain and lurched forward. As it started to get up and run, his friend yelled, "Get him!" So another shot was fired. When the deer moved once again, the man stilled it with a third shot. Only as the men ran toward the deer did they discover that it was their friend, not a deer. The friend was dead.

The deer-hunting mind-set precipitated this tragedy. What we expect to see and hear affects what we do see and hear. We derive schemas from previous experiences and use them to interpret new experiences. Sometimes interpretations are biased. We interpret information based on our schemas and this then becomes our sense of reality. Sporting events illustrate this principle nicely. If a fight erupts in a baseball game between the Los Angeles Dodgers and the New York Mets, the Dodgers fans usually see the fight as instigated by the Mets, whereas Mets fans will place the blame on the Dodgers. When basketball star Charles Barkley played for the Philadelphia 76ers, Phoenix Suns fans assumed that his impetuous behavior caused most of the fights in which he became embroiled. When Barkley joined their hometown team, they soon realized he was a victim of vicious taunts by other players and could rarely be considered culpable for his actions.   In addition to distorting perceptions of events, schemas can produce erroneous or distorted views of ourselves and others—sometimes with devastating effects. Does that mean our schemas are irrational? Is Sylvia's *Undesirable* schema irrational or crazy? No. Sylvia's *Undesirable* schema makes sense if we view the world through her experiences.

Since Sylvia was a little girl, her mother had discouraged her from eating second helpings or desserts. Sylvia loved desserts, but she came to view that as a shameful weakness. She loved to play sports and was a successful athlete in school, but in her mother's eyes Sylvia's achievements paled next to her sister's cheerleader status. Sylvia's mother and older sister were tall and thin. Both were obsessed with their weight, although Sylvia never remembers either of them as having been an ounce overweight. Both were lifelong dieters and complained endlessly about any real or imaginary weight gain. They both openly criticized Sylvia's weight and appearance, as well. They loved to shop and idealized the anorectic women on television and in magazines. Sylvia was not interested in shopping or fashion.

Is it any wonder that Sylvia developed a self-schema of *Undesirability*? She has been bombarded with criticism about her appearance since early childhood. Therefore, this schema has long been in existence and cannot be discarded easily. If you were raised in a culture that speaks Spanish, Spanish will always be your native language. You can learn new languages, but you will not forget your native tongue. So too with the schemas developed throughout your life. All the reassurance in the world from her husband and doctor had no impact on Sylvia's *Undesirable* schema.

In future chapters we'll show you how Sylvia reshaped her *Undesirable* schema instead of her body. In those same chapters, you will see what Steven did to build a new foundation of self-worth and how Lynn diminished her feelings of abandonment. You also will discover your own schemas and learn which ones are helpful and which are problematic. You may be surprised.

Perhaps Sylvia's, Steven's, and Lynn's self-schemas sound like distorted beliefs you have read about in other self-help books. In a limited way they are. But most people think of beliefs as a passive thing, something you either have or don't have. Beliefs also sound like something that can be changed rather easily.

Schemas, on the other hand, reach out and grab incoming data. Then they transform and reprocess that information, just as you could gather a bushel of apples, add some ingredients, and turn it all into applesauce. The resulting product only slightly resembles the original ingredients. Furthermore, schemas, unlike mere beliefs, evoke astonishing anxiety when we attempt to change them.

THE ASTONISHING POWER OF SELF-SCHEMAS

To appreciate the influence of schemas, consider this example. In several studies, cats spent their first months of life in an experimental environment—a tube-shaped cage with vertical lines painted on the curved walls. The cats became incapable of seeing horizontal lines. Their brains organized their visual receptors to perceive what seemed essential—namely, what had existed in the environment.

The human response may be surprisingly similar. If you place two lines of equal length next to each other, one vertical and one horizontal, a slight majority of Americans report that the horizontal line is the longest. Members of the Suku tribe in Zaire, on the other hand, almost always choose the vertical line as the longest. Why do they choose the vertical line to a far greater extent than Americans? Suku tribe members live in African grasslands where the horizon is always visible. Because survival depends on accurate vertical information, their brains organize input to enhance this ability. You may think that you would not fall prey to the influence of schemas and the expectations they create. Much in this book will focus on dissuading you of that notion.

Below are some examples of self-schemas. Notice how the examples cause dramatically disparate reactions, depending on a person's self-schema. The word *reality* itself may acquire a new meaning for you.

Do You See What I See?

One of the best ways to think about how schemas work is to consider them as a lens through which we look at the world. We see everything through that lens. Unfortunately, the lens can cause wilder distortions in what we "see" than eyeglasses that are too powerful or too weak. In these examples, an *activating event* is something that happens to you that relates to or triggers one of your schemas. Once you have viewed the event through the schema lens, you will react or respond to it. That reaction could include thoughts, emotions, or behaviors. Let's see how this works.

Activating Event #1

Our first activating event involves someone whose spouse launched a verbal rampage upon discovering an overdrawn checking account for the second time that year. Notice how this leads directly to the reaction shown because of the schema lens through which the event is viewed.

The first lens below contains the self-schema of *Inadequate*, which we have defined as "I feel I have failed or am inadequate compared with my peers in areas of achievement such as school, career, sports, or other activities. I often believe I do not have the intelligence, talent, or abilities to succeed." Note how this schema logically causes the following reaction to the activating event: "I never do anything right. I don't understand how I can be so stupid. What's wrong with me?"

Activating Event #1	Schema Lens	Reaction
Husband raged at his wife's error in handling the checkbook.	**Inadequate**	"I never do anything right. I don't understand how I can be so stupid. What's wrong with me?"

In this next case, we used the same activating event but a different schema inside the lens. In this case, the schema is *Other-Centered*, defined as "I focus on meeting others' needs, even at the expense of my own needs and preferences. I might at times resent those in my care. I am far more likely to take others' perspective than my own. When others are upset, I think it is up to me to do something about it."

Activating Event #1	Schema Lens	Reaction
Husband raged at his wife's error in handling the checkbook.	**Other-Centered**	"Actually, I am not sure how this happened. But I know I have to find ways to please him better. Maybe I can take bookkeeping courses and make him a special dinner tonight."

In this third example, the activating event is the same again, but the schema inside the lens is *Accepting*. "I realize that, as a human being, I am going to make mistakes. I can accept responsibility for my mistakes, and I can apologize comfortably to others. Although I may choose to try to change, I do not make myself feel overly guilty."

Activating Event #1	Schema Lens	Reaction
Husband raged at his wife's error in handling the checkbook.	**Accepting**	"Maybe I did mess up the checkbook. If so, that's too bad, but I know I don't deserve this kind of verbal abuse."

In each case, the same event led to completely different reactions, depending on which schema lens was at work. It's almost as though the people were looking at different events. As you can see, each schema lens dictates your interpretation of events. You don't question your view, because you don't even know the lenses are there. Have you ever been surprised by the way someone interpreted something you said? Were you puzzled by their reaction? The next time this happens, try asking which schema lens the person is looking through. The more you study schemas in yourself and others, the more you'll see how much they organize everyone's perceptions.

Activating Event #2

This next situation will also be interpreted quite differently, depending on the schema employed. This event involves just having given a presentation to fifty colleagues at work. After the presentation, the applause seems lukewarm.

The first lens below contains the self-schema of *Inadequate*, which we will again define as "I feel I have failed or am inadequate compared with my peers in areas of achievement such as school, career, sports, or other activities. I often believe I do not have the intelligence, talent, or abilities to succeed."

Activating Event #2	Schema Lens	Reaction
Lukewarm applause	**Inadequate**	"I know I gave a terrible presentation. I'll never be good enough at these things."

The second lens we will use for Activating Event #2 is *Entitled:* "I feel I should have whatever I want. I don't always think about whether my wants are reasonable or what they would cost others. Sometimes others think I walk over them. Nothing less than the best is good enough for me."

Activating Event #2	Schema Lens	Reaction
Lukewarm applause	**Entitled**	"I can't believe they aren't applauding louder. I know I did a great job and I deserve it. My colleagues are never appreciative enough of me"

Are you getting the idea of how decisively schemas govern your attention to different aspects of events? Here's the kicker—the people responding to the events listed earlier have no doubt that they perceive the situation correctly. In fact, they believe the situation has once again demonstrated the truth of their assumptions. You'll be impressed by the bedeviling power of schemas as you learn more about them. Remember, *awareness* is the first step toward change.

Activating Event #3

To further your understanding, we'd like you to look over Activating Events #3 and #4. Ask yourself how someone with different schemas would react. Then fill in a likely reaction you would have to those events. The first lens represents *Abandonment:* "I worry a lot about losing people close to me. I am afraid they will leave or be taken away from me through death or other circumstances. I need a great deal of reassurance to feel secure, but the reassurance never seems to last. I sometimes test other people's emotional commitment in ways that are not necessarily constructive. I am very sensitive to rejection."

Activating Event #3	Schema Lens	Reaction
Your spouse took one-and-a-half hours longer shopping one evening than she said she would.	**Abandonment**	

Now, imagine your reaction if you had the self-schema of *Avoidant:* "I don't feel the need to become emotionally involved. I generally keep people at a distance."

Activating Event #3	Schema Lens	Reaction
Your spouse took one-and-a-half hours longer shopping one evening than she said she would.	**Avoidant**	

Here are a few possible responses to those scenarios, using the same schema lenses shown above for Activating Event #3. Keep in mind that other responses might fit equally as well. They just need to follow reasonably from the definition of the schema lens.

Activating Event #3	Schema Lens	Reaction
Your spouse took one-and-a-half hours longer shopping one evening than she said she would.	**Abandonment**	"I guess she's having an affair. She'll probably want a divorce next."

Activating Event #3	Schema Lens	Reaction
Your spouse took one-and-a-half hours longer shopping one evening than she said she would.	**Avoidant**	"Great! Time for myself. I hate it when she wants to hang around the house and talk all the time."

Activating Event #4

Now try Activating Event #4 in which you feel your heart skip a beat. Your first schema lens involves feeling *Vulnerable*: "I often worry about terrible things happening to me or to those close to me. I worry about issues such as finances, health, crime, or natural calamities."

Activating Event #4	Schema Lens	Reaction
Heart skips a beat	**Vulnerable**	_____ _____ _____ _____

It is also possible that you may have the schema of *Invulnerable:* "I believe I am virtually immune to harm or illness. I don't worry about how I eat, exercise, or protect myself. What other people think of as high risk (hang gliding, parachuting, etc.), I often find exhilarating."

Activating Event #4	Schema Lens	Reaction
Heart skips a beat	**Invulnerable**	_____ _____ _____ _____

The following represent possible responses to those scenarios:

Activating Event #4	Schema Lens	Reaction
Heart skips a beat	**Vulnerable**	"Oh, God, I'm having a heart attack!"

Activating Event #4	Schema Lens	Reaction
Heart skips a beat	**Invulnerable**	"I'm healthy as a horse. I don't think I need to worry about my health at all. And I don't need to worry about that pressure in my chest. It's just a little stress."

CONCLUSION

The influence of schemas may be more engulfing than you realized. Few people even know they see the world through schema lenses. Instead, most blithely assume that they see what everyone else sees—the one and only "correct" version of reality. Perhaps the next time you have a disagreement with a friend, you'll consider which schema lens your friend looks through and better understand your friend's perspective. In the next chapter, you will learn more about how schemas work.

2

Why You Keep Getting the Opposite of What You Want: Paradox and Chaos Applied to Schemas

Man can only attain his desire by
passing through its opposite.
—*Søren Kierkegaard*, The Journals
of Søren Kierkegaard: A Selection

Perhaps you have taken a psychological test at some time in your life. If so, your psychologist probably gave you some interesting information about yourself. Most of these tests do a fair job of assessing characteristics such as assertiveness, extroversion, dependency, inhibition, anxiety, paranoia, and so on. In other words, they attempt to describe your personality, or your *traits*, as psychologists often call them. These traits are usually assigned a single, stable point along a straight-line continuum. Thus, if you took a test designed to measure your level of assertiveness, you would obtain a single score along a continuum such as the one below:

No Assertiveness   **High Assertiveness**

0   50   100

That's all there is to it. Your score on assertiveness might be 78, indicating that you are more assertive than the average person. Consistently. Every time. That's who you are. Just one problem. That's not who you are. People are not that consistent.

Julie, a forty-three-year-old paralegal, has come to us because of problems in her relationships. One day she is unusually distraught. She says, "I just don't understand what's wrong with me. Sometimes, I feel so safe and secure in my relationship with Brent. He is caring, kind, and wonderful to me. He's never given me reason to worry. In general, I trust him and feel positive he's the one for me. But then the slightest thing can set me off. He might have a bad day at work and look a little stressed out. Or maybe he'll mention a female friend he had lunch with. Suddenly, I become a raving maniac. I accuse him of wanting to leave or say that he has never really loved me in the first place. I believe it was a mistake ever to have gotten involved with him. His few flaws and foibles suddenly become monstrous. Later, I manage to calm down and everything goes back to normal again. I must be *insane.* I'm acting *crazy.* What's wrong with me?"

Insane? Crazy? Why can't we handle the idea of inconsistencies, even opposite aspects in ourselves without resorting to terms such as these? Possibly because psychological tests and the theories underlying them have not yet acknowledged that we can possess more than one trait along a particular continuum or dimension at the same time. Which one we demonstrate at any given moment *depends upon circumstances.* In sum, you simply can't capture personality with a few traits.

OPPOSITION: THE BASIS OF
HUMAN NATURE AND PERCEPTION

Clearly, we all demonstrate inconsistent, even opposing characteristics such as passivity and aggression, introversion and extroversion, anxiety and relaxation, and so on. Traditional tests and theories of personality have given short shrift to the idea that we fundamentally perceive the world in terms of opposites and sometimes even flip between them in different situations. Instead, theories and tests tend to focus on one trait or characteristic at a time, as though it exists in isolation with no contrasting trait.

Yet opposing dualities form the basis of how we perceive life, nature, behavior, and existence. Linguists have observed that in a totally blue world, it would be impossible to understand the concept of blueness. A fish probably cannot comprehend the concept of wetness, having known nothing else. In a word association test, the most common response to *hot* is *cold.* Darwin observed that a hostile dog—discernible by its erect tail, bared teeth, and bristled hair—assumes an opposite posture when approaching its master. In these examples, the concepts of blueness, wetness, heat, and hostility only become meaningful when juxta-posed with their opposites.

Human physiology functions largely through opposition. At the cellular level, neurons communicate through a simplistic on-and-off mechanism. The immune system has a delicate balance between activating and deactivating forces. The central nervous system consists of a sympathetic system that controls arousal functions and a parasympathetic system that counteracts arousal. Opposites also permeate physics. All forces have counterforces, all atoms possess a positive and a negative charge, and matter is counterbalanced by antimatter.

Polarities refers to phenomena that involve opposite properties, characteris-tics, or attributes. The following list illustrates how pervasively polarities influence life and nature.

Love and Hate

Yin and Yang

Matter and Anti-Matter

Sympathetic and Parasympathetic Nervous Systems

Thesis and Antithesis

Liberal and Conservative

Light and Dark

Introvert and Extrovert

Pain and Pleasure

Manic–Depressive

Constriction and Expansion

Creation and Destruction

Life and Death

In fact, you can take the following as a fundamental principle:

**In order to be understood—possibly even to exist—
most things must have an opposite.**

Why should human personalities and behavior be any different? We don't think they are. We'll show you later that our model of personality appreciates that polarities and dualities are fundamental to self-understanding. But first, let us tell you how opposites work.

Are Opposites Truly Opposite?

Opposite. Totally different. Antagonistic and irreconcilable. Most of us find it eas-ier to think of opposites in *linear* terms, as a straight line from point A to point B. Because it's easiest to think in linear terms, we might readily believe that twice as much of something good will deliver twice as much pleasure, even though it rarely does. Taking twice the prescribed medication dosage isn't likely to cure you twice as fast; rather, it's more likely to inflict harm. How about love and hate, dependence and independence, vulnerability and invulnerability, pleasure and pain? You're probably accustomed to thinking of these concepts as complete opposites. If so, we may end up changing your view of the world.

From Eastern mysticism to physics, clues for understanding the duality of human nature abound. The concepts of yin and yang have permeated Eastern thinking for centuries. Briefly, yin refers to the intuitive, receptive, complex, feminine side, whereas yang describes the rational, direct, masculine side. Imbalance in the two is believed to cause both illness and political instability. The figure below depicts the relationship of yin and yang and demonstrates how, in a sense, opposites whirl into each other. *Once something nears its extreme, it contains the seeds for its own opposite* (as represented by the dots).

Nonlinear thinking embedded within the new physics theory of chaos can help us understand the Eastern perspective on opposites. Chaos theory has given us a better way to interpret the patterns of weather, clouds, economics, stock markets, and water turbulence. Any phenomena such as these that respond to multiple stimuli tend to form chaotic systems. Chaos theory acknowledges that although patterns exist in nature, so do random influences. Consequently, both patterns and disorder coexist. Random influences decrease the predictability of our world, of course. Hence, chaos theory relies on nonlinear formulas to improve prediction and control of such variable systems. These formulas assume that equal changes in value or intensity can cause very different effects. For example, being exposed to the sun for one-and-a-half hours versus forty-five minutes more than doubles your tan.

Most of the things we count on in life work in a nonlinear fashion. Initially, linear logic applies reasonably well; that is, as things move apart, they become increasingly different from each other. Accordingly, the ends of a straight line appear to move further apart as it grows longer. Note, however, that the ends eventually meet—whether the line is drawn on the Earth or across the universe. This applies to emotions, as well. For example, being "in control" looks very different from being "out of control" and at certain points it is. Yet if you strive for control over all aspects of your life, at times you will find yourself abysmally out of control. Failure to understand this nonlinear principle will ensnare you in a never-ending quest for the unobtainable, giving you the opposite of what you seek, making you controlled by the very forces you wish to control. Like Sisyphus in Greek mythology, you'll eternally strain to push a boulder up a long hill, only to find it rolling back down just as you reach the top.

The Paradoxical Trap of Opposites

Remember Lynn from Chapter 1? She is the marketing analyst who frantically tries to avoid abandonment and to fulfill her needs yet always ends up with the opposite of what she works so hard to get. She remains mystified as to what she is doing wrong. Lynn keeps falling into a trap created by the typical, linear view of opposites. This view underlies many of life's paradoxes—ideas that seem to contradict common sense. Paradoxes repeatedly seduce us into making the wrong moves, choices, and decisions and exert unrecognized havoc on our lives. Their effects can show up unexpectedly and often. Try pondering some of our favorite examples:

▷   **The more you strive to "have it all," the less likely you are to discover what truly makes life worthwhile.**

▷   **The things you hate the most in the short run often enhance your life in the long run.**

▷   **Freedom often comes from rules and limits.**

▷   **The more you rebel against authority, the more you will be ultimately controlled by authority.**

▷   **The more vehemently you argue for your position, the less you will be heard.**

▷   **The more you must have someone, the less they will want you.**

▷ **Usually the best time to invest in the stock market is when almost everyone advises against it.**

▷ **The more open you are about your vulnerabilities, the more invulnerable you become.**

▷ **The more you exclusively focus on the needs of others, the less you will be able to meet their needs.**

▷ **Medical advances are producing harder-to-treat diseases (as seen with antibiotics that are creating new strains of bacteria, resistant to any known drug).**

Like all paradoxes, these likely strike you as counterintuitive, if not downright illogical. Until recently we saw them that way, too. Now we believe a basic principle underlies most paradoxes. Underlying most befuddling paradoxes, schemas, and emotions is the *polarity paradox*, which refers to the following nonlinear idea:

The more opposite two phenomena appear,
the more they become the same.

Opposites form two sides of the same reality. These sides must be integrated and balanced for optimal functioning. The two hemispheres of the brain must be coordinated in order for a person to approach tasks effectively. The immune system also requires balanced integration. If it is too active, autoimmune disorders such as scleroderma or lupus develop; if it is too inactive, colds, flu, or cancer may emerge. The parasympathetic and sympathetic nervous systems must also be kept in balance or one will suffer from excessive fear and overarousal or from fatigue, lethargy, and underarousal. When opposing mechanisms achieve coordinated integration, they flow together as smoothly as a well-edited film. When integration breaks down, it creates a choppiness, as if scenes were appearing one frame at a time.

SCHEMAS AND NONLINEARITY

Schemas are best understood in terms of their opposites and, as you have seen, opposites may not be as different as they appear. In our model, each schema continuum consists of a negative maladaptive schema at one extreme (–), a positive maladaptive schema at the other extreme (+), and an adaptive schema (∗) between the two:

We have depicted the continuum as circular. This allows us to place the extremes more closely together and further from the adaptive schema, thus reflecting their nonlinear relationship. Note how the extreme ends of the nonlinear, circular continuum almost touch.

Here is an example of a self-schema continuum:

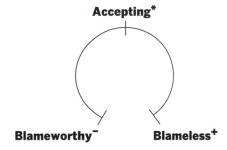

We define each of these schemas as follows:

Blameworthy⁻ "I feel I often deserve punishment or harsh criticism. I tend to be excessively critical or punitive of myself when I make mistakes."

Accepting* "I realize that, as a human being, I am going to make mistakes. I can accept responsibility for my mistakes and I can apologize comfortably to others. While I may choose to attempt change, I do not make myself feel overly guilty."

Blameless⁺ "I feel I have to be right. It is hard for me to admit I am wrong or that I have made a mistake. It is hard for me to say I am sorry."

Again, note how polarities *wrap back onto themselves*. Perhaps this depicts something fundamental about nature and human existence. Many physicists now construe space and the universe in a similar manner and predict that if you had an infinitely powerful telescope, you would peer into the heavens until you actually viewed your own back. And leading contemporary physicist Stephen Hawking speculates that although time is running forward as the universe expands, some-day the universe could contract and time may then run backward. Color percep-tion demonstrates a similar relationship. For example, the wavelengths of red and violet differ the most among all the colors, yet to the eye these two colors appear to be far more similar to each other than either does to the color green, which has an intermediate wavelength.

Negative maladaptive schemas (–) portray a harsh, critical view of oneself and the world and produce negative expectations. They consist of global, rigid, inflexible thinking. People with negative maladaptive schemas might feel *Inadequate⁻*, *Blameworthy⁻*, *Undefined⁻*, *Dependent⁻*, *Undesirable⁻*, *Acquiescent⁻*, and *Vulnerable⁻*. When activated, these schemas create feelings of overwhelming hope-lessness, despair, tension, helplessness, and anxiety, thus becoming all-consuming.

Positive maladaptive schemas (+) look like a different matter and in some ways they are. These schemas reflect a rigid, overly positive view of the self in all three zones, and these views produce unrealistically positive expectations. Yes, too positive. In spite of everything you've heard about the "power of positive thinking," it is possible to overshoot the mark. Positive maladaptive schemas that make people behave as though they are *Blameless⁺*, *Entitled⁺*, and *Invulnerable⁺* or that lead them to be *Self-Centered⁺*, *Aggrandizing⁺*, and *Domineering⁺* should make that clear. When taken to the extreme, these schemas lead people to belittle others or focus exclusively on their own needs, which doesn't exactly do wonders for their relationships. People with excessively positive maladaptive schemas often become enraged, tense, or anxious when someone challenges their puffed-up views of them-selves. Maintaining positive maladaptive schemas also takes a lot of effort. Let's face it—everyone slips and slides on the muddy road of life. Pretending you don't depletes your resources.

Possibly out of failure to recognize the importance of opposites, the field of mental health has not paid as much attention to those who have a predominance of positive maladaptive schemas. For obvious reasons, such persons don't often come to psychologists' offices seeking help for their problems—they seldom think they have flaws or foibles. The diagnostic system therefore pays these people scant atten-tion. Psychologists write fewer articles about them, and psychological tests do not assess them effectively. That is unfortunate, because positive maladaptive schemas cause considerable harm to those who have them. And those who possess a pre-dominance of negative maladaptive schemas need to learn about the other polarity, because they often get into destructive relationships with people displaying these positive maladaptive schemas.

Why do we claim that positive and negative maladaptive schemas are similar? They certainly appear as different as two things could be, so how could the polarity paradox possibly apply? That is, how could two opposites almost become the same? First, intense emotional reactions and rigid, inflexible thinking characterize both maladaptive ends more than the adaptive middle. With both types of maladaptive schemas, people grossly distort information about themselves and others. They are inflexible and impenetrable to data that could contradict their perspectives.

The second and possibly most important similarity of seemingly opposite, maladaptive schemas is that both types ultimately cause misery and negative consequences. In fact, the consequences of positive and negative maladaptive schemas are far-ranging and often surprisingly similar. For example, both these psychological extremes likely damage health. Studies increasingly show that hostility, aggression, and dominance (characteristic of those with positive maladaptive schemas) increase the risk of cardiovascular disease. One study recently found that people with a high degree of self-serving bias and distortion (also similar to those with an abundance of positive maladaptive schemas) showed increased cardiovascular responsiveness to stress. Other studies have found that loneliness, depression, and pessimism (more characteristic of those with a preponderance of negative maladaptive schemas) harm the immune system. Of course, much more remains to be learned about how both types of maladaptive schemas affect health. But enough evidence has amassed that psychologists H. S. Friedman and S. Booth-Kewley recently declared; "Personality may function like diet: Imbalances can predispose one to all sorts of diseases. Such a conclusion is supported by the considerable evidence emerging from physiological studies."

Although opposite traits may not cause identical consequences, they usually evoke strikingly similar outcomes. For example, one who suffocates a partner with insatiable demands for intimacy will end up estranged just as surely as one who maintains distance and avoids intimacy at all costs. You'll discover other fascinating similarities in the consequences of both types of maladaptive schemas as this book unfolds.

Adaptive schemas (*) differ qualitatively from both types of maladaptive schemas. Involving a complex integration of both positive and negative data about you and your world, adaptive schemas manage to process this information in a more tolerant way. They avoid extreme views of the self, others, and the world. Adaptive schemas allow recognition that few events or people are completely good or bad, black or white. People with adaptive schemas appreciate the subtle ambiguities of life and tolerate the frustration of uncertainty.

When using adaptive schemas, you take longer to pass judgment and are more willing to change your viewpoint with new information. Because such schemas contain a mix of positive and negative information, less emotional intensity results. The greatest benefit may be to your health. In the past ten years, a variety of studies have shown that flexibility (the ability to integrate highly divergent aspects of the self) as well as tempered responses to stress provide positive boosts to overall health and well-being.

This kind of integrated balance, characteristic of adaptive schemas, also has positive effects in a variety of other areas. For example, several decades of research have consistently supported the value of finding a "middle ground" in raising children. Permissiveness must be balanced with discipline. Attention must be provided, but not in overabundance. Gross imbalances easily lead to profound problems in all three life zones. Too much attention lays the foundation for the positive maladaptive schema of *Entitled*⁺, whereas too little leads to the negative maladaptive schema of *Unworthy*⁻.

By now you can see the importance of schemas in our functioning. They influence our expectations, perceptions, decision making, actions, and emotions. But the impact in these areas differs for adaptive and maladaptive schemas, as the table below shows.

Schema Characteristics

Adaptive Schemas	Both Types of Maladaptive Schemas
Are complicated	Are simplistic
Are balanced	Are one-sided
Consider circumstances	Disregard circumstances
Are flexible	Are rigid
Produce moderate views	Produce extreme views
Integrate new information	Cannot integrate new information
Produce realistic expectations of oneself and others	Produce unrealistic expectations of oneself and others
Affect relationships constructively	Damage relationships
Produce moderate moods	Produce extreme moods
Allow for behavior change—view change as possible and useful	Inhibit behavior change—view change as hopeless or unnecessary
Benefit health	Harm health

Adaptive schemas serve as the quintessential goal in psychotherapy. For good reason. When life hurls obstacles in your path—and it will—you'll find yourself less distressed if you have adaptive schemas. You'll be calmer and more at peace . . . able to be the person you want to be . . . happier and more satisfied with life . . . possibly even healthier to boot. That's not a bad package, and it's not out of reach. With time and nurturing of your new adaptive schemas, it can happen.

As you go through this book, it will be important to appreciate the adaptive schemas you already have, Psychological tests and self-help books almost never emphasize the idea of strengths, concentrating instead on problems and weaknesses. *We think it's critical to realize what you do right.* Throughout the book, we will emphasize the need to appreciate your existing strengths, your adaptive schemas.

Within each of the three life zones, there are four continua that we believe to be important. Each one contains the three types of schemas we have described above—a negative maladaptive schema, an adaptive schema, and a positive maladaptive schema. Note that each schema is followed by a superscript: a minus (−) sign identifies a negative maladaptive schema, a plus (+) sign identifies a positive maladaptive schema, and an asterisk (∗) identifies an adaptive schema. Throughout the book we will use these superscripts to categorize each schema.

Self-Worth Zone

	−	∗	+
Acceptance continuum:	Blameworthy	Accepting	Blameless
Desirability continuum:	Undesirable	Desirable	Irresistible
Worthiness continuum:	Unworthy	Worthy	Entitled
Adequacy continuum:	Inadequate	Adequate	Perfectionistic

Empowerment Zone

	−	∗	+
Assertiveness continuum:	Acquiescent	Assertive	Domineering
Capability continuum:	Dependent	Capable	Stubbornly Independent
Empowerment continuum:	Powerless	Empowered	Omnipotent
Resilience continuum:	Vulnerable	Resilient	Invulnerable

Relationship Zone

	−	∗	+
Centeredness continuum:	Other-centered	Centered	Self-centered
Intimacy continuum:	Abandonment	Intimate	Avoidant
Self-definition continuum:	Undefined	Defined	Aggrandizing
Trust continuum:	Distrusting	Trusting	Naive

31

SCHEMA FLIPPING: OUR MULTIPLE SELVES

Elaine, a thirty-four-year-old high school drama teacher, displayed an abundance of both positive and negative maladaptive schemas throughout her life, sometimes flipping from one schema to another on the same continuum like a clock pendulum swinging back and forth. She was an attractive child and received endless compliments for her appearance from friends and relatives. Her father, whom she most wanted to please, rarely gave her attention. He was too busy struggling to get ahead and make a living. The family barely scraped by during her formative years. Later, her father's efforts paid off and they acquired significant wealth. Elaine acquired the *Unworthy⁻* schema because of her relationship with her father and the family's lack of income. Due to the attention she received for her strikingly good looks, she came to believe she was *Irresistible⁺*.

These schemas caused Elaine to go from one relationship to another, because she craved attention to make up for her sense of unworthiness. Elaine flipped from a schema of *Unworthy⁻* to the opposite schema of *Entitled⁺* after her family became wealthy and as men deluged her with attention. Elaine left each relationship whenever the attention she received started to wane to the slightest degree, which offended her *Entitled⁺* schema. But she never left her current partner until she found someone else, because she felt that any attention was better than none.

Elaine repeated this cyclical pattern for years, going from one man to the next. Something surprising happened when she reached her thirty-first year. Right in the middle of an exciting new relationship, Larry dumped her. No one had ever dumped Elaine. She was stunned. The opposite schemas of *Irresistible⁺* and *Entitled⁺* were suddenly activated: *Undesirable⁻* and *Unworthy⁻*. The depression associated with her *Undesirable⁻* and *Unworthy⁻* schemas finally provided the impetus for her to go into therapy. After a year of therapy focused on her schema-related difficulties, Elaine finally developed a stable relationship that resulted in marriage. She no longer craved the intense attention and excitement of serial relationships. Her therapy helped her develop stable adaptive schemas on those two continua, thus remarkably decreasing her schema flipping.

We also find it intriguing that when one schema on a given continuum becomes active (such as *Inadequate⁻*), any other schema on the same continuum (such as *Adequate** or *Perfectionistic⁺*) seems to submerge itself deeply below awareness. For example, a colleague that normally drives himself hard, achieves great success, and has considerable confidence in his abilities surprised himself by falling into a temporary state of utter inadequacy. A few months ago, he appeared on a panel of prestigious psychologists. Suddenly, he found himself believing he didn't belong in the same room with these other presenters, much less on a panel discussing cutting-edge ideas to a national convention. Although he performed well, it took him the better part of a day to regain his usual confidence.

Sometimes, minuscule events cause the flip from one schema possibility to another. Chaos theory suggests that small inputs can create large effects. So, too, with schemas. A mere raised eyebrow or a sideways glance from others can trigger a flip from one point on a schema continuum (like *Adequate**) to another (*Inadequate⁻*). That's what happened to our colleague. When one member of his panel looked at him with what he interpreted as disdain, he found his *Inadequate⁻* schema spewing self-doubt.

Would you say our colleague is confident or lacking in confidence? We believe both to be true. When our colleague finds himself lacking in confidence, all knowledge concerning his true talents remains distantly out of reach, as though it never existed. When a schema on a given continuum (such as *Inadequate⁻*) activates, it's almost as though your mind is reading information about you from a single-topic CD-ROM disk. Other information concerning your actual adequacy remains on another disk, inaccessible and invisible. Once you eventually activate the other disc (*Perfectionistic⁺* or *Adequate**), it may seem odd that you ever felt especially inadequate. Consistent with this analogy, psychologist Henry Ellis has demonstrated in numerous experiments that people recall information that is consistent with their mood more easily than information that is discordant with that state. In other words, when we feel happy, we remember the good times; when we feel sad, the bad times are all we can recall.

So thinking affects emotions, and emotions affect thinking. If you have a strong emotional reaction in a particular schema domain, the strength of your emotions alone can cause you to think in a more simplistic, even childlike style. Reason and clarity do not abound when emotions peak. Think of the last time you experienced inordinate anger or anxiety. Could you use your best problem-solving skills? Could you effectively listen to new input or ideas? Were you able to reflect calmly and weigh all the options available? Most people cannot. At such times, most of us respond as though we have only two extreme options. So perhaps opposites do attract (just as schema polarities wrap back onto themselves).

Within our Schema Polarity Model, consistency and inconsistency coexist. People can possess multiple schemas on any given continuum, although only one is usually active at a time, while the others remain dormant. Once a schema activates, a person will act consistently within the confines of that particular schema. However, flipping between schemas on the same continuum happens often, as the seeming inconsistencies in the examples above suggest. Evidence now supports the idea that we all have "multiple possibilities." We all engage in schema flipping. Perhaps the so-called multiple personality disorder doesn't lie as far outside the normal sphere as we used to think.

Multiple possibilities exist in the animal world as well. For example, we can cause a complete reversal of complex patterns of male and female sexual behavior in many species simply by administering the hormones of the opposite sex. It seems unlikely that the hormones themselves carry information concerning such complex behavior patterns. Rather, both possibilities probably exist within the animals' repertoire, with the hormones only serving as the trigger for switching from one pattern (or schema) to another.

Of course, human sexual patterning remains complex and controversial. However, humans demonstrate equally interesting and dramatic switches from one mode or schema to another. A quiet, passive person might suddenly commit mass murder. Under certain circumstances, one person may exhibit altruism but at other times a blatant disregard for humanity. Another may feel emotionally deprived and undeserving, yet flip into a state of rageful entitlement when needs are left unmet. You'll find more of these examples throughout the book. They simply represent the multiple possibilities within all of us.

Do these ideas strike you as a bit disturbing? Perhaps they should. It means that people aren't always what they seem. How sublimely simple it would be to count on someone's character, like money in the bank. A nice, linear, cleanly categorized world would be more predictable and easier to navigate. But when you assume that people and things are consistent, you'll make more than your share of mistakes. Searching for and accepting the multiple possibilities in everyone will save you grief in the long run.

Jerome discovered this lesson the hard way. He always fell in love at the drop of a hat. All a woman had to do was show affection and a little adoration. Time and time again he found himself disillusioned and bitterly disappointed. Sometimes he found himself singed by a woman's startling shift into another persona. His last relationship illustrated this problem well. Tricia initially threw herself at him—behavior he always sought in a woman. He ignored Tricia's abysmal history with men—she always searched for new affairs within a few months of starting a relationship. She admitted all of this to Jerome but said that he was completely different, that she would never do something similar to him. Her constant affection and adoration soothed any concerns that began to creep into his consciousness. Tricia presented a perfect picture.

We suppose you won't be shocked to learn that she played out her typical scenario with him. Four months after she moved in with him, she started an affair with his best friend. What you may not realize is that Tricia was indeed sincere in the beginning. She actually wanted Jerome to be the one for her forever. But her schema of *Entitled*⁺ caused her to crave someone new and more adoring when the initial passion showed the slightest sign of fading. Jerome found himself once again burned because he only looked at the surface presentation rather than what might have lurked underneath. Neither he nor Tricia had been truly aware of her "multiple possibilities."

CONCLUSION

At this point, we have provided the essentials of the Schema Polarity Model. We explained what schemas are and how they work. Then we showed you why we see them as opposites that aren't as different as they appear. Realizing that people possess schemas at multiple places along a given continuum may have shaken up your view of yourself and others. That's OK. We'll show you what to make of all that as we go along.

We belong to a small but rapidly growing group of professionals trying to apply nonlinear principles to psychological issues. We believe that the schema theory begs for a nonlinear approach based on polarities. Understanding this fact subtly but sharply clarified our ability to understand our clients, ourselves, and even many of life's enigmas and paradoxes. Once we started using these notions, we found it hard to stop thinking about them.

Our Schema Polarity Model has been surprisingly helpful in our work with clients. They seem to understand themselves better, are more open to changes, and more easily accept and even appreciate their remaining flaws and foibles. The focus on schemas represents a new development in psychotherapy, and our idea of construing them as opposite polarities with an intriguing relationship between the extremes is even more recent. You can use the model to identify the vexing issues in your life more quickly. These are the schemas that repeatedly prevent you from feeling content, hopeful, and secure about yourself. They may drag you down, dissolve your joie de vivre, block you from getting what you want out of life, and make it difficult if not impossible to reach your potential.

Now you are ready for a journey of discovery—of your schemas, both adaptive and maladaptive, and their origins. Insight alone isn't sufficient to generate meaningful change most of the time. But it helps and it sets the stage for change. In the next three chapters, you will discover your own multiple possibilities and identify both your helpful and hurtful schemas in the three zones: Self-Worth, Empowerment, and Relationships.

3

Self-Assessment in the Self-Worth Zone

If you don't understand yourself
you don't understand anybody else.
—*Nikki Giovanni*, A Dialogue

Understanding the Self-Worth Zone is a key component in developing a new life plan, because feeling good about yourself is fundamental to everything. If you have poor self-esteem, you probably struggle to feel empowered (the Empowerment Zone) and your relationships (the Relationship Zone) likely suffer as well. Like the circles shown below, the three zones overlap and interact with each other.

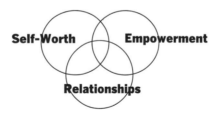

We recommend that you shore up your problems in the Self-Worth Zone first, because improving your self-esteem will help you deal with the other two zones. To do that, you must understand where your problems in this area lie. The purpose of this chapter is to help you learn about your schemas in the Self-Worth Zone.

Recognizing your schemas is not always easy. Many are formed in the preverbal stage of life when we have not developed a capacity to label or tag our feelings. These early impressions are what we call "feeling-dominated" schemas—emotionally triggered sensations experienced in reaction to events. By learning to stay with discomfort when it arises and by carefully considering what you are reacting to, you will likely find the basis for your feelings. You may even be able to attach images from childhood to your feelings to account for their origins.

For example, you may notice you often get a queasy feeling in your stomach and a sensation of pressure in your chest whenever you encounter a group of people. You may recall times in childhood when you felt the same way, such as when other kids unmercifully made fun of your clothes, which were different from what others wore. This connection may help you realize how you formed and maintained the *Undesirable⁻* schema. Once you link all of this information together, you will know where to direct your efforts to change. Your task will be to learn ways to appreciate your desirability, whether you look a little different or not.

It takes careful examination of each schema to know whether it truly applies to you. Feelings and bodily sensations are a part of this examination. You may think you don't have the schema of *Entitled⁺*, but how do you feel and how does your body react when your needs are ignored? Does rage start to simmer? Perhaps you feel tightness in your chest and your teeth clench. Reflect on these sensations. It's often useful to "sit with them" for a while. Study what they are telling you about your reactions to such schema-relevant events. The feelings may help you see that your body is acting as if you believe in the schema, whether you *think* you do or not. Indeed, tapping into your feelings will make it much easier for you to recognize the schemas that you hold. We often try to ignore such information; when we do, it makes change difficult.

Awareness is the first step in learning to change your schemas.

Each of the three schema zones contains four schema continua. Every continuum ranges from a negative maladaptive schema (−) to an adaptive schema (∗) to a positive maladaptive schema (+). For each continuum, we have provided a definition for each schema along with a few quotes we have collected from clients, friends, and colleagues. The quotes only typify someone who has the schema in question; agreement with any one quote does not prove that you have that schema. The statements could have been made in a context that would not suggest the schema's general existence. For example, if you were waiting for the results of an important medical test, the statement "I'm worrying every second something is wrong with my heart" might mean something very different than if you had those thoughts while waiting for a bus.

Read the descriptions of each schema continuum within the Self-Worth Zone. Next to each of the three schemas along a continuum, record the number that fits you. Before you decide whether you agree with the schema definition, reflect on how you feel, behave, and react in situations that relate to the schema. If the schema definition rarely applies to you; choose 0; 4 indicates that you believe the schema almost always describes you.

For every schema you record as three or four, pencil in examples of how that schema has affected your life. You may have many maladaptive schemas or only a few powerful ones. Perhaps you will find that all three schemas (negative maladaptive, adaptive, and positive maladaptive) on a given continuum describe you fairly often. Don't worry—there is a reason for this vacillation, as we will explain later.

Once you have identified your maladaptive schemas, it may seem as though they represent perfectly reasonable reactions to how the world treats you. You might even think that any other interpretation of things is laughable. We'll show you why that idea doesn't hold water. Later, we'll help you design a personal change plan.

DIRECTIONS:

Consider how the following schemas have an impact on your life. After reading each definition, record the number (0–4) that best describes your feelings. Then calculate your scores to identify the schemas that strongly influence your life. The quotations below each schema definition typify someone who has the schema in question; however, do not use them in selecting your number. Use only the schema definition.

SELF-WORTH ZONE
Acceptance Schema Continuum

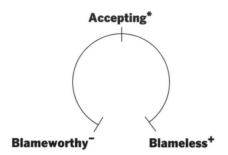

Accepting*

Blameworthy⁻   **Blameless⁺**

(–) Blameworthy: I feel I often deserve punishment or harsh criticism. I tend to be excessively critical or punitive of myself when I make mistakes.

"When I make the slightest mistake at home, work, relationship, etc., it bothers me to the point that it interrupts my sleep, thoughts, etc. I have been told by many I am too critical of myself and that I can be my own worst enemy."

"If I have to do something (like go to traffic court), the judge suddenly makes me feel like I'm eight years old again when I melted the crayons on the carpet!"

0	1	2	3	4	Score
Almost Never Describes Me	Occasionally Describes Me	Sometimes Describes Me	Usually Describes Me	Almost Always Describes Me	

Examples of your own

_____

_____

_____

(∗) *Accepting:* I realize that, as a human being, I am going to make mistakes. I can accept responsibility for my mistakes and I can apologize comfortably to others. Although I may choose to try to change, I do not make myself feel overly guilty.

"I never obsess about it when I make a mistake. I may not like it, but I think of mistakes as an opportunity to learn."

"I appreciate myself and everyone else better because we all make mistakes. If we didn't, we would all be a bunch of computers."

0	1	2	3	4	Score
Almost Never Describes Me	Occasionally Describes Me	Sometimes Describes Me	Usually Describes Me	Almost Always Describes Me	

Examples of your own

_____

_____

_____

(+) *Blameless:* I feel I have to be right. It is hard for me to admit I am wrong or that I have made a mistake. It is hard for me to say I am sorry.

"The simple fact of the matter is I usually am right, and it annoys me when others try to suggest otherwise."

"When people criticize me, I get very upset because it's usually completely unjustified."

0	1	2	3	4	Score
Almost Never Describes Me	Occasionally Describes Me	Sometimes Describes Me	Usually Describes Me	Almost Always Describes Me	

Examples of your own

_____

_____

_____

SELF-WORTH ZONE
Desirability Schema Continuum

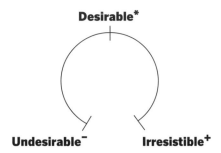

Desirable*

Undesirable‾   **Irresistible+**

(−) *Undesirable:* I feel I am in some way outwardly undesirable to others, either because I am unattractive, poor in social skills, boring, or have other flaws that are visible to people.

"Whenever I walk into a room, I feel others are looking at me and judging me poorly in some way."

"I'm told I am not, but I really believe I'm boring."

0	1	2	3	4	Score
Almost Never Describes Me	Occasionally Describes Me	Sometimes Describes Me	Usually Describes Me	Almost Always Describes Me	

Examples of your own

_____

_____

_____

(*) *Desirable:* **I am comfortable with my looks, social skills, and other visible characteristics.**

"I enjoy meeting new people and feel at ease with them. I don't really think much about how others are looking at me."

"I know there are more attractive people in the world, but I think I look just fine."

0	1	2	3	4	Score
Almost Never Describes Me	Occasionally Describes Me	Sometimes Describes Me	Usually Describes Me	Almost Always Describes Me	

Examples of your own

_____

_____

_____

(+) *Irresistible:* **I believe I am highly desirable to others in terms of looks, social skills, or other visible characteristics.**

"My greatest pleasure is being told how good I look."

"I turn heads everywhere I go, and I like it."

0	1	2	3	4	Score
Almost Never Describes Me	Occasionally Describes Me	Sometimes Describes Me	Usually Describes Me	Almost Always Describes Me	

Examples of your own

_____

_____

_____

SELF-WORTH ZONE
Worthiness Schema Continuum

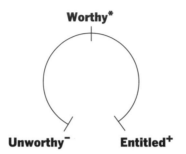

Worthy*

Unworthy⁻   Entitled⁺

(−) *Unworthy:* I feel I do not deserve attention, concern, or consideration from others or deserve to have my needs met. If, on occasion, I believe I deserve it, I still do not expect that my needs will be met. I feel there is something about me or my background that is defective or inferior.

"Even though I know I am worthy of something, I don't feel I deserve whatever it is."

"I don't really expect my wife to show me a lot of affection. I realize she grew up with a difficult background."

0	1	2	3	4	Score
Almost Never Describes Me	Occasionally Describes Me	Sometimes Describes Me	Usually Describes Me	Almost Always Describes Me	

Examples of your own

_____

_____

_____

(*) *Worthy:* I feel I am worthy of having my needs met but not at unnecessary expense to other people. I feel I am as good as anyone else.

"I really enjoy having my partner doing things for me and I like to reciprocate."

"I have done pretty well in life and I think I deserve it, but it has been because of hard work, not because I am something special."

0	1	2	3	4	Score
Almost Never Describes Me	Occasionally Describes Me	Sometimes Describes Me	Usually Describes Me	Almost Always Describes Me	

Examples of your own

_____

_____

_____

(+) *Entitled:* I feel I should have whatever I want. Sometimes I don't think about whether my wants are reasonable or what they would cost others. Sometimes others think I walk over them. Nothing less than the best is good enough for me. I feel there is something about me or my background that is superior to others.

"My father told me I could have whatever I want, and I believe it."

"I couldn't believe my best friend wouldn't lend me her china, linens, silver, and furniture for my party. It was a big event."

0	1	2	3	4	Score
Almost Never Describes Me	Occasionally Describes Me	Sometimes Describes Me	Usually Describes Me	Almost Always Describes Me	

Examples of your own

_____

_____

_____

S E L F - W O R T H   Z O N E
Adequacy Schema Continuum

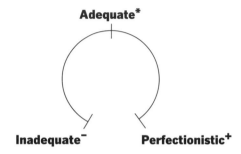

Adequate*

Inadequate⁻   Perfectionistic⁺

(–) *Inadequate:* I feel I have failed or am inadequate compared with my peers in areas of achievement such as school, career, sports, or other activities. I often believe I do not have the intelligence, talent, or abilities to succeed.

"I feel I have failed in that my marriage didn't last and there are always times I doubt I am capable of raising my three kids."

"I feel I lack skills in my sales position and that everyone can do better than me. I want to appear very professional, but I just don't see myself that way."

0	1	2	3	4	Score
Almost Never Describes Me	Occasionally Describes Me	Sometimes Describes Me	Usually Describes Me	Almost Always Describes Me	

Examples of your own

_____

_____

_____

(*) *Adequate:* I am adequate and feel good about myself regardless of my accomplishments.

"I have been fairly successful in life, but it surely isn't what makes me happy."

"Having a good relationship is more important to me than reaching the top of the corporate ladder."

0	1	2	3	4	Score
Almost Never Describes Me	Occasionally Describes Me	Sometimes Describes Me	Usually Describes Me	Almost Always Describes Me	

Examples of your own

_____

_____

_____

(+) *Perfectionistic:* I tend to pursue high standards and expectations relentlessly in the areas of achievement, recognition, status, money, or any activity in which I am involved. This pursuit is often at the expense of happiness, health, pleasure, and relationships.

"I strive so hard for perfection that people at work are always hoping I'll make an error."

"Sure, I work a sixty-five-hour workweek, but there is no way around it. My family just has to realize that."

0	1	2	3	4	Score
Almost Never Describes Me	Occasionally Describes Me	Sometimes Describes Me	Usually Describes Me	Almost Always Describes Me	

Examples of your own

_____

_____

_____

Sylvia's Score Sheet: The Self-Worth Zone

Negative Maladaptive Schemas (−)	Adaptive Schemas (*)	Positive Maladaptive Schemas (+)
2 Blameworthy	4* Accepting	0 Blameless
(4) Undesirable	0 Desirable	0 Irresistible
1 Unworthy	3* Worthy	1 Entitled
1 Inadequate	3* Adequate	0 Perfectionistic

What do these scores tell us about Sylvia? First, Sylvia clearly has several strengths. She has a strong *Accepting** schema; that is, when she makes mistakes, she usually forgives herself. You might be wondering how someone can be self-accepting with such a strong *Undesirable⁻* schema. Remember, you need to pay attention to our definitions of each schema, not just the label. The definition of the *Accepting** schema focuses on the issue of mistakes. It refers to your capacity to forgive yourself when your performance does not meet your expectations. Occasionally, Sylvia feels blameworthy when she strays from her eating and exercise routine, but in most instances she accepts her fallibility.

Sylvia also has a strong sense that she is *Worthy** (score of 3). She feels good about who she is and believes she is as worthy of respect as anyone else. But when she "falls off the wagon" on her exercise or dietary regimens, she feels a little *Unworthy⁻* of positive regard. Likewise, when she has been excessively conscientious about these regimens, she feels just a bit self-indulgent (*Entitled⁺*).

Sylvia has a powerful *Adequate** schema (score of 3). She feels good about her roles as a wife and mother and her active participation in church and community activities. She is a dependable person and a good leader, but she is just as willing to be a group member. She does not need a lot of recognition to feel good about herself; she is well liked and likes herself. Yet, in spite of her strong *Adequate** schema, Sylvia's weaker *Inadequate⁻* schema kicks in on occasion. For example, she sometimes feels that other women view her with contempt because she is unemployed. But Sylvia was a successful legal secretary before the first of her three children was born. She and her husband always planned that, if they could afford it, she would stay home full-time with the kids. She feels good about

50

that decision and loves devoting herself to her husband, the kids, and the various activities that she finds worthwhile. She knows that eventually she will return to the workplace, but she is doing what she wants in this stage of her life. Not bringing in a paycheck means having fewer luxuries, but neither Sylvia nor her husband view that as a loss compared with all the benefits the family derive from this arrangement.

Sylvia's motivation to invest so much of her life in exercise waned after she married and had children. She still runs for an hour three or four times a week, but her weight remains the same: okay for the doctor, not okay for her. Sylvia has never thought about what her obsession with her appearance has cost her over the years, so she agrees to do a cost-benefit analysis of her *Undesirable⁻* schema.

A *cost-benefit analysis* is exactly what it sounds like. Sylvia lists all of the advantages and disadvantages of the *Undesirable⁻* schema, both past and present. Yes, maladaptive schemas do have benefits, at least on the surface and sometimes in practice. The purpose of a cost-benefit analysis is to see if the current benefits outweigh the costs. Unless the costs are substantial, you will not be motivated to try to change a maladaptive schema. A thorough, honest evaluation is therefore necessary. It does not matter what your friends or even your psychologist thinks. If you do not believe that the costs significantly exceed the benefits, trying to change that particular schema will be a waste of effort on your part.

Sylvia's Cost-Benefit Analysis: *Undesirable⁻*

Benefits
My exercise and dieting have kept me healthy. I'm seldom sick. My cholesterol is always under 200.

I learned how to apply makeup and dress well to compensate for my body. People often compliment me on my appearance. I like compliments, but I rarely believe them.

Costs
In the past I spent a lot of money on various weight loss programs and different exercise gimmicks. Even if I did lose some weight, the weight always came back . . . but my money never did.

I think about what I should or shouldn't eat all day long. When I fix cookies or cake for the family, I struggle to avoid having any. When I do eat a dessert, I beat myself up for it the next day. My family loves to eat out, but up until the moment we leave, I worry about whether I will eat too much.

51

My mood every morning is affected by how much I weigh. If I weigh a pound less than normal, I am cheerful. If I weigh the same, I am sad. If I weigh more, I am crabby. My husband, Jack, has threatened to throw out the scales. Since he insisted that I come for therapy, I have noticed that my depressed moods are almost always the result of my thoughts about my appearance.

My oldest daughter, who is eight, is becoming very weight-conscious and her weight is normal. This has happened even though I have never criticized her. I do not want to do to her what my mother did to me. But I know my obsession with my appearance will influence all three of my kids destructively. I do not want any of them to become anorexics or bulimics. I need to stop this.

Because I am unhappy with my body, I do not feel sexy. This has created a lot of friction between Jack and me. Jack says he finds me very desirable, but I think he says that to not hurt my feelings. He says it hurts his feelings that his opinion doesn't matter. Well, his opinion does matter, but I just don't believe him. My sexuality has been badly damaged by my negative view of my body. Jack said he is often afraid to approach me sexually because I usually go into a long lament about how undesirable I am.

I think Jack is about to give up on me. This obsession has almost damaged our relationship beyond repair. He has always been devoted to me, and I have taken that for granted because I have been so absorbed in my appearance.

Sylvia is stunned that she can only find two benefits to this obsession about her desirability, but she is even more struck by the costs to herself and her family. She expresses anger at herself for not being able to change. She says she does not want to continue to be the source of such unhappiness for her husband or their kids. She does not want them to "walk around on eggshells" because she has gained a pound. She does not want to spoil happy occasions by whining about her weight and pouting through meals. Doing the cost-benefit analysis makes Sylvia realize that her focus on weight is draining the joy out of her life and the lives of those she loves.

Steven

Next, let's look at the self-worth zone scores for Steven, our forty-two-year-old physician.

Steven's Score Sheet: The Self-Worth Zone		
Negative Maladaptive Schemas (−)	**Adaptive Schemas (*)**	**Positive Maladaptive Schemas (+)**
__1__ Blameworthy	__2__ Accepting	__(3)__ Blameless
__2__ Undesirable	__2__ Desirable	__0__ Irresistible
__(3)__ Unworthy	__1__ Worthy	__0__ Entitled
__2__ Inadequate	__2__ Adequate	__(4)__ Perfectionistic

The Self-Worth Zone is difficult for Steven. His most severe schemas are *Perfectionistic*[+], *Unworthy*[−], and *Blameless*[+]. His ratings of 1 or 2 on all the adaptive schemas show that although he believes in his own worth, both his positive and negative maladaptive schemas can easily eclipse this belief.

Steven says his *Unworthy*[−] schema was worse when he was younger but decreased since he became a doctor. When not in his physician role, he feels uncomfortable around others. His "doctor" title is a fragile facade of status—it might convince others he is worthwhile but it hasn't convinced him. Steven notes that his moderate *Undesirable*[−] schema (score of 2) was even stronger before he could afford to dress well and drive an expensive car. Even with his high standard of living, he still worries about his appearance and about being out of place in social situations.

Steven rates his *Perfectionistic*[+] schema (score of 4) as the most severe. He believed he had to be perfect academically to earn a scholarship to college and then to medical school. Academics were his highway out of poverty and shame. The endless hours he put in as a student and then as a resident continued with his practice. He remains extremely conscientious about his work and admits his fear that if he makes a mistake, he will be sued for malpractice. Any damage to his professional reputation would destroy him emotionally, because he feels his only legitimate worth derives from his role as a doctor. When he makes a rather rare mistake, he feels inadequate, temporarily losing all confidence in his medical skills. Steven's perfectionism even extends to his family. He becomes upset when his children don't do their best in academics or other activities. Both his wife and kids have accused him of being unrelenting in his expectations of them. They have even said they could not be as "perfect" as he is.

Steven also describes his *Blameless*[+] schema (score of 3) as a source of stress for himself and others. It is very hard for him to admit mistakes, and he compulsively avoids making any. He realizes he is quick to fault others in order to avoid being blamed. Both his family and his staff are tense in his presence, and he knows that comes from their fear of his harsh criticism.

In spite of Steven's unrelenting perfectionist efforts over the last forty-two years, his deep sense of worth remains impaired. As he describes his past and reviews his schemas, he breaks down and cries. He says he feels as if he has been struggling against despair forever. He is exhausted at having to be perfect. He just can't do it anymore.

Let's look at Steven's cost-benefit analysis of his *Perfectionistic*[+] schema.

Steven's Cost-Benefit Analysis: *Perfectionistic*[+]

Benefits
I don't make many mistakes.

I am admired by others.

I have a high standard of living. My kids will never know the shame and poverty that I did.

I get great feedback for what I do.

Costs
I had very little fun in high school or college because I was always so obsessed with studying. I still never relax. I am so exhausted on vacations, I sleep much of the time. I do not know how to do anything except work.

I have no close friends. Friends take time away from my work, but then I often feel lonely. But I also have the fear that if someone gets to know me well, they will know that I am not perfect and think less of me.

I cannot relax or get my mind off my work. When I am not on call, I sometimes drink too much to relax.

The pressure I feel is unrelenting. It makes me irritable and short-tempered. I say things angrily that I regret later.

I never sleep well. I clench my teeth all night long.

I beat myself up mercilessly when I do make a mistake, even over little things.

My kids never confide in me, for fear I'll be disappointed in them. My wife feels the same way. Sometimes I think they dread having me come home. And I don't blame them. Good grief! I don't like myself either. I am miserable being this way.

Reviewing the costs and benefits of his *Perfectionistic*[+] schema is an emotional experience for Steven. He sobs as he acknowledges that the costs are staggering—pressure, exhaustion, misery, and the alienation of his family—but Steven even questions the validity of some of the benefits. He says that his perfectionism sometimes does not prevent mistakes, because the pressure reduces his efficiency and causes occasional lapses in judgment. Although many people admire him, he knows that some resent his perfectionism and are quietly delighted when he makes a mistake. Steven admits that the great feeling he gets from being "perfect" never lasts very long. It is like a "fix" for a drug habit. As for his income, he never has time to enjoy his beautiful home or to drive his expensive car except to work. He hesitates to take time off from work for fear that something will go wrong. He always needs to stay in control to make certain things run perfectly.

The costs for Steven have been excessive. Yet some of the benefits are real: His perfectionism helped him out of poverty and earned him a respectable professional status. These benefits certainly were not insignificant. But they have been expensive. Seeing the costs, Steven feels ready to make a change. Whenever his motivation to change wanes, however, Steven reviews his cost-benefit list. He carries the list in his wallet to remind himself of how much he has sacrificed to be "perfect." It has been too much.

Lynn

What can we learn from Lynn's self-worth zone scores?

55

Lynn's Score Sheet: The Self-Worth Zone

Negative Maladaptive Schemas (−)	Adaptive Schemas (*)	Positive Maladaptive Schemas (+)
_0_ Blameworthy	_2_ Accepting	(3) Blameless
_0_ Undesirable	_2_ Desirable	(3) Irresistible
_0_ Unworthy	_1_ Worthy	(4) Entitled
_1_ Inadequate	_1_ Adequate	(3) Perfectionistic

Lynn has only modestly developed adaptive schemas on all four continua in the Self-Worth Zone. Unfortunately, she also has strong positive maladaptive schemas on those same continua. Although she can sometimes forgive her own mistakes, she has a very hard time acknowledging that she makes any mistakes in the first place. Seldom do the words *I'm sorry* or *my fault* pass her lips. Lynn is also proud of her looks, to the point that she thinks many men find her irresistible. And many men do—at least for a while. Lynn admits to being a perfectionist about her work and her appearance, and she is proud of that trait. Lynn describes herself as "a high-maintenance woman" and enjoys the attention her efforts produce. Since Lynn does not seem to have much insight into her impact on other people, we ask her to do a cost-benefit analysis of her *Entitled⁺* schema.

Lynn's Cost-Benefit Analysis: *Entitled⁺*

Benefits
If you expect the best, you get it. Life is too short to settle for less. That says it all.

Costs
Other people often are jealous of me. Women envy my looks. They exclude me from conversations. At work some of my co-workers think I got my promotions by playing up to my supervisors, but that's ludicrous. I got the promotions because I was better than they were. I deserved them. But their comments hurt.

56

I don't have any really close friends. I don't get along well with women. I think most other women feel inadequate around me, because I am more competent and sexier.

Some of my boyfriends have said that they can't meet my expectations. I don't understand that. My expectations are not unreasonable. More than one has complained that they cannot "afford" me. Well, I guess they couldn't.

Nobody seems to be able to live up to my expectations.

As you can see, Lynn has little insight into her impact on other people or much apparent compassion. Her absence of insight is even more glaring in the Relationship Zone. Before Lynn will be willing to make an effort at changing, she will first have to understand that her current positive maladaptive schemas are hurting her. At this point, she is not convinced that the problem originates with her maladaptive schemas. All the costs Lynn lists do not outweigh the one benefit she attributes to her *Entitled*⁺ schema. Lynn still believes the problem lies with other people. She does not need to change; others must change to accommodate her. Lynn's *Entitled*⁺ schema is firmly entrenched, unswayed by her cost-benefit analysis.

COST-BENEFIT ANALYSES: HOW MUCH PAIN DO THESE RASCALS PRODUCE?

A cost-benefit analysis can illuminate the pain that your maladaptive schemas produce. This realization can be a powerful incentive for you to change. But commitment to change is difficult to maintain, and without that commitment, change will not happen. Before you can benefit from the suggestions for change in this book, you will have to make a commitment to the process.

You must take two initial steps before you can make a commitment to change a schema. The first step is awareness. To gain this awareness, you must honestly face up to what your schemas are about. You have already taken that first step in identifying your schemas in the Self-Worth Zone earlier in this chapter. We also think it will be helpful if you ask one or two close friends or family members to review the schema list to see if they view you differently. If they disagree with your list, this does not mean that they are right. But they may have noticed something that you have overlooked about yourself. A word of caution: Do not share your list unless you can accept a different viewpoint from your own. That is, if you think you will be hurt or angry with them if they see you differently than you see yourself, you may not be ready for this exercise or you may not have anyone in your life right now that you trust enough to do this exercise in a con-structive way.

The second step is a thorough cost-benefit analysis of your maladaptive schemas. You have already seen the cost-benefit analyses that Sylvia, Steven, and Lynn did. You saw how each maladaptive schema had advantages and disadvan-tages for the person with that schema. An accurate cost-benefit analysis will determine whether change is needed. If you have a maladaptive schema that is mildly annoying, you will be unlikely to want to invest the time and energy to change. And that makes sense. We all have a few maladaptive schemas that are similar to a scratchy seam on the inside of a shirt that we occasionally wear. Irritating but tolerable. But if you left several sharp pins in the shirt when you unwrapped it, every time you put it on, it will draw blood. You cannot wear it without experiencing pain. When a schema cost-benefit analysis reveals substan-tial pain or disruption in your life, then you need to consider if you can make a commitment to change that schema. We will discuss commitment further in a later chapter. But we hope you can see how important your cost-benefit analysis will be in determining whether change is worthwhile.

CONCLUSION

Now you know something about the Self-Worth Zone and what, if any, schemas are disrupting your sense of well-being. You may also be starting to realize that troubles with self-worth can spill over into problems with your relationships and your sense of empowerment. Each life zone overlaps with the others. Sylvia, Lynn, and Steven all experience considerable relationship difficulties because of the severity of their self-esteem problems. In their misguided attempts to shore up their fragile sense of self-worth, they have managed to drive away their partners.

You can stop the self-destructive cycle of maladaptive schemas. But first, you must assess what they are costing you. None of us would maintain problem-atic schemas if we didn't believe in some way that they protected us from nega-tive outcomes or that they helped us obtain something positive. An objective, hard-nosed cost-benefit analysis will help you see that the few benefits that your maladaptive schemas bring are not worth the pain. You will need to come to that realization in order to have the motivation to change. You may have to remind yourself frequently of the results of your cost-benefit analysis to stay on the path of self-improvement. Only then will you stop getting the opposite of what you really want. Following are some exercises that we suggest you try as a prelude to changing your schemas.

UNDERSTANDING YOUR SCHEMAS
IN THE SELF-WORTH ZONE

1. Appreciating Your Adaptive Schemas

You have already identified all of your schemas in the Self-Worth Zone. Now make a list of the adaptive schemas that you think you have. Describe how they have been helpful to you.

An example of Sylvia's response to this exercise appears below:

Adaptive Schema	Ways in Which This Schema Has Been Helpful
*Accepting**	I am not overly hard on myself when I make mistakes.
	I am willing to try new things.
	I am not overly critical of my family or other people.

Adaptive Schema	Ways in Which This Schema Has Been Helpful
_____	_____
_____	_____
_____	_____
_____	_____

2. How New Adaptive Schemas Would Be Helpful

You may not hold all or any of the adaptive schemas in the Self-Worth Zone. This exercise is to help you see how having those adaptive schemas would be beneficial to you. List each adaptive schema from the Self-Worth Zone that you rated as 0 or 1. Describe how you would benefit if you had them. Lynn's response to this exercise follows:

New Adaptive Schema	Ways in Which This Schema Would Be Helpful
Worthy[*]	I wouldn't make outrageous demands of my boyfriends anymore.

I wouldn't spend so much money, and I could start saving. |

New Adaptive Schema	Ways in Which This Schema Would Be Helpful
_____	_____
_____	_____
_____	_____
_____	_____

3. Schema Cost-Benefit Analysis

Now it is time for you to do a cost-benefit analysis of each of your maladaptive schemas in the Self-Worth Zone. List each maladaptive schema from the Self-Worth Zone that you rated as a 3 or 4. Then list the advantages and disadvantages of that schema. Reviewing the cost-benefit analyses of Sylvia, Steven, and Lynn may be helpful.

Maladaptive Schema	Costs	Benefits
_____	_____	_____
_____	_____	_____
_____	_____	_____
_____	_____	_____
_____	_____	_____
_____	_____	_____

4. Schema Diary

Before you begin to change a schema, you need to know what impact the schema has on your life. The easiest way to discover this is to keep a schema diary. Start a schema diary now. You will need this information for the schema-change chapters ahead. If you record your schema examples each day at some regular time, you will have half a dozen examples of your schema in a short time. You will need that many examples to analyze a maladaptive schema. For your convenience, we have included a schema diary in Appendix B. Please turn there now and write down at least one example of your maladaptive schema. If you skip the diary now, you still will need to do it before you can apply the schema-change procedures. You can do it now or you can do it later, but as Nike would say, "Just do it."

4

Self-Assessment in the Empowerment Zone

It is a strange desire, to seek power, and to lose liberty;
or to seek power over others, and to lose power over a man's self.
—*Francis Bacon, "Of Great Place,"* Essays

Empowerment represents the second major area you must learn to balance in order to achieve what you want from life. Once again, you will find that too little or too much in this area can wreak havoc with life satisfaction. As with the Self-Worth Zone, problems in the Empowerment Zone can sow seeds of disharmony in the other two zones. For example, if you feel powerless to control the events in your life, your self-worth will be negatively affected (Self-Worth Zone) and you may feel taken advantage of by others, including loved ones, which may ultimately unravel the fabric of your relationships (Relationship Zone). On the flip side, an excessive sense of control and power can also damage your relationships by causing you to run over those who are important to you.

It's time to learn how empowered you are. We have listed the four schema continua of the Empowerment Zone, each of which includes a negative maladaptive schema (−), an adaptive schema (*), and a positive maladaptive schema (+). We have provided you with a definition of each of the three types of schemas along the continuum, along with a few quotations we have collected from clients, friends, and colleagues. And again, we have presented the quotations as examples of things that someone who has the schema in question might say. You should not use these comments to determine whether the schema applies to you; instead, use the definition of each schema in making that decision.

Remember that you must also carefully examine each schema to know if it fits. Use your feelings, sensations, and actions to make this determination. For example, you might think that the *Domineering*⁺ schema does not apply to you. In fact, you might believe it is objectionable for anyone to dominate others. But how do you *feel and react* when others try to exert their will and desires over you? Do you respond with a calm firmness accompanied by a willingness to make a rea- sonable compromise? Or do you become enraged and vociferously argue for your position, viewing compromise as a defeat? If it's the latter, a *Domineering*⁺ schema may be controlling you.

Now, let's assess your schemas in the Empowerment Zone. Read the descriptions of each schema continuum within the Empowerment Zone. Once again, next to each of the three schemas along the continuum, record the number that best fits you. The number 0 suggests that the schema definition rarely, if ever, applies to you; 4 indicates that you believe the schema almost always describes you. For every schema you record as a 3 or 4, pencil in examples of how the schema has affected your life. Remember that it is possible for you to find that all three schemas on any given continuum describe you fairly often.

DIRECTIONS:

Consider how the following schemas have an impact on your life. After reading each definition, record the number (0–4) that best describes your feelings. Then calculate your scores to identify the schemas that strongly influence your life. The quotations below each schema definition typify someone who has the schema in question; however, do not use them in selecting your number. Use only the schema definition.

EMPOWERMENT ZONE
Assertiveness Schema Continuum

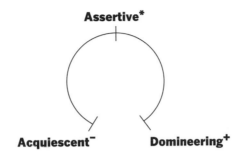

Assertive*

Acquiescent⁻   **Domineering⁺**

(–) *Acquiescent:* I tend to give in to others' preferences and decisions. I try to avoid conflict whenever I can.

"I find my thoughts turn to scrambled eggs whenever someone argues with me."

"I hate to rock the boat. I want to be liked."

0	**1**	**2**	**3**	**4**	**Score**
Almost Never Describes Me	Occasionally Describes Me	Sometimes Describes Me	Usually Describes Me	Almost Always Describes Me	

Examples of your own

_____

_____

_____

65

(*) _Assertive:_ My decisions and preferences are important, and I will express them readily. It is also important for me to listen to the decisions and preferences of others. I will work out compromises whenever possible. I will not let others walk over me and won't take advantage of them.

"I certainly know how to stand up for myself. I also don't like to take advantage of people."

"I look for win-win solutions to conflict."

0	1	2	3	4	Score
Almost Never Describes Me	Occasionally Describes Me	Sometimes Describes Me	Usually Describes Me	Almost Always Describes Me	

Examples of your own

_____

_____

_____

(+) _Domineering:_ I like to be in control. I am often critical of other people's decisions and preferences and can discount them easily. Basically, I like to have my own way.

"Compromise is for wimps."

"It's a dog-eat-dog world. Other people have to look out for themselves because I'm certainly not going to do it."

0	1	2	3	4	Score
Almost Never Describes Me	Occasionally Describes Me	Sometimes Describes Me	Usually Describes Me	Almost Always Describes Me	

Examples of your own

_____

_____

_____

EMPOWERMENT ZONE
Capability Schema Continuum

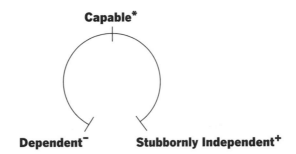

Capable*

Dependent⁻   **Stubbornly Independent⁺**

(–) *Dependent:* **I often feel incapable of handling everyday decisions and responsibilities. I usually seek help from others.**

"I can hardly imagine making a decision on something without checking it out with someone else."

"Without someone to depend on, I'd just shrivel up and die."

0	1	2	3	4	Score
Almost Never Describes Me	Occasionally Describes Me	Sometimes Describes Me	Usually Describes Me	Almost Always Describes Me	

Examples of your own

_____

_____

_____

(*) *Capable:* I believe I am capable of handling most everyday decisions and responsibilities. However, when I do need help, I don't hesitate to ask for it.

"I'm capable of making responsible decisions regarding my life. But on occasion I ask others for their opinions, just to consider all of the alternatives."

"I really enjoy taking on new things and learning new skills. I don't know everything, but that's OK too."

0	1	2	3	4	Score
Almost Never Describes Me	Occasionally Describes Me	Sometimes Describes Me	Usually Describes Me	Almost Always Describes Me	

Examples of your own

_____

_____

_____

(+) *Stubbornly Independent:* I believe I can handle almost anything. It is hard for me to ask for help. Sometimes I will even refuse appropriate and essential assistance.

"It's hard for me to ask for help because I don't want people to think I'm needy. I always want to be able to handle everything on my own."

"There is nothing I can't do myself. Other people just get in the way."

0	1	2	3	4	Score
Almost Never Describes Me	Occasionally Describes Me	Sometimes Describes Me	Usually Describes Me	Almost Always Describes Me	

Examples of your own

_____

_____

_____

EMPOWERMENT ZONE
Empowerment Schema Continuum

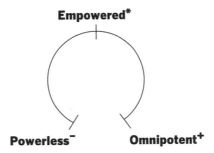

Empowered*

Powerless‾   **Omnipotent⁺**

(–) *Powerless:* I often feel I can do little to change things. Frequently, I feel overwhelmed by life's events and powerless to do much about them.

"I feel I am trapped in my marriage, powerless to do much about it."

"I just don't think there's much of anything I can do to make a difference in the way things come out in my life."

0	**1**	**2**	**3**	**4**	**Score**
Almost Never Describes Me	Occasionally Describes Me	Sometimes Describes Me	Usually Describes Me	Almost Always Describes Me	

Examples of your own

_____

_____

_____

69

(*) *Empowered:* **I believe there are many outcomes I can influence to one degree or another. At times, there are things I can't change and I can accept that.**

"Jobs are scary nowadays. The economy is changing, society is changing, and I don't know what will happen from week to week, day to day. And yet, somehow, I have the feeling I can find a way to make it."

"I know I can't change the world, but I can do my part to make a difference."

0	**1**	**2**	**3**	**4**	**Score**
Almost Never Describes Me	Occasionally Describes Me	Sometimes Describes Me	Usually Describes Me	Almost Always Describes Me	

Examples of your own

_____

_____

_____

(+): *Omnipotent:* **I believe I can make almost any situation come out the way I want it to.**

"I can make anything come out the way I want it to—my marriage, my job, arguments, any-thing."

"There is absolutely nothing I couldn't do, be, or become if I wanted to."

0	**1**	**2**	**3**	**4**	**Score**
Almost Never Describes Me	Occasionally Describes Me	Sometimes Describes Me	Usually Describes Me	Almost Always Describes Me	

Examples of your own

_____

_____

_____

EMPOWERMENT ZONE
Resilience Schema Continuum

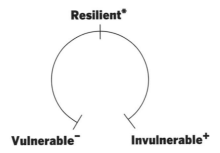

Resilient*

Vulnerable⁻   **Invulnerable⁺**

(−) *Vulnerable:* I often worry about terrible things happening to me or to those close to me.

"I guess it mainly is financial issues. I worry from week to week and pray that somebody doesn't get sick or hurt, because we can't afford it. Being in that position makes me sad and angry."

"Sometimes I really worry about the safety of my family, to the point of paranoia."

0	1	2	3	4	Score
Almost Never Describes Me	Occasionally Describes Me	Sometimes Describes Me	Usually Describes Me	Almost Always Describes Me	

Examples of your own

_____

_____

_____

(∗) *Resilient:* I recognize that harm and illness will occur at various points in my life, and I take reasonable precautions to prevent them. I also believe that when these things happen, I can bounce back.

"I work hard to keep myself in good health and do everything to protect myself and my family against harm. On the other hand, things happen. When they do, you just have to deal with them."

"The awareness of our own strength makes us modest." —Paul Cézanne, Letters

0	1	2	3	4	Score
Almost Never Describes Me	Occasionally Describes Me	Sometimes Describes Me	Usually Describes Me	Almost Always Describes Me	

Examples of your own

_____

_____

_____

(+) *Invulnerable:* I believe I am virtually immune to harm or illness. I don't worry about what I eat or exercise or about my personal safety. What other people think of as high-risk (hang gliding, parachuting, etc.), I find exhilarating.

"There is no greater thrill to me than taking a risk. Bungee jumping, rollerblading, hang gliding, you name it. I think it's all great!"

"I don't know why people worry about things like how much fat is in their food, how much they exercise, whatever. People are just paranoid about those things. I figure, fate is fate. What's going to happen to you is going to happen."

0	1	2	3	4	Score
Almost Never Describes Me	Occasionally Describes Me	Sometimes Describes Me	Usually Describes Me	Almost Always Describes Me	

Examples of your own

_____

_____

_____

Score Sheet: The Empowerment Zone

Negative Maladaptive Schemas (−)	Adaptive Schemas (*)	Positive Maladaptive Schemas (+)
_____ *Acquiescent*	_____ *Assertive*	_____ *Domineering*
_____ *Dependent*	_____ *Capable*	_____ *Stubbornly Independent*
_____ *Powerless*	_____ *Empowered*	_____*Omnipotent*
_____ *Vulnerable*	_____ *Resilient*	_____ *Invulnerable*

The above list reflects the four schema continua within the Empowerment Zone. Although these continua are laid out in a linear manner for convenience, remember that they are circular, as shown below. Both the negative maladaptive schemas (−) and positive maladaptive schemas (+) share more with each other than they do with adaptive schemas (*), because both extremes entail a pattern of rigid thinking that usually leads to negative consequences. We will show how destructive these negative consequences can be in examples to follow.

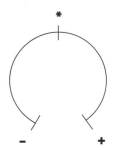

Circle any negative maladaptive or positive maladaptive schema that you recorded as a 3 or 4. These represent the areas you will want to target for change. Put an asterisk (*) by any adaptive schema you recorded as a 3 or 4. These represent your psychological strengths, so keep careful track of them as well.

SCHEMA FLIPPING

Remember that medium to high scores on more than one point on a continuum mean that you sometimes flip between schemas. For example, Tracy initially gives herself a score of 4 on *Acquiescent⁻*, a 0 for *Assertive**, and a 0 for *Domineering⁺*. From those scores you would assume that she habitually backs down from conflict, while exuding the demeanor of Milquetoast. She notes that this description fits most of the time. When we push Tracy to remember whether she ever acted differently, she admits that she exhibited bouts of uncontrollable rage with her parents whenever they wanted to discuss her spending. At such times, she yelled accusations, threatened to disown the family, and slammed the front door behind her. Thus, in most situations she backs down, but with her parents she feels safe to explode in rage. As a result of this exploration, Tracy changes her score for *Domineering*$^+$ to a 2 because this schema certainly applies to her "sometimes."

Only later does Tracy understand that her rage from the *Domineering*$^+$ schema is closely related to her score of 4 on *Acquiescent*$^-$. As long as she acts like a doormat, her anger increases until she reaches the breaking point, like a balloon too full of air. Only when she learns to be assertive will she be able to stop flipping from one end of the continuum to the other.

SCHEMA PORTRAITS

Now, let's take a look at the scores in the Empowerment Zone.

Jake

Fifty-two-year-old Jake who also flips from one end of a schema continuum to another.

Jake's Score Sheet: The Empowerment Zone

Negative Maladaptive Schemas (−)	Adaptive Schemas (*)	Positive Maladaptive Schemas (+)
_1_ Acquiescent	_4_* Assertive	_0_ Domineering
_0_ Dependent	_2_ Capable	_(4)_ Stubbornly Independent
_2_ Powerless	_3_* Empowered	_(3)_ Omnipotent
_(4)_ Vulnerable	_1_ Resilient	_(3)_ Invulnerable

Jake gives himself scores of 3 on *Empowered** and *Omnipotent*$^+$, 4 on *Stubbornly Independent*$^+$, and 3 on *Invulnerable*$^+$. For most of his life, Jake thought of himself as powerful, independent, and virtually immune to illness or health problems. He was proud of his body and excelled in sports in high school. He claimed he could perform more work than any two other plumbers in the company put together. His boss seemed to agree and often sent Jake by himself to handle even the most difficult job. Jake rarely feels the need to dominate anyone (he gives himself a 0 for *Domineering*[+]). So why does he give himself a score of 4 on *Vulnerable*[−]? That trait hardly seems to fit someone like Jake.

Jake always felt immune to life's hard knocks—until the day he sustained a herniated disk while trying to carry a huge section of pipe. It should be obvious why he didn't ask for help (he scores a 4 on *Stubbornly Independent*[+]) and why his *Invulnerable*[+] schema (on which he would have scored a 4 before the accident) influenced him to ignore preventive measures. After the injury, Jake found his *Invulnerable*[+] schema shattered. He struggled arduously to believe he would heal completely, fully regain his former strength and capabilities, and feel totally invulnerable again. Yet every ache and pain filled him with the fear that he would never be the man he had been in the past. For Jake, it was "all or nothing"; either he could do the work of two men or he had no value.

During his rehabilitation program, his occupational therapists puzzled over why Jake seemed to magnify and complain about his pain far more than most. They didn't know that every pain reminded Jake of his feared *Vulnerable*[−] schema. Jake's progress stalled until we helped him identify his troublesome schemas and plan the changes he needed to make in the future. And although Jake had to give up his job as a plumber, he nevertheless managed to recreate a satisfying life and job as a safety inspector for the city water department.

Sylvia

How does Sylvia, the housewife we met earlier, fare in the Empowerment Zone?

Sylvia's Score Sheet: The Empowerment Zone		
Negative **Maladaptive Schemas (−)**	**Adaptive** **Schemas (*)**	**Positive** **Maladaptive Schemas (+)**
(3) Acquiescent	2 Assertive	0 Domineering
2 Dependent	3[*] Capable	0 Stubbornly Independent
2 Powerless	3[*] Empowered	0 Omnipotent
0 Vulnerable	4[*] Resilient	0 Invulnerable

75

Sylvia shows strong adaptive schemas in the Empowerment Zone. She feels capable of handling most situations. However, she says her modest *Dependent⁻* schema (score of 2) really developed after she left her job. Although she and her husband make all of their financial decisions together and view their income as jointly earned, Sylvia still feels dependent on him for financial support. She has a strong sense of empowerment except when it comes to managing her weight, an area that seems to be the focus of her modest *Powerless⁻* schema (score of 2).

In the Empowerment Zone, Sylvia's only truly problematic schema is *Acquiescent⁻*, which appears a little stronger than her *Assertive** schema. Sylvia says that in the past, her *Acquiescent⁻* schema was much stronger than her *Assertive** schema, but she became much more assertive after working as a legal secretary. Initially, she was upset at how rude and intimidating other lawyers and even some clients could be. When her boss realized her distress, he taught her how to handle people assertively on the phone and in person. He even role-played different situations with her and gave her lots of praise for her progress. Today, she reports that she has slipped into increased acquiescence over the years since she left her job. Because this is her primary maladaptive schema in the Empowerment Zone, Sylvia does a cost-benefit analysis of her *Acquiescent⁻* schema.

Sylvia's Cost-Benefit Analysis: *Acquiescence⁻*

Benefits
Most everyone likes me, because I try to be agreeable.

People are rarely mad at me. I don't like conflict, so in disagreements I often give in.

Costs
I am overcommitted, because I can't say no. I am the one who drives the kids in the neighborhood to school, bakes the goodies for brownies and scouts, arranges the camping trips, and substitutes for the teacher's helper when other mothers don't show. I even end up providing free day care for several kids in the neighborhood whose moms work. While expressions of gratitude feel good, I am getting tired of this. Jack gets frustrated with me for not telling these other mothers no. He's right, too.

This is especially problematic with my mother when she and my dad visit. She criticizes me for baking occasional treats for the kids and Jack. She tries to discourage the kids from eating them. This annoys Jack as much as me, but he won't say anything if I don't since she's my mother. She also comments on the way I let the kids dress and, of course, on how I dress. I dread her visits. It is not by accident that we moved two thousand miles away after we got married.

Sylvia can see from her cost-benefit analysis that her Acquiescent⁻ schema is costing her family as much as it is costing her. She wants to work on increasing her assertiveness, and she feels optimistic that she can do it because of her previous experience with her boss.

Steven

Now let's review the Empowerment Zone scores for Steven, the forty-two-year-old physician described earlier.

Steven's Score Sheet: The Empowerment Zone

Negative Maladaptive Schemas (−)	Adaptive Schemas (*)	Positive Maladaptive Schemas (+)
_1_ Acquiescent	_2_ Assertive	_(3)_ Domineering
_1_ Dependent	_3*_ Capable	_2_ Stubbornly Independent
_1_ Powerless	_3*_ Empowered	_2_ Omnipotent
_(3)_ Vulnerable	_1_ Resilient	_0_ Invulnerable

Steven shows some strong adaptive schemas. He feels he can handle most situations he encounters (*Capable**, score of 3); yet, on occasion, it is hard for him to ask for help (*Stubbornly Independent⁺*, score of 2). He has a strong belief that he can influence most outcomes (*Empowered**, score of 3), especially in medicine. For instance, he knows he cannot make his patients follow his recommendations, but he feels most of them are compliant. At times, he feels that people owe him respect because he is a doctor and that being a doctor enables him to exert more influence over others (*Omnipotent*[*], score of 2). Yet when patients deteriorate in spite of his best efforts, he occasionally feels powerless. He also has felt powerless to change his perfectionism and his unyielding sense of unworthiness.

Steven has a strong *Domineering*[+] schema (score of 3). He is in charge in his office and with his patients, but he realizes that his domineering attitude extends to most other situations. He feels a need to be in control; yet in regard to hospital staff meetings, Steven sometimes acquiesces to the majority opinion because he dislikes conflict. He does not want to alienate his colleagues, so he always tries to accommodate their requests for the on-call schedule. This often causes friction at home, particularly when his family has to change their plans or go without him.

Steven's *Vulnerable*[−] schema (score of 3) is also quite powerful. In spite of his substantial wealth, he has never felt wealthy and always worries about finances. He has worried about money since he was a little boy. He worked odd jobs even then to give his mom some extra money. On more than one occasion, his family was evicted because they could not pay the rent. When his dad developed cirrhosis from his alcoholism, the family became dependent on state Medicaid. Steven often drove his dad to the county clinic for his medical visits, where some of the staff treated his father scornfully. Although his dad was an alcoholic, he was never unkind to Steven or his mom, and it hurt Steven deeply to see the way others treated his father.

Because of his large loans for medical school and private practice, Steven and his wife lived on a very tight budget until his third year of practice. Any unexpected expense always pushed them to the edge of financial disaster. He still feels that a huge malpractice suit could do the same thing, even though he has hefty malpractice insurance. Steven has also witnessed some of his patients' families having to declare bankruptcy due to medical catastrophes and nursing home expenses.

Now let's examine the cost-benefit analysis of Steven's *Vulnerable*[−] schema.

Steven's Cost-Benefit Analysis: *Vulnerable*[−]

Benefits
I am cautious with my money. I save most of it.

I know how devastating illnesses can be to people, so I exercise and eat a low-fat diet.

I don't take chances. I have seen the losers in the emergency room. I know that money buys better medical care, so I have excellent insurance coverage even though it is expensive.

Costs

I feel guilty whenever I spend money on nonessential things, which destroys the joy of giving or getting nice presents.

I am so worried about avoiding future disasters that I don't enjoy today.

I can't sleep until I hear the kids come home. They claim that I am overprotective, and I am, but I just can't help it. That generates a lot of arguments between them and me. They think I am just being mean.

I worry so much about one of my family members' becoming ill that I don't enjoy them now.

I feel guilty whenever I stray from my diet or exercise routine. It impossible for me to just have fun.

As with any strong schema, there must be benefits, or it would have disappeared long ago. Steven's *Vulnerable⁻* schema has made him a cautious, responsible man, but also a very worried one. In truth, he does not enjoy anything. What he does have—a family, good health, and a sound retirement plan—he worries about losing. His wife and he have frequent arguments about what she sees as his miserliness. And she and the kids complain frequently that he has no sense of fun. Steven realizes that if he does not change this schema, he will consume his whole life worrying, because he could never have enough savings or good enough health to protect him from every conceivable disaster. No one does. He knows he has to change this schema, and he wants to change it, but he is terrified at the prospect of changing. He has found over time that reviewing his cost-benefit analysis helps calm his fears.

Lynn

Lynn, the marketing analyst you first met in Chapter 1, has schema scores on the Empowerment Zone that might surprise you.

Lynn's Score Sheet: The Empowerment Zone

Negative Maladaptive Schemas (−)	Adaptive Schemas (*)	Positive Maladaptive Schemas (+)
_1_ Acquiescent	_2_ Assertive	(3) Domineering
(4) Dependent	_2_ Capable	_0_ Stubbornly Independent
(3) Powerless	_2_ Empowered	_2_ Omnipotent
(3) Vulnerable	_2_ Resilient	_0_ Invulnerable

How can she have a strong *Domineering*[+] schema (score of 3) along with powerful *Dependent*[−], *Vulnerable*[−], and *Powerless*[−] schemas? A glimpse at her past may answer that question. Lynn was five years old when her father left. She never saw him again. Her mother was devastated and so was Lynn. Her dad showered her with affection and laughter. She does not remember that her parents ever fought. Then one day, he just disappeared, and with him went the attention she enjoyed and needed. Her mother was so overwhelmed by the task of supporting them financially and coping with her own loss that she became emotionally unavailable. Lynn became her mother's comforter. After a short time, Lynn and her mother moved into a garage apartment, where they lived until her mother remarried a year later. Her stepfather supported them well financially, but he was a stern, domineering man. When Lynn cried in protest, her mother scolded her for not appreciating what he had done for them and reminded Lynn of how dreadful life above the garage had been. Her mother's mantra became "A family cannot survive without a man."

Lynn does not believe she can survive on her own, in spite of the fact that she has supported herself for the past eight years and, at times, has provided for her boyfriends as well. She desperately believes she needs a husband to take care of her; yet none of her relationships last. She feels powerless to secure a long-term relationship. Her modest *Empowered** schema (score of 2) reflects how successful she has been in her work and in making situations turn out the way she wants. She has been so successful that, on rare occasions, she actually feels omnipotent. But her stronger *Powerless*[−] schema reflects her lack of success in relationships. In spite of her strong *Dependent*[−] and *Powerless*[−] schemas, Lynn readily admits that she has a strong *Domineering*⁺ schema: "I've had to be in charge ever since my dad left. No one else watched out for me. I am always the stronger one, the responsible one. Other people even ask me to take charge, and then they complain that I am too domineering." Lynn admits that she also feels safer being in control, because she sees the world as dangerous and unpredictable—just as it had been for that little girl whose world was turned upside down the day her dad disappeared. You can see how Lynn's negative maladaptive *Vulnerable*⁻ and *Powerless*⁻ schemas have fueled her *Domineering*⁺ schema.

Since Lynn's *Dependent*⁻ schema is so strong, she does a cost-benefit analysis of it.

Lynn's Cost-Benefit Analysis: *Dependent*⁻

Benefits
If I can depend on someone, then I am not alone.

Other people take care of me when I act dependent. I can't handle a lot of things.

When things don't work out, then someone else can help me. I won't feel so overwhelmed.

Life is not as scary when I am able to depend on others.

Life is easier if someone else handles things.

When things don't work out, it's not my fault.

Costs
When I depend on others, they get annoyed. I have been criticized for acting like a little girl instead of an adult.

Some of my co-workers have felt that I used their help to get ahead.

I also have been criticized for acting helpless to get other people to do my work.

People resent spending time trying to help me figure out a problem when I don't follow their advice.

When I have depended on others too much, things have often not worked out as well as if I had just tried to handle the situation on my own.

If I want a promotion, I have to change this. Being too dependent and not having enough self-confidence were criticisms on my last evaluation.

I have gotten into every relationship with the expectation that I could depend on my boyfriend, and inevitably they end up depending on me.

Lynn can see how damaging her *Dependent⁻* schema has been. People have felt used by her and lost respect for her. Lynn also respects herself less when she acts help-less. Now, her future goal to be division vice president is threatened: "Even though I have been successful, I actually believe it is because other people have helped me. I really do have doubts about my own ability to handle a lot of things. In new situations, I often panic, even if I don't show it. I ask for other people's opinions, because I think they'll have better ideas than I have. But most of the time, my own ideas are better, so then I only tick them off when I don't take their advice."

Lynn's *Dependent⁻* schema has played a part in every relationship she has had. She shares her mother's mantra "A family cannot survive without a man." But when she was dependent in past relationships, the situation backfired. For instance, Lynn and one boyfriend pooled their money, and she let him handle their financial matters. That fiasco brought her close to bankruptcy and back to separate accounts. Although intellectually Lynn can see that her dependency in relationships has been counterproductive, she acknowledges that emotionally she still believes she needs to depend on others.

The Empowerment Zone can inflict its share of damage, can't it? Sylvia, Steven, and Lynn all suffer under the burden of their positive and negative mal-adaptive schemas. And they remain helpless to do anything about it until they begin to understand where change needs to occur in their lives.

THE EMPOWERMENT COST-BENEFIT ANALYSIS

The cost-benefit analysis for the Empowerment Zone can be challenging. When it comes to the negative maladaptive schemas (*Acquiescent⁻*, *Dependent⁻*, *Powerless⁻*, and *Vulnerable⁻*), our clients sometimes object by saying, "But there are no benefits to my negative maladaptive schemas. All I want to do is get rid of them. How could they be beneficial?" Trust us, there are ways in which they at least seem to be useful. For example, Sylvia believes that the benefit of her *Acquiescent⁻* schema is that people like her better than her more assertive friends. So ask yourself, From what negative consequences do your maladaptive schemas seemingly protect you?

Our clients usually have the opposite objection when analyzing their positive maladaptive schemas. At first, they can't believe that these schemas actually cause harm and misery to themselves or others. *Stubbornly Independent⁺*, *Domineering⁺*, *Omnipotent⁺*, and *Invulnerable⁺* schemas, for example, are seductive and provide the illusion that they can convey great power and protection from harm. The illusion crumbles under the scrutiny of a cost-benefit analysis.

To illustrate, let's start with Jake's cost-benefit analysis of his *Stubbornly Independent⁺* schema. In this case, Jake easily thinks of advantages for this schema. It takes him longer to come up with disadvantages, but once he gets started, the disadvantages come to mind easily.

Jake's Cost-Benefit Analysis: *Stubbornly Independent⁺*

Benefits
I can feel more like a man.

My boss sees me as important.

I do a better job than anyone I would ask help from.

I never have to look stupid asking for help.

Only wimps ask for help, and I am no wimp.

My life could go a lot easier if I could learn to ask for help as easily as I give it to others.

Costs
I injured myself trying to do the work of two people. This thing could ruin my health.

Sometimes I have spent lots of unnecessary time trying to figure something out when someone else could have helped.

Sometimes I look more stupid not asking for help.

> My wife gets really mad at me when I won't ask for directions or get help when I need it.
>
> My wife thinks I don't ask for help because I am insecure, and maybe she is right.

Once Jake gets over his initial mental logjam, he finds that his costs column add up quickly. He is struck by how much his *Stubbornly Independent*⁺ schema extracts from his life. In reviewing both lists, he also concludes that the so-called benefits of his *Stubbornly Independent*⁺ schema seem insignificant after he starts to sift through it. For example, he realizes that even if his boss did see him as more important, that is not worth the cost to his health. He also finds that his wife sees him as less of a man when he fails to ask for help and thinks he looks stupid, if not ridiculous, when he stubbornly perseveres on a project that is obviously way over his head. Jake begins to see flaws in his old criteria for "manliness" and understands that being a man has nothing to do with being excessively independent.

HOW IS YOUR SELF-ASSESSMENT COMING ALONG?

Now you have reviewed two of the three zones, Self-Worth and Empowerment. How is your self-assessment coming along? Have you found yourself overwhelmed with maladaptive schemas? Or have you found yourself unable to discern any trouble spots in these zones?

If you are beset with numerous maladaptive schemas, remember that schemas are not based on a mental disease model. A schema is based on something quite different—an information-processing model. Rather than assuming people act and feel the way they do because of mental illness or disease, the schema information-processing model proposes that we form schemas as a way of making sense out of our life experiences. The brain's primary task is to perceive, interpret, and organize information. A well-functioning brain automatically creates schemas from our experiences. Maladaptive schemas simply represent a normal reaction to abnormal life experiences. Schemas are formed by what we experience. You have already begun to see how Sylvia, Steven, and Lynn formed maladaptive schemas from their experiences. None of them has a mental disease. Of course, there are biological processes and diseases that affect brain functioning. Psychosis, schizophrenia, bipolar disorders, and some types of depressions are examples of problems that have biochemical bases. But even people with these biological disorders form schemas.

So what does it mean if you discovered numerous maladaptive schemas or almost none at all? After reviewing her problematic schemas in all three zones, Carla lamented, "I have almost all the negative maladaptive schemas and a few of the positive maladaptive schemas to boot. What's wrong with me? Am I hopeless?" If you are feeling as down as Carla, it's important to stop berating yourself. It is not unusual to discover several problematic schemas, and it certainly does not make you hopeless. It does mean you have a lot of work to do. Fortunately, when you successfully tackle a few maladaptive schemas, others also will begin to change, because schemas overlap and interact with each other. It's basically a chain reaction, like the way a pebble thrown into a pond will cause ripples to emanate from the center.

Carla also complained, "If I have this many maladaptive schemas, I must really be one sick puppy." We take exception to terms such as *sick* and *mental case*. They come from the old mental illness or disease model that we find troublesome and logically flawed for most of the problems our clients experience. You don't need the burden of pejorative labels that add nothing to the understanding of your problems. Everyone has schemas and everyone has at least a few maladaptive schemas. Perfect people do not exist.

Ron represents the other extreme from Carla. He can't find a single maladaptive schema in the Empowerment and Self-Worth Zones. (Most people will find one or two trouble spots after completing the first two schema questionnaires.) Some people with a preponderance of positive maladaptive schemas tend to be overly defensive, have a hard time acknowledging any negative data about themselves, and strive to be "on top." Ron does not want to admit that anything about himself is maladaptive. He has only come to therapy because his wife has delivered an ultimatum: "Come into marital therapy with me or I will divorce you! I have already gotten an attorney, and I mean it. If therapy doesn't work for us, our marriage is history." He is certain that he can convince the psychologist that his wife has all the problems and that she just needs to be "fixed."

Ron is wrong. His desperate attempts to maintain his flawless self-image are obvious. When he starts to respond to the schema self-assessment, he can't bring himself to acknowledge the presence of his destructive positive maladaptive schemas. Then he is pushed to think hard about situations relevant to each schema continuum. For example, he is asked to think about how he felt each time his wife disagrees with him about an important issue. Does he respond with calmness or with righteous indignation and counterattacking (suggestive of a *Domineering*[+] schema)? Does he ever say he is wrong or apologize in disagreements with his wife (suggestive of a *Blameless*[+] schema)? It doesn't take too many questions for Ron to realize (with some shock, we might add) that he has quite a few positive maladaptive schemas. His wife is equally shocked. In all their married life, she has never heard him acknowledge a personal problem or flaw.

Once he begins, Ron is able to admit to other problems. He is unhappy, tense, and insomniac. His high blood pressure is also probably related to his positive maladaptive schemas. Ron's marital therapy is a true success story. His wife gives him more support than he has imagined possible as he lets his guard down. She feels closer and more loving toward him. And he is able to give her support because he no longer needs to keep himself on top of an imagined hierarchy.

An honest self-assessment is essential. Too much or too little self-criticism will lead you astray. The goal is to acknowledge your trouble spots while avoiding self-blame and punitiveness. Only then will you be ready to move ahead.

After you have completed a cost-benefit analysis of your schemas in the Empowerment Zone, you will have finished two-thirds of your self-assessment. You may find that your maladaptive schemas have cost you dearly. We believe that neither type of maladaptive schema ever pays off in the long run. You would be better off putting money on the odds of winning a million dollars in a state lottery than getting a positive payoff from your maladaptive schemas. The benefits look real, but they always prove to be an illusion.

CONCLUSION

Now you have learned about both your strengths and weaknesses in the Empowerment Zone. And you probably continue to see how the zones interact with each other. If you have excessive problems in the Empowerment Zone, it is hard to imagine how those would not affect your self-esteem or relationships. You truly can stop your self-destructive cycles in this zone. But the first step is to conduct your cost-benefit analysis. That will give you the motivation to change. Once you feel motivated, we will provide you with many ideas for changing your problematic schemas. Following are a few exercises to start preparing you to change your schemas.

UNDERSTANDING YOUR SCHEMAS
IN THE EMPOWERMENT ZONE

1. Appreciating Your Adaptive Schemas

You have already identified all of your schemas in the Empowerment Zone. Now make a list of your adaptive schemas in this zone. Describe how they have been helpful to you. Steven's response to this exercise appears below:

Adaptive Schema	Ways in Which This Schema Has Been Helpful
Capable*	I usually feel I can handle any of life's problems.
	I rarely feel unable to make a decision in a crisis.

Adaptive Schema	Ways in Which This Schema Has Been Helpful
_____	_____
_____	_____
_____	_____
_____	_____

2. How New Adaptive Schemas Would Be Helpful

You may not hold all or any of the adaptive schemas in the Empowerment Zone. This exercise is to help you see how having those adaptive schemas would be beneficial to you. List each adaptive schema from the Empowerment Zone that you rated as 0 or 1. Describe how you would benefit if you had those schemas. Jake fills out this exercise in the following manner:

New Adaptive Schema	Ways in Which This Schema Would Be Helpful
Resilient*	I would quit worrying about having to be Superman.
	I would work to take care of my health, but not panic over every ache and pain.

87

New Adaptive Schema	Ways in Which This Schema Would Be Helpful
_____	_____
_____	_____
_____	_____
_____	_____

3. Schema Cost-Benefit Analysis

Now it is time for you to do a cost-benefit analysis of each of the maladaptive schemas in the Empowerment Zone that you rated as a 3 or 4. List those maladaptive schemas. Then list the advantages and disadvantages you have experienced from that schema. Reviewing the cost-benefit analyses of Sylvia, Steven, and Lynn may be helpful.

Maladaptive Schema	Costs	Benefits
_____	_____	_____
_____	_____	_____
_____	_____	_____
_____	_____	_____
_____	_____	_____
_____	_____	_____

4. Schema Diary

Before you can begin to change a schema, you need to know what impact it is having on your life. The easiest way to do this is to begin a schema diary. Start keeping a schema diary now, so you will have the information you need for the schema-change chapters. For your convenience, we have included a schema diary in Appendix B.

5

Self-Assessment in the Relationship Zone

*It is only when we no longer compulsively need someone
that we can have a real relationship with them.*
—*Anthony Storr*, The Integrity of the Personality

How many self-help books on relationships are there? A bunch! Relationships can be our primary source of joy at times and, at other times, the bane of our existence. Gender wars. Marital conflict. Divorce. These terms are littered throughout magazines, newspapers, and general conversation like weeds that will not die. With divorce rates hovering around 50 percent, we must be doing something wrong. But what could that be? Some of us work harder at this part of our lives than at anything else and still find ourselves alone. As one relationship after another fails, we remain totally perplexed about the cause.

We cannot overemphasize the importance of the Relationship Zone. Study after study has shown that it isn't money, the kind of house you live in, or the model of car you drive that determines your sense of well-being. It's the quality of your relationships. Although it is largely true that you have to learn to be happy by yourself before you can be happy with anyone else, most people report that their greatest source of satisfaction stems from their relationships with their partner, family, and friends.

If you are thinking that maladaptive schemas are the root of most problems and conflicts in relationships—bingo, you're right. Relationship battles usually represent unintentional schema wars rather than deliberate assaults on each other (we'll discuss schema wars later in this chapter). Maladaptive schemas represent people's "hot buttons," and all of us can push them easily and unintentionally. In this chapter, we'll show you how this works and what to do about it. But first, let's explore the problematic schemas that may plague you in the Relationship Zone. Then we'll show you how they operate behind the scenes.

As we have said repeatedly, awareness is the first step. You have to know where to aim your efforts if you want to change something about yourself. We have listed the four schema continua of the Relationship Zone, each of which includes a negative maladaptive schema (–), an adaptive schema (*), and a positive maladaptive schema (+). Definitions for each of the three schemas along the continuum appear, along with more quotes collected from clients, friends, and colleagues. Remember, you should not use these quotes to determine whether the schema applies to you; instead, use the *definition* of each schema to make that decision.

Remember, also, to examine your feelings, actions, and sensations carefully to see if the schema fits. For example, you might *think* that the schema of *Self-Centeredness*+ does not apply to you. You might *think* of yourself as someone who cares about others. But how do you feel and react when someone asks for your help? Do you find yourself bristling with a sense of resentment when someone wants you to donate your scarce free time? Do you feel put out? Do you only respond because you know you might look selfish to others if you don't? If so, that's a pretty good indicator of the *Self-Centered*+ schema. Now, let's assess your schemas in the Relationship Zone.

DIRECTIONS:

Consider how the following schemas have an impact on your life. After reading each definition, record the number (0–4) that best describes your feelings. Then calculate your scores to identify the schemas that strongly influence your life. The quotations below each schema definition typify someone who has the schema in question; however, do not use them in selecting your number. Use only the schema definition.

RELATIONSHIP ZONE
Centeredness Schema Continuum

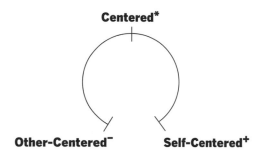

Centered*

Other-Centered⁻   **Self-Centered⁺**

(−) *Other-Centered:* **I focus very much on meeting the needs of others, even at the expense of my own needs and preferences. I might, at times, resent those in my care. I am far more likely to take the perspective of other people than to consider my own. When others are upset, I think it is up to me to do something about it.**

"As a single mother, I don't have any time to devote to myself."

"With my cultural upbringing, I was taught to be a martyr—someone who takes care of others, a superwoman. As a young mom and full-time employee, I would stay up until all hours baking, making doll clothes, etc., so my children could have everything their friends with non-working moms had."

0	1	2	3	4	Score
Almost Never Describes Me	Occasionally Describes Me	Sometimes Describes Me	Usually Describes Me	Almost Always Describes Me	

Examples of your own

_____

_____

_____

(*) *Centered:* I take responsibility for meeting my own needs. However, I am considerate of the needs of others. I can empathize and care about others without necessarily taking responsibility for or taking care of them.

"If I am not for myself who will be? If I am only for myself, what am I? If not now, when?"
—Rabbi Hillel

"People used to take advantage of me, but I have learned it costs too much. I don't want to step on them, but I'm not going to allow that to continue."

0	**1**	**2**	**3**	**4**	**Score**
Almost Never Describes Me	Occasionally Describes Me	Sometimes Describes Me	Usually Describes Me	Almost Always Describes Me	

Examples of your own

_____

_____

_____

(+) *Self-Centered:* I believe my own perspective is sufficient for understanding. I don't worry a lot about how other people look at things. People can take care of themselves. I don't have to worry about their needs.

"I have enough to take care of with myself. Other people can take care of themselves and that's that!"

"I'm really puzzled when my partner gets upset with me. I have no idea why he thinks the way he does."

0	**1**	**2**	**3**	**4**	**Score**
Almost Never Describes Me	Occasionally Describes Me	Sometimes Describes Me	Usually Describes Me	Almost Always Describes Me	

Examples of your own

_____

_____

_____

RELATIONSHIP ZONE
Intimacy Schema Continuum

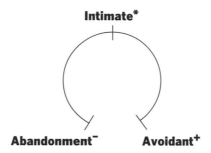

Intimate*

Abandonment⁻   Avoidant⁺

(–) *Abandonment:* **I worry a lot about losing a person or persons close to me. I am afraid they will leave or be taken away from me through death or other circumstances. I need a great deal of emotional reassurance to feel secure. Reassurance never seems to last. I sometimes test the emotional commitment of others in ways that are not necessarily constructive. I am very sensitive to rejection.**

"I worry all the time that my therapist is not really interested in me. When he goes on vacation, I am sure that he'll return and tell me he can no longer work with me."

"I can't figure out why my wife stays with me. I know she'll leave eventually. Sometimes I find myself acting the worst I possibly can just to see if she'll put up with it."

0	1	2	3	4	Score
Almost Never Describes Me	Occasionally Describes Me	Sometimes Describes Me	Usually Describes Me	Almost Always Describes Me	

Examples of your own

_____

_____

_____

(*) *Intimate:* I enjoy and feel comfortable getting emotionally close to some people. I realize it would be very painful to lose those people, but I don't spend a lot of time worrying about that possibility, because I know I could cope.

"I enjoy getting to know the inner thoughts and feelings of my partner and my best friends."

"Sometimes it is hard, but I like to open up the vulnerable parts of me with people. I usually find they are amazingly accepting."

0	1	2	3	4	Score
Almost Never Describes Me	Occasionally Describes Me	Sometimes Describes Me	Usually Describes Me	Almost Always Describes Me	

Examples of your own

_____

_____

_____

(+) *Avoidant:* I don't feel the need to become emotionally involved. I generally keep people at a distance.

"Frankly, I just don't need anybody. I'm self-sufficient and closeness seems foreign to me."

"My life is plenty complete by itself. I don't need anyone else to make it better."

0	1	2	3	4	Score
Almost Never Describes Me	Occasionally Describes Me	Sometimes Describes Me	Usually Describes Me	Almost Always Describes Me	

Examples of your own

_____

_____

_____

RELATIONSHIP ZONE
Self-Definition Schema Continuum

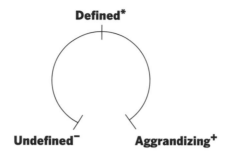

Defined*

Undefined⁻   **Aggrandizing⁺**

(–) *Undefined:* I don't have a strong sense of who I am. I define myself in terms of the people who are close to me (that is, my partner or my children). I tend to adopt their beliefs, attitudes, and identities. When I have no one else close to me, I often feel empty.

"I guess I tend to identify with whomever I am close to at the time. I need them to find my own strength."

"Sometimes I've been called a chameleon. Maybe I even feel that way. I find my opinions and thoughts on things change, depending on whomever I'm around."

0	1	2	3	4	Score
Almost Never Describes Me	Occasionally Describes Me	Sometimes Describes Me	Usually Describes Me	Almost Always Describes Me	

Examples of your own

_____

_____

_____

(*) *Defined:* I have a clear sense of who I am. I am aware of my purpose, attitudes, beliefs, and values. However, I don't expect those close to me always to agree with my beliefs. People who love me are free to disagree with me within reasonable limits.

"I know where I am headed in life, and I know my identity. I have a career and goals. I am close to my husband, and I know who I am, separately from him."

"I identify myself with my work. I also identify myself with my partner and my children. And yet, at the same time, I have a sense of who I am separate from all of these things."

0	1	2	3	4	Score
Almost Never Describes Me	Occasionally Describes Me	Sometimes Describes Me	Usually Describes Me	Almost Always Describes Me	

Examples of your own

_____

_____

_____

(+) *Aggrandizing:* I know who I am. I have such a strong sense of identity and purpose that others often adopt my beliefs, attitudes, and values. Those close to me generally look up to me, sometimes to the point of adoration.

"My ideas are important. I am important. I expect others to recognize that fact."

"It is hard for me to deal with somebody if they aren't looking up to me."

0	1	2	3	4	Score
Almost Never Describes Me	Occasionally Describes Me	Sometimes Describes Me	Usually Describes Me	Almost Always Describes Me	

Examples of your own

_____

_____

_____

RELATIONSHIP ZONE
Trust Schema Continuum

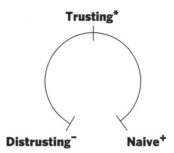

Trusting*

Distrusting⁻   **Naive⁺**

(−) *Distrusting:* **I do not trust other people's motives. I often believe that other people intentionally hurt, abuse, cheat, lie, manipulate, or take unfair advantage of me.**

"I think my past hurts have made me more cautious than I should be."

"I think basically other people are out to get you. You have to be really careful to keep yourself from getting cheated or abused."

0	**1**	**2**	**3**	**4**	**Score**
Almost Never Describes Me	Occasionally Describes Me	Sometimes Describes Me	Usually Describes Me	Almost Always Describes Me	

Examples of your own

_____

_____

_____

(*) *Trusting:* **I generally trust people, unless they give me a reason not to. However, I do show reasonable caution, which has prevented me from being taken advantage of very often.**

"I think I have a great group of employees. I am not going to spy on them. On the other hand, I am not going to overlook indiscretions either."

"Look, I trust my wife. She's given me no reason not to. She thinks I'm wonderful and she lets me know it all the time. Why should I be jealous if she has lunch with a male colleague or has a few casual male friends?"

0	1	2	3	4	Score
Almost Never Describes Me	Occasionally Describes Me	Sometimes Describes Me	Usually Describes Me	Almost Always Describes Me	

Examples of your own

_____

_____

_____

(+) *Naive:* **I believe most everyone can be trusted. I don't believe there is a need to question other people's motives. Sometimes I don't even take reasonable precautions to protect myself in relationships.**

"I believe that everyone has a good side and should be given a chance. I trust just about anybody."

"Sure, I know my husband has been out late, sometimes until 2:00 or 3:00 in the morning. And yeah, his reasons have seemed pretty strange. But I can't imagine he would fool around on me, even if we have been having a lot of problems the last year or two."

0	1	2	3	4	Score
Almost Never Describes Me	Occasionally Describes Me	Sometimes Describes Me	Usually Describes Me	Almost Always Describes Me	

Examples of your own

_____

_____

_____

Score Sheet: The Relationship Zone

Negative Maladaptive Schemas (−)	Adaptive Schemas (*)	Positive Maladaptive Schemas (+)
_____ *Other-Centered*	_____ *Centered*	_____ *Self-Centered*
_____ *Abandonment*	_____ *Intimate*	_____ *Avoidant*
_____ *Undefined*	_____ *Defined*	_____*Aggrandizing*
_____ *Distrusting*	_____ *Trusting*	_____ *Naive*

Once again, circle the 3's and 4's on any negative maladaptive schema or positive maladaptive schema that you recorded above. These are your trouble spots. Put an asterisk (*) by any adaptive schema you recorded as a 3 or 4. These describe your psychological strengths. Don't forget about those. Your scores should help you see if you have maladaptive schemas in this zone. Don't let the linear layout of the score sheet deceive you. Remember, as shown below, we consider the negative and positive maladaptive schemas to be much closer to each other than they are to the adaptive schemas:

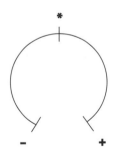

You might wonder how the *Abandonment⁻* schema could be more similar to the *Avoidant⁺* schema than to the *Intimate** schema. Here's an example of two people with opposite schemas that experienced the essentially same outcome. Cathy possessed an intense *Abandonment⁻* schema. She wanted to keep a relationship with a man desperately, and she held on as tightly as she knew how. She watched vigilantly for any hint that her newfound love might stray and she rarely let him out of her sight. The guy eventually began to "choke" from the constant togetherness and surveillance and felt compelled to leave.

Ryan sounds completely different than Cathy at first. He was a forty-four-year-old electrical engineer who complained of loneliness yet avoided committed relationships. The *Avoidant*[+] schema was a core issue for Ryan. As a child, he had learned to keep a distance from his mother, who constantly criticized him. As an adult, he assumed that the way to deal with women was to maintain a wide berth. He admitted that he thought women were great to hang out with or have sex with but that they overwhelmed him in a relationship.

Ryan and Cathy possessed two totally opposite schemas (*Abandonment*[−] and *Avoidant*[+]), yet they acquired the same result over and over again: estrangement and loneliness. The intensity of both Ron and Cathy's "opposite" maladaptive schemas inevitably caused negative and surprisingly similar outcomes.

So what did your self-analysis tell you about your relationships? If you scored well on the adaptive schemas, congratulations! That may indicate that you have good, satisfying relationships with your partner, family, and friends. If you gave yourself higher scores on the maladaptive schemas, then you need to make a choice; you can strengthen your adaptive schemas so that you can develop good relationships with others, or you can continue as you have been.

SCHEMA FLIPPING

Once again, high scores on more than one schema on any specific continuum reflect a tendency to flip between beliefs. Let's look at Theresa, a twenty-nine-year-old customer service agent for the phone company, as an example of someone who has flipped between negative and positive maladaptive schemas with unwanted results.

Theresa's Score Sheet: The Relationship Zone

Negative Maladaptive Schemas (−)	Adaptive Schemas (*)	Positive Maladaptive Schemas (+)
(4) Other-Centered	1 Centered	(3) Self-Centered
(4) Abandonment	2 Intimate	(3) Avoidant
(4) Undefined	1 Defined	0 Aggrandizing
(3) Distrusting	2 Trusting	1 Naive

These scores tell us a lot about Theresa. Her most troublesome schema is not easily apparent from the raw numbers alone. But, after she has talked with us in therapy, it becomes clear that the *Undefined⁻* schema has controlled her life like a gun held to her head. Theresa has no clue who she is outside of a relationship. Her additional negative maladaptive schemas, *Abandonment⁻* and *Other-Centered⁻*, support her *Undefined⁻* schema by keeping her focused on others rather than developing her own needs. Thus, she clings to each new relationship, doing anything to please her partner, anything at all. If he asks where she wants to go to dinner, she inevitably replies: "Wherever you want, dear." And she takes the same approach with *everything*—movies, sports, opinions about politics, etc.—whatever he says, she agrees. Her boyfriends often find this behavior pleasing at first. They feel flattered as she pours on the attention, compliments, and adoration. They feel special when she tells them how much she thinks of them, and they revel in her agreement with their ideas. They believe it when she says how smart they are and how much she respects everything about them.

Yet, inevitably, a disquieting feeling slowly unfolds. After a while, they feel bored with her constant fawning agreement. They start to crave someone with whom they can *really* talk about ideas. They want a relationship, not just a mirrored reflection of themselves. Thus, Theresa continually finds herself alone, dazed and wondering what she has done wrong. After all, she has given the man everything she imagined he wanted. But one thing has been missing—*herself*—because she doesn't really know who she is.

Theresa has rarely expressed her own opinions and actually has few she could even call her own. Through therapy, however, Theresa gradually constructs a sense of herself. Outside of therapy, she works on developing her own interests, opinions, ideas, and tastes. You might think someone as undefined as Theresa sounds implausible. Surely everyone knows what they like and don't like, right? Actually, many of our clients have sometimes paid little attention to their own development in the quest for a relationship with another. Some people misguidedly believe that they can adopt someone else's life as their own and that a relationship, any relationship, can quell all of their life's misery and pain.

As Theresa makes progress with her *Undefined⁻* schema, she sometimes finds herself flipping between the extremes on one or the other continua. Initially, she is unaware that she possesses any needs or wants or her own, indicative of her *Other-Centeredness⁻* (score of 4). After a couple of months, she begins flipping between her *Other-Centered⁻* and a new *Self-Centered⁺* schema. She has become acutely aware of the needs she has suppressed over the years and feels a rage surging within her. That rage causes her to express her needs at the expense of her significant other, who ultimately leaves her. Fortunately, Theresa eventually acquires the *Centered** schema and a stable, long-term relationship.

SCHEMA PORTRAITS

Sylvia

What can we learn about Sylvia from her Relationship Zone scores?

Sylvia's Score Sheet: The Relationship Zone

Negative Maladaptive Schemas (−)	Adaptive Schemas (*)	Positive Maladaptive Schemas (+)
③ Other-Centered	_1_ Centered	_2_ Self-Centered
_1_ Abandonment	_3_* Intimate	_0_ Avoidant
_1_ Undefined	_3_* Defined	_0_ Aggrandizing
_0_ Distrusting	_4_* Trusting	_0_ Naive

We see strong adaptive schemas for Sylvia. She is comfortable being emotionally close to people (indicated by her score of 3 on *Intimate**). She acknowledges that she is sensitive to rejection, but feels that this is not too much of a problem for her (indicated by her score of 1 on *Abandonment*$^-$). She has a strong sense of her own identity and purpose, but there are a few times when she feels so absorbed in her roles as mother and wife that she loses sight of her individual identity (a score of 1 on *Undefined*$^-$). She feels most people can be trusted but still uses reasonable caution (a score of 4 on *Trusting**). Sylvia's score sheet indicates that her most problematic schema is *Other-Centered*$^-$, which sometimes alternates with her *Self-Centered*$^+$ schema. She somewhat reluctantly admits that being *Other-Centered*$^-$ might be a problem for her, but she isn't completely convinced. So she does a cost-benefit analysis of the *Other-Centered*$^-$ schema to get a clearer picture of its role in her life.

Sylvia's Cost-Benefit Analysis: *Other-Centered*$^-$

Benefits
My family needs me. I take such good care of them that they say they cannot manage without me.

102

My family and friends come to me to solve their problems. They respect me.

By taking care of everything, I have more control over what happens—what we eat, what we do, where we go.

Other people view me as a supermom. I kind of like that. Actually, I like that a lot.

Costs

Taking care of everybody can be exhausting.

When I do ask for help, Jack and the kids don't know what to do, because I have never taught them.

I do not have much time for myself. When I want to do something for me, everybody acts terribly inconvenienced.

At times I feel taken for granted, and then I get mad. I say I am not going to do everything for such lazy people anymore, and I go on strike for a day and sulk. I have done that so often that they now ignore me. It used to get them worked up and more attentive. I know I have trained them to take me for granted.

I am tired of being the crying towel for my friends. They seldom take my advice anyway. So I hear the same sob story two weeks later. They feel better after talking to me, and I end up feeling frustrated and irritable. And they never ask about my problems. They even tell me I don't have any problems. They say we are the perfect family, so why would I ever be upset?

When I quit to stay home, my boss told me that he would give me a raise when I came back, if I took some classes in paralegal training. I started a class last fall that met two nights a week, but Jack complained about having to handle the kids after working all day, and the kids complained about my being gone, so I quit after three weeks.

Before Sylvia does her cost-benefit analysis, she does not think her *Other-Centered⁻* schema is much of a problem; afterward, she changes her mind. She has expected

103

other people to meet her needs just as she tried to meet theirs. She sees that she often feels resentful when others do not reciprocate. She also wants more time for herself. But she recognizes that it is she who has trained her family and friends to rely on her. If the situation is going to change, she will have to be the catalyst.

Steven

What are Steven's scores in the Relationship Zone?

Steven's Score Sheet: The Relationship Zone		
Negative **Maladaptive Schemas (−)**	**Adaptive** **Schemas (*)**	**Positive** **Maladaptive Schemas (+)**
_2_ Other-Centered	_1_ Centered	_(3)_ Self-Centered
_2_ Abandonment	_1_ Intimate	_(3)_ Avoidant
_2_ Undefined	_3*_ Defined	_2_ Aggrandizing
_2_ Distrusting	_2_ Trusting	_0_ Naive

Steven admits that he is too *self-centered* with his family (indicated by a score of 3 on *Self-Centered*[+]). He thinks that whenever he is home, his needs should come first because he works so hard. His wife tries to be understanding, but his kids accuse him of being selfish. In professional situations, he flips to his *Other-Centered*[−] schema. He is overly accommodating to the requests of his patients and colleagues. He tries to avoid their disapproval at all costs, but he often resents them.

Steven also flips between the schemas of *Abandonment*[−] (score of 2) and *Avoidant*[+] (score of 3). He sometimes worries that something tragic will happen to his wife and kids. He frequently seeks reassurance from his wife that she loves him and is happy in their marriage. Yet he also keeps his wife and children at a distance, not sharing with them his own feelings of inferiority, because he is afraid they will disrespect him. He also keeps others at a distance, making his relationships superficial. None of his colleagues ever really get to know him personally.

Steven has a strong *Defined** schema (score of 3). He has a firm sense of who he is professionally, but at home he adopts whatever interests or pursuits his wife has, revealing a weaker *Undefined⁻* schema (score of 2). His modest *Self-Aggrandizing⁺* schema (score of 2) sometimes influences others around him to adopt his beliefs and values because he holds them so strongly and because he believes that he is "right."

He holds a moderately strong *Trusting** schema, balanced by a *Distrusting⁻* schema of equal strength (each scored a 2). He wants to trust people but he is afraid of being hurt. He feels that some people treat him with respect because he is a doctor and that they would treat him differently if he were a grocery store clerk. Steven questions the motives of some of his colleagues. He has seen them back-stabbing each other frequently, so he doesn't trust many of them.

Let's review Steven's cost-benefit analysis of his *Avoidant⁺* schema.

Steven's Cost-Benefit Analysis: *Avoidant⁺*

Benefits
I don't get involved in hospital intrigue or rumors.

People don't dump their problems on me and use up my time.

I feel safer, because people do not know me well enough to be critical of me.

I don't get as upset when a patient dies.

Costs
I have been accused of being cold and unfeeling.

Sometimes I feel left out, because my family and staff do not confide in me.

After patients die, I feel guilty that I was not able to talk with them and their families about their concerns about dying.

I have few friends. I have always felt lonely.

I am seldom invited to casual parties. I do not feel liked.

My wife and kids feel cut off from me and feel that they don't really know me. I feel alone.

105

Some of the benefits from Steven's *Avoidant*[+] schema are real. Emotional involvement with people does take time and energy. But the flip side is that the lack of emotional involvement creates a deep sense of loneliness and isolation in Steven. He is so afraid of revealing personal weaknesses that he cannot completely confide in anyone, not even his wife. At times, this makes her feel that she is unimportant to Steven and could easily be replaced. On the occasions when Steven has shared his fears with her, she has told him that she feels closer to him and more loving. He has felt that too, but it is still scary to be that open all of the time. Steven also realizes that his avoidance of intimacy makes his patients find him cold and indifferent. Because he is afraid they will become upset, he tries to communicate in a matter-of-fact tone, which he knows often frustrates them. Sometimes he feels guilty afterward. He wishes he could relax and let people confide in him more easily.

Steven is highly motivated to change this schema. His wife doesn't want to continue in a relationship with someone who seems close to her only sporadically, and she is about to give up on him. But Steven doesn't want to be cut off anymore either, not from her or their kids. He wants friends, too. He knows he will have to take risks to change this schema.

Lynn

What do Lynn's scores in the Relationship Zone tell us?

Lynn's Score Sheet: The Relationship Zone

Negative Maladaptive Schemas (–)	Adaptive Schemas (*)	Positive Maladaptive Schemas (+)
1 Other-Centered	1 Centered	③ Self-Centered
③ Abandonment	1 Intimate	2 Avoidant
2 Undefined	3[*] Defined	2 Aggrandizing
2 Distrusting	2 Trusting	2 Naive

Again, we see adaptive schemas counterbalanced with maladaptive schemas. Lynn has a strong *Defined** schema; that is, she knows what she wants and where she wants to go. But she occasionally alternates between her modest *Undefined⁻* and *Aggrandizing⁺* schemas. At times, she feels she needs a man for her life to be complete, while at other times she feels that people adore or envy her because of her professional success and looks. Lynn also vacillates on the Trust Schema Continuum; she is *Naïve⁺* at the beginning of her relationships, then *Trusting**, and finally *Distrusting⁻* by the end of the relationship. Lynn is unapologetic about her *Self-Centered⁺* schema. She takes care of herself and feels that others should, too.

Lynn sees her maladaptive schemas on the Intimacy Continuum as problematic. She flips between her *Abandonment⁻* and her *Avoidant⁺* schemas like some people "channel surf." So Lynn does a cost-benefit analysis of her *Abandonment⁻* schema.

Lynn's Cost-Benefit Analysis: *Abandonment⁻*

Benefits
I feel better when I am reassured that the other person cares. But the feeling doesn't last very long.

I do get more attention.

Costs
Over time my boyfriends have all been exasperated by my need for reassurance. Some of them have even been insulted that I had so little faith in them.

Some of my boyfriends have complained that I smother them and am too possessive. I am like that. I also am terribly jealous. I have had a lot of arguments with them about that. Some of them have said that if I am going to accuse them of being unfaithful, they might as well be. I ended up driving them away when all I wanted was their reassurance that they loved me.

I am so sensitive to rejection that once I ended a relationship before I thought a boyfriend would. Later I found out that he was very hurt by me, but then it was too late. He wouldn't even talk to me. I avoided being the rejectee, but I really cared about him. Maybe it wouldn't have ended if I had talked to him about my feelings.

I have hurt some of my boyfriends by trying to make them jealous to see if they cared. I knew that was immature, but I did it anyway. And sometimes they have retaliated by going out with other women.

Lynn's *Abandonment⁻* schema has been a destructive force in her life. Instead of creating a closer bond, it has driven her partners away. She has begun to see the answer to her question, "Why can't I get what I want?"

TYING IT ALL TOGETHER

Perhaps you have found yourself wondering about schemas from the other two zones (Self-Worth and Empowerment) that may have damaged your relationships as well. For example, if you have an extreme *Dependent⁻* schema from the Empowerment Zone, it might drive your partner crazy because you so often ask for excessive, unneeded help. That's why we showed you earlier that schemas overlap like the circles below.

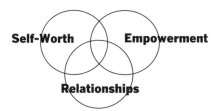

We presented the schemas in the Relationship Zone that *consistently* cause chaos in relationships. It's hard to imagine how schemas from the Relationship Zone such as *Self-Centered⁺*, *Abandonment⁻*, *Distrust⁻*, or *Aggrandizing⁺* would not disrupt your relationships. Schemas in the other zones (such as *Dependent⁻*, *Entitled⁺*, *Inadequate⁻*, *Blameworthy⁻*, or *Omnipotent⁺*) often inflict harm on relationships as well, but not always. Again, all three zones frequently interact with each other.

Shelly illustrates this point nicely. Her schemas in the Relationship Zone mostly consisted of adaptive schemas and she had only a little trouble with the two negative maladaptive schemas, *Other-Centered⁻* (score of 3) and *Abandonment⁻* (score of 2). Yet her relationships usually fell apart within six months. That's because her Self-Worth Zone was pockmarked with severe negative maladaptive schemas of *Blameworthy⁻* (4), *Undesirable⁻* (3), *Unworthy⁻* (4), and *Inadequate⁻* (3). Men usually liked her a lot at first. When they saw she had low self-esteem, they tried to build her up. Because of her schemas she resisted those attempts mightily. Eventually, most men burned out trying to shore up her fragile self-worth. They usually felt quite guilty about it, but they left her because they felt drained by her negative maladaptive schemas in the Self-Worth Zone.

SCHEMA WARS: THE REAL CULPRIT BEHIND CONFLICT

Maladaptive, surreptitious schemas deserve the blame for relationship difficulties more than any single factor we can name. You have already seen a glimpse of what they can do in the brief vignettes of Theresa, Sylvia, Lynn, and Steven: They generate conflict, havoc, and unhappiness. That's why we call such conflicts *schema wars*. For example, Linda and Ethan often quarrel over Linda's relationships with her co-workers, primarily because Linda has several male colleagues. Whenever she talks about them or has to stay an hour late at work, Ethan goes berserk as a result of his powerful schema of *Distrust⁻*. Linda loves him very much, has no romantic interest in her friends at work, and does not share his *Distrusting⁻* schema, so she can't understand why Ethan gets so angry. Their fights are not based on mutual antipathy; they originate in Ethan's profound schema of *Distrust⁻*.

If you find yourself embroiled in repetitive, endless fights with a partner, co-worker, spouse, or friend, you need to reflect on whether maladaptive schemas—your own or those of your partner—are responsible for this upheaval. Let's take a look at Will and Marta to see how this works. Will, a thirty-two-year-old stockbroker and Marta, a thirty-four-year-old real estate salesperson, have been married for six years. Together, they earn about $120,000 per year. They have much in common: Both like to travel, hike, go camping, and attend the opera. Will and Marta reported feeling a strong attraction for each other almost from the moment they met. All things considered, they seemed to "have it made." But two years into the marriage, they found themselves fighting incessantly. What about? Money and sex, two of the all-time favorite topics for arguments.

Will constantly harangued Marta about her tendency to spend money excessively. He frequently exclaimed, "My God, all we have is money in our 401K plan at work and the other two retirement plans we set up through our financial planner. That's it. We don't have another dime in savings, not a dime. Not only that, we often carry a thousand dollar or more balance on our credit card! That's the worst interest rate you can pay. But we have to, because of the way you spend money. This *has* to stop! Furthermore, I just don't understand why you never want to have sex anymore. I'm beginning to think you don't love me. What's wrong with you anyway?"

Marta's typical reply was, "All you ever think about is money. You feed your precious retirement plans like they were prize pigs for the state fair. *Nobody* pumps that much money into retirement. And why would I want to have sex with you? All you do is nag me about money." This same theme repeated itself over and over again. As long as Will and Marta stuck with the content of their argument, they got absolutely nowhere. They desperately needed to find out the true cause of their conflicts, or their marriage was soon headed for the garbage bin.

As a last resort, they sought marital therapy and learned what was really going on with their constant squabbling. Marta discovered that her intense *Unworthy⁻* schema from the Self-Worth Zone had caused her to flip into the *Entitled⁺* schema when she finally acquired some money. She described it as "trying to fill the void" she had felt inside since childhood, because her needs had generally been ignored and her family had rarely given her attention, time, or things. Now she wanted it all. Slowly she learned that she didn't really need to have it all to feel OK. A little less spending was all right, because she could get by and be fine on less. She also realized that the reason she felt so little sexual desire had to do with her anger at Will for not giving her all she wanted. It finally dawned on her that no one could give her all she wanted—that was a futile quest. What she *really* wanted was intimacy, and that was obstructed by her anger.

Don't let yourself think that Marta's schemas bore the sole responsibility for their marital problems, not by any means. For instance, Will began to see that he poured all of his resources into his retirement plans because of an intense *Vulnerable⁻* schema from the Empowerment Zone. This schema started when he was twelve years old and his family faced financial ruin after his father died. Will was forced to find any job he could to help support the family. They lived on welfare for years, and he was terrified to think he might ever be in such dire straits again. Thus, although his retirement account already had a high six-figure balance, it felt like chicken feed to him. Input from his therapist and his financial adviser convinced him that he was going overboard on the retirement quest. He "loosened the reins" financially, eased up a little at work, and made more time for Marta. Not surprisingly, she began to feel closer to him, and her sexual desire began to return. Their marriage gradually pulled back from the brink of disaster.

Here's another scenario that may sound familiar. Nancy and Barry were driving across town to a party when it became clear to Nancy that they were hopelessly lost. They had been driving around for almost forty-five minutes, and she was sure they had passed the same gas station three or four times. Finally, Nancy blurted out, "Why don't you stop being so damn stubborn and admit you're lost? Let's stop and ask someone for directions. This driving around is making me crazy!" Barry responded, "Look, I know how to find this place. Quit bugging me. I don't need to stop and ask for directions." After another half-hour of driving around, he finally stopped and had Nancy ask someone for directions. On the way home, feeling humiliated, he attacked Nancy, telling her that she tried to upstage him at the party by telling lots of engaging stories. She said she was trying to help him make a connection with some important people.

Guess what? This fight also stemmed from maladaptive schemas. Nancy wasn't too surprised by Barry's revelation in marital therapy that he had the excessive positive maladaptive schemas of *Stubbornly Independent*⁺ and *Perfectionistic*⁺, but she was surprised to learn where they came from. Barry had never told her that, as a child, he had heard constant messages from his father that he needed to make his own way in the world and that real men don't need others to help them. Whenever he messed up on his homework or any other project, his father forced him to work at it again and again until he got it right. His father never once helped him out. He often told Barry that men have to carry the load in life and that he shouldn't expect anyone to help him. Barry's positive maladaptive schemas of *Stubbornly Independent*⁺ and *Perfectionistic*⁺ flourished with these messages serving as the catalyst. Furthermore, he was scared to death that if he didn't always live up to his father's ideals, he might appear pathetically *Dependent*⁻ and *Inadequate*⁻ (the opposites of Barry's positive maladaptive schemas of *Stubbornly Independent*⁺ and *Perfectionistic*⁺).

Nancy said it helped a lot to realize what Barry's seeming "insanity" was really about. She still didn't like it, but she learned to deal with his issues more gently and with less anger. Barry then found it easier to relax the unrelenting standards that he held for himself. He even realized he could turn to others for help, particularly Nancy. He decided that it was time to reevaluate some of his father's messages.

OK, we can almost hear you thinking, "Barry sounds like *all* men. None of them can ever stop and ask for directions!" Well, we have found that men probably do possess some positive maladaptive schemas (such as *Stubbornly Independent*⁺) to a slightly greater degree than women, whereas women possess some negative maladaptive schemas to a slightly greater degree than men. But you should note that although schema differences probably account for part of what we have labeled the *gender wars*, you should not overgeneralize or make too much of the differences between the sexes. It's the differences in schemas between the two individuals in a couple that matter most. Often, those differences don't follow the stereotyped differences between the sexes.

Also, be aware that schema wars can be stopped. The first step is learning to recognize your own maladaptive schemas that may be problematic in your relationships, just as Marta realized that her spending habits sometimes went out

111

of control as a result of her *Entitled*⁺ schema. The second step is to recognize that your partner's schemas are causing him or her to react intensely. By learning this fact, you can pull back and not take the attack so personally, because it often really isn't about you as a person. It has to do with the other person's "hot buttons" or schemas. Marta said it helped her to know that Will got so angry because he actually felt intensely vulnerable, an issue that had existed for him since childhood. Will felt better knowing that Marta's desire to spend stemmed from an emptiness she had felt inside since childhood. The door to compromise opened, and the key to unlocking it came from understanding each other's schema-based issues. Most contentious issues can end in productive compromise, as long as you know the schemas operating in the background.

Compromise in the midst of schema wars can also come about more easily when you learn to look for the piece of truth in the other person's point of view. Sometimes it seems impossible to believe that the other person might have a valid point when your own maladaptive schemas are blinding you to the possibility of finding truth in anything but your own position. When emotions boil over, back off; don't communicate until you have calmed down. We recommend that you invent a nonverbal time-out signal with your partner. Use the time-out period to calm down. Then go back and analyze what schemas might be responsible for the fight. Be sure to reengage the issue with your partner and resolve it through compromise. Will and Marta learned to do exactly that. Will learned that Marta actually had a point in that his miserliness controlled their lives like a jail guard, and Marta came to understand that saving for retirement does make sense.

Of course, not all schema wars can end in compromise. In some cases, you may simply need to know your personal limits and boundaries and make sure you do not allow yourself to be pummeled into submission. You might need professional help for dealing with such issues.

CONCLUSION

Now we must ask you to be patient. You are likely aware of most of your problematic maladaptive schemas in all three zones, and you are no doubt anxious to rid yourself of these nefarious beasts once and for all. If only it were that simple, but it's not. We have found that it is important to approach the change process one step at a time. You have completed the first phase by becoming *aware* of your trouble spots. The exercises below will help you look at your relationship schemas even more closely.

UNDERSTANDING YOUR SCHEMAS IN THE RELATIONSHIP ZONE

1. Appreciating the Adaptive Schemas You Have

You have already identified your schemas in the Relationship Zone. In the space below, list the adaptive schemas that you think you have and describe how they have been helpful to you. Sylvia's response to this exercise follows:

Adaptive Schema	Ways in Which This Schema Has Been Helpful
Intimate*	I can tell my husband my inner thoughts without being afraid he will take advantage of me.
	It helps me form close friendships easily.

Adaptive Schema	Ways in Which This Schema Has Been Helpful
_____	_____
_____	_____
_____	_____

2. How New Adaptive Schemas Would Be Helpful

If you gave yourself low scores on the adaptive schemas in the Relationship Zone, this exercise is to help you see how having those adaptive schemas would be beneficial to you. In the space below, list the adaptive schemas from the Relationship Zone that you scored as 0 or 1 and describe how you would benefit from stronger adaptive schemas. Lynn filled out this exercise in the following manner:

New Adaptive Schema	Ways in Which This Schema Would Be Helpful
Centered*	I would quit burning my boyfriends out with my constant demands.
	People would like me more if I showed more interest in them sometimes.

113

New Adaptive Schema	Ways in Which This Schema Would Be Helpful
_____	_____
_____	_____
_____	_____
_____	

3. Schema Cost-Benefit Analysis

Now it is time for you to do a cost-benefit analysis of your maladaptive schemas in the Relationship Zone. In the space below, list each maladaptive schema that you rated as a 3 or 4 and the advantages and/or disadvantages you have experienced as a result of that schema. Reviewing the cost-benefit analyses of Sylvia, Steven, and Lynn may be helpful to you.

Maladaptive Schema	Costs	Benefits
_____	_____	_____
_____	_____	_____
_____	_____	_____
_____	_____	_____
_____	_____	_____
_____	_____	_____

4. Schema Diary

Before you can begin to change a schema, you need to know what impact it is having on your life. The easiest way to do this is to keep a schema diary such as the one in Appendix B.

5. Relationship Review

Look for the trends. Are you acting like a moth drawn toward a deadly candle flame?

For those of you who are not currently in a satisfying relationship, this exercise can prepare you to change repetitive destructive patterns that may inadvertently hamper your efforts. Start by listing the five most important relationships in your life that ultimately went awry. Next, write down what the primary problems or conflicts were in the relationship, as well as which schemas might have been involved for you and your partner. We'll start by showing you what Gerald came up with on this exercise.

Gerald's Review: Relationships

Partner's Name	Core Problem(s)	Partner's Schema(s)	My Schema(s)
Sue	She was married.	*Avoidant*[+]	*Abandonment*[−]
	She focused on her needs too much.	*Entitled*[+]	*Unworthy*[−]
			Distrusting[−]
		Self-Centered[+]	*Other Centered*[−]
Terri	She lived in another state.	*Avoidant*[+]	*Abandonment*
	She rarely called.	*Irresistible*[+]	
		Self-Centered[+]	*Other Centered*[−]
		Distrusting[−]	
		Unworthy[−]	
Carole	She had a history of unfaithfulness.	*Entitled*[+]	*Unworthy*[−]
		Irresistible[+]	
	She was a lousy listener.	*Avoidant*[+]	*Abandonment*[−]
	Sometimes she lied to me.	*Stubbornly Independent*[+]	*Distrust*[−]
		Self-Centered[+]	*Other Centered*[−]

Gerald listed three or four additional relationships, but he got the point after these three. He was astonished to learn that he had been unconsciously choosing partners that fit his schemas "like a glove." His *Abandonment*[−] schema especially stood out; it had led him to *expect* that women would avoid intimacy and eventually leave him. He groaned, "God, I am always going for women who are unavailable. It's like I am drawn to them. How do I stop doing this?"

We'll give you more ideas about the answer to that question in later chapters. However, we can tell you that Gerald found it helpful to know which characteristics to avoid. For starters, he decided to never again pursue anyone who was married, who lived in another state, or who had a horrendous history of unfaithfulness. His maladaptive schemas made it difficult to adhere to that decision, though.

In the space below, fill out the same chart as Gerald did.

Partner's Name	Core Problem(s)	Partner's Schema(s)	My Schema(s)

6

Where It All Began: Schema Origins

The great majority of men are bundles of beginnings.
—Ralph Waldo Emerson, Journals

You identified your adaptive and maladaptive schemas in the last three chapters. We have discovered that people tend to take their adaptive schemas for granted but become quite distressed about their maladaptive schemas. Often, they feel disgusted with themselves for having problematic schemas, as if somehow they chose them. You may be feeling that way, too. This chapter will help you realize that *people do not choose their schemas.* You did not pick your schemas because you wanted to be miserable or mean. But you can choose to change your schemas, and later we will show you how. For now, we want to help you understand that *your schemas inevitably result from your personal history and biology.*

SCHEMA INFORMATION CHANNELS

Humans are programmed to produce schemas. Remember how we explained in Chapter 1 that the brain automatically starts processing our experiences into schemas the moment we are born? To understand how schemas develop, you first need to know the four channels by which information travels to the brain. Schema information is channeled through:

▷ **How we are treated**

▷ **How we manipulate our world**

▷ **What we hear**

▷ **What we see**

117

Channel One: How We Are Treated

We derive our earliest schema information simply from the way others treat us. Schemas on the Empowerment Continuum probably develop first. An infant who cries and is then picked up, cuddled, fed, or changed out of dirty diapers will begin to acquire some sense of control in the world, thus creating the rudiments of an *Empowered** schema. If another infant's crying is typically ignored and his needs are inconsistently met, a *Powerless⁻* schema is more apt to develop. If every whimper from a third infant is acknowledged immediately with endless efforts to comfort her, an *Omnipotent⁺* schema may develop.

A child records or *encodes*, the earliest memories in the *sensorimotor system*, the system that regulates sensations and motor activity. The ability to encode visual information becomes stronger after the age of two, and the ability to encode language develops even later. So *kinesthetic sensations*—being touched and handled—are the earliest information channeled for schema development. This means that some of our schemas may have little, if any, language associated with them.

Channel Two: How We Manipulate Our World

We learn a lot by interacting with our environment. We live in both a physical and social world. As an infant grows and becomes more interactive and mobile, early schemas will increase in strength if the infant's experiences continue to be relatively consistent. A toddler's *Empowered** schema is likely to keep growing if her family responds to her verbalizations and continues to meet her needs and requests, while ignoring some behaviors and correcting others. But the child's social world is not the only source of information for a schema. A child with good motor coordination will be able to manipulate her physical world more effectively, which will add to her *Empowered** schema.

Channel Three: What We Hear

If we hear that we are smart, pretty, or athletic, the schemas of *Desirable** and *Adequate** are likely to start developing. If our parents and others around us rave about these aspects, the schemas of *Irresistible⁺* and *Perfectionistic⁺* are more apt to emerge. If our families criticize us for our mistakes and ridicule us when we try new things, the schemas of *Inadequate⁻* and *Blameworthy⁻* may arise. These same experiences might teach us that we should never make mistakes and should avoid trying anything new unless we can be successful immediately. Over time, these messages may create the *Perfectionistic⁺* and *Blameless⁺* schemas, in addition to the *Inadequate⁻* and *Blameworthy⁻* schemas.

118

Channel Four: What We See

Our ability to learn merely from observing the world around us is amazing. Most of our knowledge comes from what we observe rather than from direct experiences. If you have been around young children, you know that what you do is far more likely to be imitated than what you say. And what is imitated can be unpredictable, as with the two-year-old who refuses to use the toilet, yet claps and exclaims, "What a good girl!" whenever her mother uses the toilet.

If a child is raised in a family in which the father verbally and physically abuses the mother and then blames her for causing him to act that way, the child may develop several related schemas: The world is a violent and dangerous place (*Vulnerable⁻*); when you are out of control, it is someone else's fault (*Blameless⁺*); females are weak and men are strong (*Powerless⁻* in girls, *Omnipotent⁺* in boys).

Merely observing the parents' interactions could have provided the information for all of these schemas. Parents or parental figures present powerful role models for children, because children depend on them from the moment of their birth and because parents have the greatest exposure to the child during infancy and early childhood. These observations form the foundations of the child's developing schemas.

In addition to observing their parents, children also observe the actions of other role models: siblings, friends, teachers, athletes, coaches, and the parents of their friends. These models provide information about who can fill those roles. If a Hispanic child sees both male and female Hispanics in roles as teachers, coaches, doctors, lawyers, and pilots, that child is more likely to develop a *Worthy*** schema—that is, Hispanics can work in these professions just as well as any other race. If Hispanics are seldom seen in those roles and only appear in roles of lesser stature, the child may develop a schema of *Unworthy⁻* and come to believe that those roles are not appropriate for Hispanics. We learn who is and who is not appropriate for roles by observing who fills them and who does not.

Although we observe the people around us, the media—including television, movies, and videotapes—are a major source of vicarious learning. For the last half of this century, psychologists have repeatedly demonstrated that media modeling is as powerful as live modeling for learning. Children are as likely or more likely to imitate models on film as they are to imitate models performing the same behaviors in their presence. Children even imitate cartoon characters. Corporations do not invest millions of dollars in advertising without considerable conviction that modeled behavior influences viewers. Recently, teenagers were found to smoke the cigarette brands that have the greatest amount of advertising. Gee, what a surprise! Behaviors, attitudes, and values are all modeled through the media and all provide observers with schema information.

Another vicarious learning process is reading. We need not experience things firsthand or see them on film, because we can gain access to them through the written word. A little girl can learn that women are capable of being astronauts by reading about Sally Ride, Shannon Lucid, and other women astronauts. The sources of vicarious information are vast, including the people around us, television and movies, anything in print, and the rapidly expanding computer world.

SCHEMA INFORMATION SOURCES

Even though we all channel schema information by the four processes we have discussed, no two people have exactly the same schemas. Our own personal experiences determine our schema content, and no two people have exactly the same experiences. A variety of sources influence the content of the information channeled into our schema processes.

Schema Information Sources

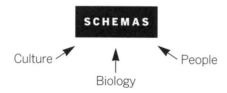

Culture

Culture affects the attitudes and structures of our families, the religions to which we are exposed, the educational opportunities that exist, and the content of the media that we see. The schemas that are viewed as appropriate in one culture may seem inappropriate in another. In the United States, research has found that outgoing children are viewed as more popular than more inhibited children, but in some cultures, such as China, uninhibited behavior is viewed as disrespectful and not to be emulated. So outgoing, gregarious behavior in the United States might be seen as part of a *Desirable*[*] schema, but in China such behavior might be part of the *Undesirable*[-] schema. Culture influences the content of schemas, and then schemas influence our perceptions and interpretations of our experiences.

Religious Background

Your religious background can contribute to your schemas. Buddhists, Christians, Jews, Muslims, and atheists all have different views of life. Religions that emphasize strict rules and the consequences of sin can produce the *Blameworthy*[-] schema.

120

A religious emphasis on a deity's forgiveness and love can contribute to the *Worthy** schema. Religions that allow only males to hold positions of greatest authority will influence schemas on the Worthiness Schema Continuum and the Empowerment Schema Continuum for both genders.

School Experiences

Academic performance is a primary source of content for schemas on the Adequacy Schema Continuum. Children who do well academically tend to develop the *Adequate** schema, whereas children who struggle in school receive repeated messages that they are *Inadequate*⁻. Thirteen years of negative feedback can produce a massive *Inadequate*⁻ schema, regardless of whether the student struggles because of learning disabilities, attention deficit problems, or a chaotic, unsupportive home life. A *Perfectionistic*⁺ schema can develop in children who are so academically successful that they never experience anything but straight A's. They can develop the belief that others will not think positively of them if they are ever less than perfect.

Schemas on the Adequacy Schema Continuum can be reinforced or contradicted by other experiences during the school years. For example, parents of a learning-disabled child can do much to support the child's work in school, regardless of the outcome, and they can praise what is often enormous effort. They also can provide nonacademic activities for success experiences, whether in athletics, music, or artistic endeavors. Those experiences will contribute to an *Adequate** schema. Even with those positive experiences, it is very difficult for a child with any significant academic disadvantage to escape the school experience without forming a slight *Inadequate*⁻ schema.

Although school experiences can shape all of our schemas to some extent, they particularly affect schemas on the Worthiness Schema Continuum. Our sense of worth can be influenced by the attitudes of teachers toward members of our race, regardless of what our race is. Those messages will come across through glances, ridicule, favoritism, or merely neglect. If a Caucasian teacher appears contemptuous of nonwhites, his nonwhite students may hesitate to ask questions or seek help when they are confused. The same is true regarding school attitudes toward gender. If the school thinks athletics are really just for boys, girls will not be encouraged to pursue those opportunities. All of these attitudes influence the schemas on the Worthiness Schema Continuum.

People

Other people obviously have a powerful impact on our schemas. We'll discuss peoples' influences under the categories of "family" and "peers and friends."

Family

Our families are typically the major content source for our schemas, and every family is unique. The number and gender of siblings, financial status, health of family members, individual personalities, education and employment experiences, attitudes, and coping styles are only some of the ways in which families vary. The negative maladaptive schemas of *Blameworthy⁻* and *Unworthy⁻* are likely in a child who is the family scapegoat. A severe chronic illness in a family member can produce the *Vulnerable⁻* schema in the family's children. A family that favors one child can produce the *Entitled⁺* and *Self-Centered⁺* schemas in that child and *Unworthy⁻* and *Other-Centered⁻* schemas in the rest of the children. A divorced mother who is too reliant on her children can influence them to develop *Other-Centered⁻* schemas.

Peers and Friends

Although teacher attitudes can influence the schemas on the Desirability Schema Continuum, peer attitudes are much more powerful. An *Irresistible⁺* schema would be hard for a child to avoid if her family always ensured that her clothes were more expensive than those of her peers. Likewise, in an upper income school district, a child from a low-income family who could not afford to wear the same type of clothes as his peers may be prone to develop an *Undesirable⁻* schema.

Friends play a major role in the schemas we develop. Our friends expose us to new ideas and interests or reinforce the ones we have. A boy who is not particularly athletic might develop a friendship with a boy who moves in next door. The newcomer may be an excellent athlete and may begin to encourage the other boy to play with him. With practice and support from his new friend, the boy may improve his physical skills and receive praise from his classmates during their recess games. If the child enjoys playing with his new friend and begins receiving positive attention from his classmates, it can reinforce his efforts to continue to improve athletically, thereby creating an *Adequate** schema.

Friends also serve as models of comparison, which can strengthen old schemas or fuel new ones. A junior high girl who always felt *Desirable** might begin to develop an *Undesirable⁻* schema if her best friend evolves into a swan, thus becoming the object of male attention and pursuit. How much of an impact this has depends on how well developed her *Desirable** schema already was. If it was quite strong, she might simply conclude that her friend is especially pretty and that this new beauty does not diminish her appreciation of her own desirability.

Biology

Humans vary biologically from the moment of birth. For instance, newborn human infants can immediately be classified as cuddlers or noncuddlers. Cuddlers love being held and snuggled. Noncuddlers enjoy being kissed and bounced but dislike physical contact that restricts their movements. Differences in cuddliness can influence schemas on the Empowerment Schema Continuum. Parents who understand cuddliness as a biological preference and respond appropriately will increase the infant's sense of power. Parents who are insensitive or ignorant to such differences can contribute to a schema of *Powerless⁻*. Noncuddlers sit unsupported and can stand and crawl earlier than cuddlers; these mobility differences can influence schemas on the continuums of Empowerment and Capability.

Our gender also affects the way others react to us and the role models we imitate. Even birth order affects our experiences. Within the same family, older and younger children are not treated identically. Physical attractiveness and resemblance to certain family members can also influence the responses a child elicits from others, thereby influencing schemas on the Desirability and Worthiness Schema Continua.

The various biological changes that occur throughout our development are potent schema influences. For example, greater motor coordination during childhood correlates with greater popularity, because of the role these skills play in typical childhood games. This can affect the schemas on the Adequacy and Desirability Schema Continua. Being too short or too tall and physically maturing early or late can influence schemas on the Desirability Schema Continuum. One of the most painful sources of an *Undesirable⁻* schema is the adolescent phenomenon of acne. In truth, any physical attribute, whether visible or invisible, can influence our schemas on the Desirability Schema Continuum. Because of an early *Undesirable⁻* schema, an adult may try to become *Desirable** or even *Irresistible⁺* by exercising, dieting, buying expensive wardrobes, or even having cosmetic surgery.

Whether you have observed baby humans, horses, cats, dogs, or marmosets, you know that any two mammals arrive in the world with their own distinct temperaments. *Temperament* is the relatively stable, basic disposition inherent in a person.

Babies show distinct temperaments in the first few weeks of life that are unrelated to the parenting styles they experience. Forty percent of infants have been found to be easy babies—they have cheerful dispositions and adapt quickly to new people, situations, and routines. Fifteen percent are slow-to-warm-up babies, who have low activity levels, tend to be somewhat negative in mood, and adapt slowly to new situations. Ten percent are difficult babies; they cry a great deal, eat and sleep irregularly, have violent tantrums, and are hard to comfort. A third of infants show a mixture of these three dispositions.

In others ways, too, individuals seem to vary from birth. Common shyness seems to be an inherited tendency that persists through adulthood. Tendencies toward leadership or dominance and obedience to authority are other behaviors that may have biological bases. These various tendencies increase or decrease the likelihood of developing certain schemas. We come into the world with different dispositional tendencies.

Our schemas, however, are not solely products of our temperament or biology any more than they are of our environment alone. Rather, the interaction of our innate dispositions and our world determines our schemas. This mutual interaction is called *reciprocal influence.*

RECIPROCAL INFLUENCE: SCHEMAS LIVE ON TWO-WAY STREETS

Reciprocal influence is a major principle of human development. From infancy, we are active agents in our world. We influence the way others respond to us, just as others influence our responses to them. A noncuddler may disappoint a mother, who may interpret this as rejection, which in turn may decrease her responsiveness to the infant. This interaction demonstrates the principle of reciprocal influence. The schemas of both the mother and the infant can influence the other's reactions. Thus, the baby may begin to develop a *Powerless⁻* schema and the mother an *Inadequate⁻* schema.

Difficult and slow-to-warm-up babies can be stressful for parents, particularly new parents, who may attribute the baby's distress to their own inadequate parenting. Merely knowing that infants vary in temperament can reassure these parents and prevent what might become a destructive cycle of reciprocal influence. Because individual dispositions differ, parenting styles and environments must also vary for the best fit for a child's development. No single type of environment or parenting style fits all infants or children, but the fit between baby and parent styles will influence the schemas that evolve.

The principle of reciprocal influence explains why psychologists have trouble answering the seemingly simple question, "Why am I like this?" No single factor causes a particular schema. This issue is an essential component of the chaos theory mentioned earlier. Multiple factors contribute to the development of any schema, and that schema then influences how a person perceives and interprets those factors in the future.

Schema Sources and the Principle of Reciprocal Influence

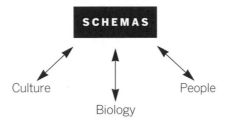

Different Experiences, Same Schemas

Two people can derive the same schemas from different experiences. A well-coordinated child may develop the *Empowered** and *Adequate** schemas in a family that encourages athletics. Another child may develop those same schemas from playing the piano in a family that enjoys and admires musical abilities. Each of these children may realize that they are not as skilled in the other activity. They may include that information in their *Empowered** and *Adequate** schemas; if they were not belittled for lacking those skills and if their families value their areas of expertise, their deficits will not undermine their adaptive schemas. Remember, adaptive schemas include both positive and negative information. The negative information is not viewed as unacceptable, and the overall balance of information in an adaptive schema is more positive.

Same Experiences, Different Schemas

In the same vein, two people can have the same experiences and can produce different schemas. No two people are exactly the same, so even if they are in the same setting, they will not experience events identically. Children reared in the same family often have very different schemas. Their schemas will depend on the reciprocal influence of their innate dispositions, biological factors, and their social and physical worlds.

Resilient children are an excellent illustration of this. Many children experience such family events as illness, accidents, death, divorce, or severe financial stress. Some children experience long-lasting adverse psychological effects from such stressful events, whereas other children rebound well. Psychologists call this latter group *resilient*. What is different about these resilient youngsters? They appear to have three protective factors. First, they are predisposed to be socially responsive and autonomous during infancy and childhood. Second, they have warm and supportive family environments. Third, they have support from peers and extrafamilial adults and positive role models. As you can see, these protective factors include both the child's innate characteristics and constructive environmental influences, again illustrating the principle of reciprocal influence. Thus, the schemas of a resilient child are not the same as the schemas of a nonresilient child from a similar environment.

The same is true for resilient adults, some of whom grew up in horrific circumstances. Resilient adults typically have above-average intelligence and special talents, have a sense of powerfulness and autonomy, are not impulsive, and have demonstrated social responsiveness and helpfulness to others since childhood. Did these adults have islands of refuge and support during their development or were they able to create them through their own predispositions? For example, a bright, engaging child from a dreadful environment may be able to attract the support of other children and adults more easily than a child who lacks those attributes. Regardless, you can see how the schemas that evolve depend on the reciprocal influence of the various factors present in any individual's life.

This example also demonstrates how schemas that develop early may not be as adaptive later in more healthy circumstances. One of the characteristics in resilient people is helpfulness to others, indicating an *Other-Centered⁻* schema. By being helpful and socially sensitive to others' needs, they may elicit support and caring. As adults, they may need to learn that they have a right to satisfy their own needs and not always focus on being responsible for others. An *Other-Centered⁻* schema may be adaptive in early difficult environments for children dependent on others' goodwill. Later, a schema that has a more balanced view of responsibility for self and others will be more useful.

SCHEMA FORMATION

Now you know the sources of content for schemas. You also understand the different channels by which our brains receive this information. Next we need to examine how the content turns into schemas. There are two primary ways we form schemas: repeated experiences and traumatic experiences.

Repeated Experiences

Most schemas form through repeated experiences on a given continuum. As with all our schemas, we receive information about our desirability from how we are treated, what we hear, what we see, and how we manipulate our world. During early childhood, if we receive feedback that we are desirable, a *Desirable** schema will begin to develop. However, schemas typically do not form in a linear fashion.

In its early stages, a schema can easily be modified in the face of contradictory information. For instance, a child may have the rudiments of a *Desirable** schema, but at daycare she may be teased for having red hair and freckles. She also may see how the staff and other children fawn over a freckle-free blond girl. Consequently, a rudimentary *Desirable** schema may be smothered if the child perceives that she is undesirable. An *Undesirable⁻* schema will grow if messages on this continuum continue in a negative vein.

Our perceptual processes favor our existing schemas. Once a schema is formed, we are more apt to notice information that is consistent with it. The little redhead will notice all the examples of people who make fun of her red hair. She will also interpret ambiguous situations in ways that support her *Undesirable⁻* schema. If two boys laugh when she walks by them at recess, she will think they are laughing at her funny red hair. They could be laughing about anything, but her *Undesirable⁻* schema interprets that situation as another example of her undesirability. As this girl does, we unintentionally gather more and more evidence for a schema once it exists.

Moreover, we spontaneously discount information that does not fit our schemas, because it does not make sense. The little redheaded girl believes that her parents compliment her pretty red hair because they are her parents and are apt to think she is pretty, no matter how she looks. We automatically assume that our schemas are accurate. Once we form beliefs and assumptions about ourselves and the world, we do not continually question them. We take them for granted and operate as if they are undoubtedly true. We could not function if we questioned every assumption and expectation that we had.

Traumatic Experiences

Most of us view the world as a relatively safe place and see ourselves as usually able to control what happens. We think that good things happen to good people and bad things happen to bad people; we believe people largely get what they deserve. If we tend to see the world as essentially benevolent, predictable, and reasonably controllable, this suggests that we tend to feel *Empowered**, *Worthy**, *Trusting**, and *Resilient**.

A traumatic event, such as an accident, death, deformity, assault, rape, or natural disaster, does not fit these schemas. A tornado that rips through your community, turning your homes into sawdust and maiming residents, is neither benevolent nor predictable. An assault or burglary is not compatible with the adaptive schemas *Empowered** or *Trusting**. A diagnosis of cancer may not fit a *Resilient** schema. One of the reasons traumas have such a brutal emotional impact is that they seldom fit our schemas. Traumas are not what we expect.

127

To some extent, whether an experience traumatizes people depends on their preexisting schemas. For example, research on crime victims found women who had viewed themselves as invulnerable to crime had more difficulty recovering from the trauma than women who viewed themselves as no more or less likely to be victimized than anyone else. This also explains why similar experiences are not necessarily traumatic for everyone.

When a traumatic experience does not fit our schemas, our brain deals with this discrepant information either through modification or construction. *Modification* either alters the information to fit the existing schemas or slightly adjusts the schema to accommodate the new information if it is not too discrepant. *Construction* creates a new schema to fit the information. Because it is much more efficient to change the details of a specific event than to create a whole new schema, our modification process is much more active than our construction process.

For instance, if a young man is robbed while walking to his car from a bar late one evening, he may tell himself that this happened because it was so late and because he was less aware of his surroundings after drinking so much. He thereby incorporates additional information into his adaptive *Empowered** and *Resilient** schemas (concluding, for example, "I can control most things that happen to me unless I am impaired by alcohol"). The modification process can therefore alter the discrepant information and slightly alter the preexisting schema, but the schema essentially remains viable.

However, modification is not always effective. In a case of date rape, a woman may tell herself that it could not have been rape, that she must have given the impression that she wanted sex. Here, she modifies the story to discount that she repeatedly said no, struggled to stop the encounter, and was overpowered by the man. Parts of the interpretation could fit her *Resilient** and *Empowered** schemas, but pieces of the memory simply do not fit. When we cannot integrate discrepant information completely, even after modification, various cues reminiscent of the event will trigger flashbacks and memory fragments. The woman is likely to experience repeated, distressing recollections of the rape. Intrusive memories and nightmares indicate that a traumatic event has not been completely reconciled with existing schemas.

When we are totally unable to modify traumatic information to fit current schemas, we construct new ones. For example, when a trusted adult sexually abuses a child, the experience is alien to the child's current schemas. If others do not view this adult as a bad person, the child decides that she is bad and deserves to be mistreated, thereby generating an *Unworthy⁻* schema. Other typical negative maladaptive schemas that children develop after suffering sexual, physical, or verbal abuse are that people cannot be trusted (*Distrusting⁻*), people cannot be prevented from being cruel (*Powerless⁻*), and intimacy is dangerous (*Avoidant⁺*).

Psychologists have found that certain schemas seem especially sensitive to any type of victimization experience. These schemas are on the continua of *Resilience, Trusting, Empowered, Worthy,* and *Intimate.* When victims cannot incorporate traumas into preexisting schemas on these continua, they generate new schemas. Sometimes, the new schemas are adaptive. When a fifty-year-old man with an *Invulnerable*[+] schema develops angina, he may generate a *Resilient*[*] schema and begin to exercise regularly and develop more healthy eating habits; he now realizes that bad things can occur when one does not take reasonable precautions. However, construction also can produce maladaptive schemas. If a rape victim generates negative maladaptive schemas of *Vulnerable*[−] and *Powerless*[−], whereas she previously held the adaptive schemas of *Resilient*[*] and *Empowered*[*], she may drastically restrict her activities and lifestyle and live in constant fear. Unfortunately, this is not an uncommon outcome of rape.

Once a trauma generates new schemas, we maintain and expand them as if they resulted from repetitive experiences. We ruminate about the experience, thereby more strongly entrenching the new schemas. We are more apt to notice information related to the trauma we experienced, and we may change our behavior because of the new schema. For instance, a rape victim may drop all her extracurricular activities and only venture out to work each day in an attempt to remain safe in a dangerous world. She may see any effort at familiarity by a male as a first step to sexual assault and may therefore keep all men at a distance. Thus, trauma-generated schemas can continue to expand, just as schemas produced by repetitive experiences do.

CONCLUSION

At this point, you have a good grasp of how schemas are formed. Four information channels supply the content from a variety of sources. Through reciprocal influence, all of these sources can interact with each other and with the schemas being formed. Repetitive experiences and traumas can create new schemas.

Now it is time to figure out how your schemas formed. This is an important step. We have found that our clients often feel less guilt and self-contempt when they realize that they did not pick their schemas. It is simply impossible for anyone with your particular experiences and personal dispositions to have developed any schemas other than the ones that you have at this moment. What you can do is change these schemas in the future, as we describe in the next chapters.

For now, these exercises should help you stop blaming yourself for your maladaptive schemas. That does not mean you should blame anyone else for your schemas, though. You inevitably have some maladaptive schemas that resulted from your parents' schemas, but your parents did not get to choose their schemas either. People are not born with malevolent schemas. The purpose of these next exercises is to expand your understanding of yourself, not to create grounds for retribution.

EXERCISES FOR UNDERSTANDING THE ORIGINS OF YOUR SCHEMAS

1. Cultural Schemas

Reread the definitions of the schemas listed in Appendix A. Then, try to identify the schemas that were encouraged by the different organizations and media in the culture where you were reared. For example, some religions encourage the *Other-Centered⁻* or *Unworthy⁻* schemas and discourage the *Self-Centered⁺* schema. What schemas did the religious organizations of your community encourage and discourage? Some schools encourage the *Acquiescent⁻* or *Capable** schemas and discourage the *Aggressive⁺* schema. What schemas did the schools that you attended encourage and discourage? You need not have developed the schemas that you identify from your culture.

Organization   **Schema**

_____   _____

_____   _____

_____   _____

_____   _____

_____   _____

_____   _____

2. Other People's Schemas

List the people who have played the most significant roles in your own development, whether that impact has been positive or negative. Then, after each name, write down the adaptive and maladaptive schemas that seem to be most characteristic of these people. List as many schemas as you think you can recognize in each person. Also try to provide an example of each schema. Include anyone you want on this list: family, friends, teachers, supervisors, colleagues, enemies, idols, fictional individuals—any figure who has had a significant impact on you in some way. Then in the last column describe how you think each of their particular schemas influenced you. If you think that some of their schemas did not affect you, just leave the columns blank for those schemas. The example illustrates how Steven, the physician, began this exercise.

Name & Relationship	Schema & Example	Their Schemas' Effect on Me
Dad Father	*Self-Centered**: He drank heavily, regardless of the impact it had on Mom and me.	Made me feel unworthy, unimportant, and powerless.
Dad Father	*Unworthy*⁻: He always put himself down, said he was never any good and that he didn't deserve Mom or me.	Made me feel unworthy, too, but also sorry for him.

Name & Relationship	Schema & Example	Their Schemas' Effect on Me
_____	_____	_____
_____	_____	_____
_____	_____	_____
_____	_____	_____
_____	_____	_____

3. Origins of the Schemas of Others

Realizing how someone else might have gotten their schemas can help decrease the anger and blame we feel toward that person for influencing our maladaptive schemas. From exercise 2, write down the people you listed there and their maladaptive schemas. Then record what might have produced their schemas. Again, the example is from Steven.

Name	Their Maladaptive Schema	How Person Might Have Developed This Schema
Dad	*Unworthy⁻, Self-Centered* *	His dad used to physically abuse all the kids and Dad's mom, who died when Dad was about eight. His dad took off and left all the kids a few years later, so the kids went to different homes, but the places Dad was sent were as bad as being with his dad had been. Nobody ever cared about him until he met Mom.

Name	Their Maladaptive Schema	How Person Might Have Developed This Schema
_____	_____	_____
_____	_____	_____
_____	_____	_____
_____	_____	_____
_____	_____	_____
_____	_____	_____

4. Repeated Experiences or Traumatic Experiences

List the five or six most dominant schemas you think you have, adaptive and maladaptive. In the second column, indicate whether each schema came from repeated experiences or traumatic experiences or both. In the third column, describe the circumstances that contributed to the development of that schema. The example is again from Steven.

Schema	Trauma or Repeated Experience or Both	Circumstances for Schema Creation
Perfectionistic[+]	Repeated experience	Was repeatedly praised and respected for getting A's throughout school. Came to believe anything less was unacceptable. Perfect grades got me scholarships to college and medical school. Mom made me feel I needed to be perfect to make up for what people thought of my dad.
Schema	Trauma or Repeated Experience or Both	Circumstances for Schema Creation
_____	_____	_____
_____	_____	_____
_____	_____	_____
_____	_____	_____
_____	_____	_____
_____	_____	_____

7

That Often Overlooked Step: Preparation for Change

We shall be better prepared for the future
if we see how terrible, how doomed the present is.
—Iris Murdoch quoted in David Crimond,
The Book and the Brotherhood

This chapter will prepare you for the sometimes frightening process of change—in this case, the process of changing your schemas. Changing schemas requires a number of phases. You completed the first by becoming aware of your adaptive and maladaptive schemas. You completed the second phase when you explored the origins of your schemas. This chapter presents the third phase: *preparation* for changing your schemas.

Perhaps you are wondering why you can't just cut to the chase and change. Well, to begin with, change is best undertaken one step at a time. And preparation for change is one of those steps. If you aren't mentally prepared, it would be like trying to win a marathon without training for it in advance—a most unlikely accomplishment. Contemplating the prospect of changing schemas can also be quite powerful and emotional. A client once stated that when he started to work on changing his schemas, he felt as if he were standing on the end of a diving board and everyone was waiting for him to dive in. The problem was, he sensed he was wearing a pair of imaginary goggles. These were magic goggles that removed the sight of the water, so all he could see was cold concrete below. He tried to listen to his therapist and the well-intentioned supporters on the side of the pool who urged him to dive in. They saw the water. He knew that he could and should dive in, but his eyes told him that disaster would result if he did.

Preparing for schema change consists of five steps. The first step involves learning more about adaptive schemas and how they are constructed. The second step is learning the balance between self-acceptance and change. Most people who want to change neglect the self-acceptance part of the equation in favor of a false but perceived dire need to change. The third step focuses on the pace and process of change, so you will know what to expect. The fourth step will explain the concept of schema maintenance. This step will help you understand why the change process can be so difficult and why you may find yourself fighting the process in a variety of ways. Finally, we will teach you about the fifth step, understanding your schema triggers. As a warm-up to these five steps, we think it will help if you remember your strengths.

AN APPRECIATION OF YOUR STRENGTHS

To help you begin the change process, we recommend that you start by appreciating what you already have. Frequently, we are struck that many people rate themselves with a different set of standards than the one they apply to others. They clobber themselves for not being attractive enough, not having achieved enough, not having found the right relationship, or for being unable to stand up for themselves when they think they should. Yet, when we ask our clients what they admire in other people, they rarely cite those sorts of things. Rather, they usually say they admire qualities such as the following:

Trustworthiness	Helpfulness
Listening skills	Kindness
Honesty	Friendliness
Sense of humor	Compassion
Dependability	Generosity
Ability to empathize	Warmth

We believe it's a good idea to use a similar set of standards in evaluating yourself. You undoubtedly have friends who are not living at the top of the corporate ladder. Nor are they stunningly attractive. Yet you would rate them very highly on basic human qualities, such as the ones listed earlier. Aren't these the things that really matter? The world has plenty of high achievers but not enough people with these characteristics. Most of our clients who have poor self-esteem usually report feeling pretty good about their basic human qualities. The bottom line is that you should rate your own worth on the same scale you use to determine the worth of other people.

So as a warm-up exercise, list the characteristics or qualities you admire in other people. Then ask yourself, "How many of these qualities apply to me?" We think you'll find that many of the items apply to yourself. Appreciate those qualities! They are, after all, your true worth as a human being. Now you are ready to go through the five steps involved in preparing to change your schemas.

STEP 1: KEY ASPECTS OF ADAPTIVE SCHEMAS

The first step in preparing to change is not to focus on core maladaptive schemas per se but to learn how the adaptive schemas can be used as future possibilities, as alternatives to your maladaptive schemas. You can think of adaptive schemas as your goals. Changing without knowing where you are headed makes as much sense as traveling around unfamiliar country without a map. The key concepts in understanding adaptive schemas are *variability, flexibility*, and *tolerance*.

Variability

Adaptive schemas can vary among people. There is no exact spot on the schema continuum that represents the ideal way to be. If there were, it would imply that there is some kind of standard to which we should all adhere. Such personality cloning seems reminiscent of the "The Stepford Wives," in which all of the women were converted into perfect, albeit robot-like homemakers. Although the circular continuum depicted in Chapter 2 might suggest that there is only one "sweet spot," as there is on a baseball bat or the head of a golf club, that just isn't true. The key is finding a happy medium between the extremes that works fairly well for you.

Flexibility

Adaptive schemas allow new data to be incorporated into your self-concept flexibly. For example, if you had the *Adequate** schema, you would feel secure with yourself and your capabilities, in contrast to the *Inadequate*$^-$ or the *Perfectionistic*$^+$ schemas, which represent the two maladaptive extremes on this particular schema continuum. At the same time, your *Adequate** schema might include the information that you have not done quite as well as your peers in a few ways.

137

You might have thought of yourself as not quite as capable as others, even though you certainly did not feel like a failure (which would indicate an *Inadequate⁻* schema). A reasonably adaptive *Adequate** schema would allow you to notice new information about yourself.

Let's pretend that you prepared a report at work that received a lot of praise for its creativity and innovative thinking. As a result, you were asked to serve on several important committees and to make presentations at other branches of the company across the country. An adaptive schema would allow you to incorporate this new information and to realize that your capabilities are somewhat greater than you had previously thought. At the same time, an *Adequate** schema would prevent this recent success from making you suddenly too full of yourself. Because of this *Adequate** schema, you would not begin to pursue higher and higher accolades relentlessly at the expense of happiness, health, pleasure, and relationships.

By contrast, maladaptive schemas are usually not nearly as accommodating to new information. For example, the *Undesirable⁻* schema might lead you to believe that you are unattractive in a host of ways. You may think you are not good-looking or that you don't know the right things to say. The resolute rigidity of maladaptive schemas forces you to discount any contradictory information. So, if an attractive, desirable person showed interest in you, your *Undesirable⁻* schema might lead you to conclude that there must be something wrong with that person. The *Undesirable⁻* schema may have prompted Groucho Marx to say, "I don't care to belong to any club that will accept me as a member."

Fortunately, adaptive schemas are considerably more flexible than that. Adaptive schemas integrate both your strengths and weaknesses without overemphasizing either one unnecessarily. An adaptive schema is not simply a midpoint between the two maladaptive extremes. Rather, adaptive schemas integrate information from the opposite extremes in a way that softens them. For example, the *Blameworthy⁻* schema might suggest that you make many mistakes and that you deserve punishment or harsh criticism on such occasions. With the opposite, *Blameless⁺* schema, you will need to be correct almost all the time; admitting to being wrong or having made a mistake is very difficult. Self-blame does not occur, because it is not relevant. The *Accepting** schema is not one in which you simply acknowledge that you are blameworthy half the time and blameless the rest of the time. Rather, with the *Accepting** schema, you acknowledge that all humans make mistakes and that errors are inevitable. You do not blame yourself. Instead, you acknowledge responsibility for mistakes and are able to apologize comfortably. Do you see how the *Accepting** schema takes information from both extremes and integrates and softens it?

Tolerance

Tolerance of yourself and others is another feature of adaptive schemas. The lack of tolerance is ubiquitous in this world—simply look at the plight of Muslims in Bosnia, Turks in Germany, Italians in Switzerland, or Haitians in the United States. Subtle differences in the social meaning of various behaviors, such as gestures or appropriate physical space between people in a conversation, can often lead to gross misinterpretations and, ultimately, to intolerance. It may seem obvious that we should become more tolerant of others in social contexts such as these. Yet you are unlikely to become more tolerant of others without becoming more tolerant of yourself.

Adaptive schemas do not lead to self-punishment or self-abuse. In a sense, they are "egoless" as they attempt to reconcile various kinds of information in ways that create reasonable self-tolerance and self-acceptance. You will see the importance of self-tolerance and self-acceptance in the step below.

STEP 2: THE ACCEPTANCE-CHANGE BALANCE

Ironically, in order to *change*, you must first learn to *accept* yourself. Does this seem like a radical idea? Aren't we all the best that we can be at any given point if you take into account our biology, genetics, and experiences? The only thing we can influence is where we are headed, not where we have been. If you cannot at least partially accept yourself as you are now, your efforts to change will be difficult, because you will be too desperate to escape yourself. Such desperation produces unnecessary stress and impulsiveness. Schema change requires a more thoughtful, calm approach.

Imagine two kinds of teachers. Teacher A is a harsh, punitive, judgmental teacher who raps students' knuckles with a ruler and makes them stand in the corner of the classroom when they make mistakes. In sum, Teacher A shows little regard for students' feelings and instead focuses on their mistakes. By contrast, Teacher B is warm, accepting, and praising of students' efforts. Teacher B sets limits and is firm with disruptive behavior, but focuses on praising positive efforts with a variety of encouragements. Which of these teachers do you think will produce students who love to learn, grow, and change? And which teacher will produce students who fear learning and will avoid it at all costs? We hope you recognized that the methods employed by Teacher B will produce superior results; that teacher's students will be motivated, will try to learn from their mistakes, and will not avoid the learning process.

Which approach do you take with yourself? You may know that the methods employed by Teacher A are not good but still adhere to the harsh approach when dealing with yourself. When you make a mistake or fail to accomplish a goal, do you berate yourself and make yourself miserable? If so, this type of self-abuse has to stop. Of course, everyone does this occasionally, but some people don't know when to quit.

We have an alternative for you. The next time you begin to punish yourself for failing to accomplish what you want or for making a mistake, ask what you would tell your own best friend in a similar circumstance. Would you be as harsh and punitive? Most people would not. Most would tell their friends to pick themselves up, dust themselves off, learn from the mistake, and move on. Not only would they tell that to their friends but they would mean it. Knowing that it is human to make mistakes, they would think no less of their friends. So try treating yourself the same way. The next time you screw up, ask yourself what you would tell your own best friend about that situation—and then do that for yourself! You probably treat your best friend with an acceptance-change balance—you accept your friend in the present while supporting any effort to make changes.

Being your own best friend might be harder to do than it sounds. It may be best simply to pick a day in which you conscientiously and religiously treat yourself as your own best friend. You might even write something like the following on a flash card:

Sample Best Friend Flash Card

> I know I'm going to make mistakes in learning to become more assertive. Everybody screws up when they try to change. When I act too passively, I'm going to ask myself, "What would I tell (name of best friend) about this situation?" I would probably say, "Sure, maybe you goofed up. Yes, being more assertive would have been better. So what? Learn from it and move on. It's not going to help if you beat yourself up." In fact, that sounds like good advice! I can learn from my mistakes. And beating up on myself just makes the process of becoming more assertive all the more difficult, because it robs me of energy and depresses me.

Write your own flash card and keep it with you. On the day you decide to treat yourself as your own best friend, you might need to read it over many times. Once you have begun to treat yourself as your own best friend, extend the trial period by a couple of days. You might be surprised at how much better you begin to feel. We are not saying you should ignore your mistakes or pretend that they didn't happen. Rather, you need to analyze and learn from your mistakes rather than dwell upon them.

Self-evaluation, in the sense of rating or grading oneself, is a pointless exercise anyway. Albert Ellis, a renowned psychologist credited with developing rational-emotive therapy, made a list of reasons that judging one's own worth can be self-defeating. We describe these reasons below.

1. Self-evaluation creates self-centeredness as opposed to problem-centeredness.

2. Self-evaluation can easily result in one-upmanship or one-downmanship. If you think of yourself as good or bad, you are likely to see other people as better or worse than you, which can cause jealousy, envy, or feelings of superiority.

3. Evaluating yourself on the basis of a few particular acts of behavior doesn't make sense. It is much better to put any given act of behavior in an overall context.

4. When you are constantly evaluating yourself, it is much harder to listen empathically to others. Full understanding probably can only come from a noncompetitive, intensive listening to the other person's point of view and worldview. This includes accepting that person's view as being valid at least for them.

5. How can we rate somebody's overall worth anyway? How would we weigh each of the individual acts throughout a person's life? What if someone performed thousands of wonderful giving, caring actions and yet one day stole some expensive silverware from a neighbor? Would this be a vile, contemptuous person, or would it be an honorable one? Obviously, there is no clear answer.

6. Time spent evaluating yourself can be put to much better use. We might add that if all of the time and energy spent on self-ratings were devoted to some more productive enterprise, it is hard to imagine what the human species might have accomplished by now.

Self-acceptance also means realizing and accepting that the process of change takes a lifetime; it never ends. As the bumper sticker proclaims, "God is not finished with me yet!" If change isn't infinite, you would have to assume there will be a place and time when you eventually will be able to declare, "I'm perfect now!" Is that really what you would want? Are you sure? Imagine a painting of a landscape that is absolutely perfect in every way. Every leaf is green, there's not a single gnarl in the bark, and every blade of grass is green and luscious. In this painting, the sky is cloudless, and there's not a clump of dirt or craggy rock. What do you think your reaction would be to the painting? Would it seem beautiful and inspiring? Or, possibly, would it seem monotonous and boring? Consider for a moment that all of life's little imperfections are part of a real landscape's interest and appeal. Indeed, they contribute to its beauty.

Is it possible that our imperfections also give us richness and make us interesting, even human? Think of the people you like most. Don't they have interesting little quirks, weaknesses, difficulties, and frailties? Do you like them less for it? Probably not. So if you don't magnify and dwell on every flaw and foible in others, why do so with yourself?

As you develop self-acceptance, you will prepare yourself for change. When we say *self-acceptance*, we don't mean self-aggrandizement and puffery. Excessive self-promotion is not a better option. A fully integrated sense of yourself includes flaws and foibles and, at the same time, strengths and positive attributes. *Self-acceptance* means a recognition and acceptance of human weaknesses. Self-acceptance will lead to a far better balance in your life.

STEP 3: THE PACE AND PROCESS OF CHANGE

The Pace of Change

How does change toward adaptive schemas occur? Do you think it's a straight, smooth line upward? Rarely. More often, change follows the path in the progress chart shown on the next page. Notice that change always progresses in an uneven course. People often expect that change will progress in a smooth, direct path upward. This never happens. Instead, there are ups and downs.

The down times can be depressing if you lose perspective. Imagine you are standing in the middle of one of the valleys in this figure. It would be easy to imagine that you have never been so low before, wouldn't it? These are not good times to evaluate the progress you are making, because things will look distorted. Keep in mind that these times present an opportunity to learn what kinds of issues and problems knock you backward. Knowing this can help you make upward moves in similar future situations. Use these down times to understand yourself better.

When you are doing well, it is much easier to look back with some objectivity and see the overall upward trend that includes some downs. However,

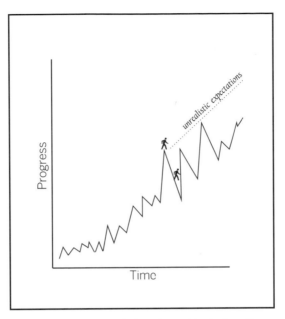

This illustration helps the patient visualize progress in therapy.

at these times, be wary of slipping into unrealistically positive expectations about the future. Such expectations can set you up for disappointment. Be satisfied with an overall trend in the right direction.

The Process of Change

Our colleagues, Drs. Prochaska, Norcross, and DiClemente, have discovered that change appears to consist of six different stages. We describe these stages below.

Precontemplation

People in the precontemplation stage often don't even realize they have a problem. For example, an alcoholic who has been arrested on two DWIs, yet maintains that he is in perfect control of his drinking, is probably in the precontemplation stage. By contrast, others can often see the self-defeating nature of the precontemplative person's behaviors. Fortunately for you, if you are reading this book, you have probably moved past this stage with respect to some important problem areas in your life.

Contemplation

People in this stage know they have a problem, but they feel overwhelmed and trapped by it. In fact, it would be common for them to spend several years in this stage. Our section on schema maintenance will show you why they stay stuck in this stage. A man who desperately wanted to commit to a relationship but felt panicked and overwhelmed every time he started to get close to a woman would be an example of someone in the contemplation stage of change if he recognized his dilemma.

Preparation

This stage precedes action. At this point, most people have given their problems a lot of thought and plan to take action soon. Many find it useful to make a public commitment about their plans to change as an additional incentive. At this time, they plot out a detailed battle plan. Some, perhaps many, of you are at this stage. After contemplating divorce for eight years, a woman who consults an attorney and a CPA is in the preparation stage.

Action

This stage is the one most obvious to others. The action stage is when you implement your plans for change, whether those plans involve cutting down on eating, facing fears, or reprioritizing your life. This stage consumes much energy. It is important, but too much emphasis on this stage can throw the acceptance-change balance out of whack if your actions don't result in successes. When the woman filed for divorce and enrolled in a paralegal course, she entered the action stage.

Maintenance

Many people are unprepared for the problems posed by this stage. They think that once they take action, their problems will be solved. This is usually not true. Most of us struggle with this stage. Continued vigilance and plans for dealing with difficult moments are crucial for a successful resolution. A man thought he had conquered his fears when he finally asked his girlfriend to marry him. He finally took action to overcome his fear of commitment, but he was surprised by the amount of anxiety his decision evoked. He found himself struggling to maintain his commitment in this stage.

Termination

This stage represents the dream for all of us—the day that temptation no longer lurks at the front door and when the struggle has ended. Unfortunately, some problems never reach this stage. People often continue to make determined efforts with their issues for a lifetime. That does not mean they haven't made excellent progress and that the quality of their lives has not improved greatly from their efforts. It just means that complete resolution of their problems may not be realistic. After having worked for a long time to achieve a measure of self-acceptance, a man finally reached the termination stage and found that making mistakes didn't grab his attention anymore. He was comfortable with criticism and could apologize with ease.

If you want to know more about these stages and how to deal with them, we highly recommend the book *Changing for Good*. For now, you need to know that flipping back and forth among these stages is not unusual. Nor is it an indication that you are hopeless. For example, many smokers move smoothly from the precontemplation stage through the contemplation and preparation stages and into the action stage and then discover themselves unable to maintain their gains. Although they may not return to the precontemplation stage, they may fall back to the contemplation phase until they are ready to try again.

Most people who change successfully have tried to change many times before. Do not forget this point. Just because you have tried and slipped back to an earlier stage does not mean that you will be unable to change successfully in the future. Think of each attempt at change as an opportunity for learning what works and does not work for you. One of our clients described this process as "falling forward." She said that each time she tried and didn't get where she wanted, she at least learned something about herself that she could use in her next attempt.

STEP 4: SCHEMA MAINTENANCE

What is it about maladaptive schemas that makes them so tenaciously resistant to change? Even in the face of exorbitant evidence that they no longer hold water, we fail to see this fact. Primarily, we hold onto them because we automatically assume that they are valid as a way of viewing the world and ourselves. As you probably know by now, with maladaptive schemas in place, we believe that bad things will happen if we break out of our patterns. For example, an *Inadequate⁻* schema can make us believe that if we try to accomplish something, we will very likely fail. Rather than working to disprove this belief, we put our energy into minimizing the schema's negative consequences. Sadly, as you will see, these efforts to minimize the consequences often seem to prove that the maladaptive schema is true.

Avoidance

Sam believed so strongly that he was an inadequate person that he avoided doing anything that would let others see how inadequate he was. As a child, he avoided athletics. As an adult, he avoided people and any situation that would draw

145

attention to his self-perceived inadequacies. Even though he was an intelligent, skillful mechanic, he did not believe that. He avoided situations that drew attention to his incompetence. Unfortunately, avoiding opportunities to display his skills meant that he also avoided the possibility of a promotion. He stayed at the bottom of the ladder in his trade for years, so his *Inadequate⁻* schema stayed intact. Sam believed that avoiding attention and shying away from extra responsibilities protected him from the shame and ridicule he would otherwise experience. The thought that his schema might be fundamentally flawed never occurred to him. Again, once a schema forms, we assume it's valid; therefore, we work hard to avoid its consequences.

The first time Dan (a newly licensed teenager) ever drove a car by himself, a truck ran through a stoplight and smashed into him, causing severe injuries that required months of prolonged recuperation. How do you think Dan approached the task of renewed driving? Was he calm and relaxed? No. He formed the *Vulnerable⁻* schema with respect to driving. Feeling horribly tense and anxious, he constantly checked his rearview mirrors and was hypervigilant every second he spent behind the wheel. Did these measures of extreme caution make Don safer? No. In fact, because he was so anxious, he was at greater risk for another accident. So why didn't he simply relax and drive normally? Because he was convinced that another disaster would immediately ensue if he did and that he had to remain hypervigilant.

The extreme anxiety associated with changing a schema comes from the assumption that the schema is true and must be followed to avoid or forestall the anticipated negative consequences. Psychologists refer to this process as *avoidance conditioning*, a learned response that is one of the most difficult patterns to change. Avoidance conditioning was first observed in animals. Assume that an experimenter administers an electric shock to a rat every time the rat wanders into a certain corner of the cage. Obviously, the rat quickly learns to avoid that corner. The experimenter then tries teaching the rat to overcome this fear by never shocking it in that area again. The attempt fails. Why? The rat has, in essence, formed a schema about that corner. The rat "believes" that it successfully avoided the shock every time by avoiding the corner. The rat will not venture into the corner even if the experimenter puts food there. This example illustrates why changing avoidance behavior is so hard. Once avoidance behavior results in perceived safety, the rat or person will not try alternatives that *seem* dangerous, even if they are perfectly safe.

But, you might object, most schemas don't involve matters of physical pain or injury. Perhaps not. But they can be very painful emotionally, and sometimes, particularly from a child's point of view, schemas *do* involve issues of life and death. For example, a child would die if completely abandoned by any and all competent caretakers. That fact might suggest that we are hardwired as a species to be sensitive to such issues as abandonment. John became extremely abandonment fearful from the age of five when his mother left without warning. She left a terse note, but otherwise she took everything that belonged to her while John and his dad were fishing. Neither John nor his father ever saw her again.

Unfortunately, schemas like John's persist even after conditions have changed, and conditions usually do change after childhood. At that point, the schemas have become maladaptive and self-defeating because their validity is never questioned. For example, John was no more likely to be abandoned as an adult than anyone else. Yet he assumed that anyone important to him would eventually leave. John felt that if he relaxed and stopped believing in his schema, the most feared consequence would come true—his wife would leave him. Believing in his *Abandonment⁻* schema led him to think that he could prevent his wife from ending their marriage by constantly checking her fidelity. We hope it's becoming clear to you why people don't give up their schemas easily.

For now, we want you to appreciate fully that avoidance is a primary schema maintenance strategy. Sam, the mechanic, thought he avoided ridicule and shame by not taking on responsibilities. Dan attempted to avoid another horrible accident through hypervigilant driving habits. John thought he could hold onto his wife a little longer. And the rat tried to avoid electric shocks. In each case, avoidance not only wasn't necessary but also had the unfortunate consequence of perpetuating the schema because it seemed to work—it appeared to prevent the dreaded negative outcome. These perceptions were illusory. More often than not, the consequences would not have occurred and the costs of avoidance were high. Sam lost out on promotions, Dan experienced extreme stress, John worried all of the time, and even the rat lost freedom.

Compounding the problem, the avoidance pattern is sometimes so extreme that it actually causes the very thing the person fears. Because of John's powerful *Abandonment⁻* schema, he experienced unwarranted jealousy. He questioned where his wife was going, when she would be back, and who would be with her. If she arrived more than a few minutes late, he grilled her for hours about where she had been and what she had been doing. And he rarely believed her answers. His wife eventually felt suffocated. These feelings drove her out of the house more often, which made John even more jealous. Eventually, she left for good. John's exhaustive efforts to ensure that his wife would not abandon him ended up driving her away and reinforced his belief that anyone important would eventually leave.

Procrastination is a particularly insidious form of avoidance. For example, it might be tempting to skip the "best friend" flash card exercise we suggested, because doing so means that you must acknowledge a few weaknesses. We have known students who put off finishing their doctoral degrees in clinical psychology for years, because beginning their practice might challenge their *Inadequate⁻* schema. Others delay learning new skills such as assertiveness, because they fear they will arouse others' anger if they make the attempt. Submissiveness may not achieve their goals, but it avoids the anxiety associated with anger. Be on the lookout for procrastination; don't let it foil your attempts to reach your goals.

Rejection and Revision of Contradictory Evidence

We stubbornly maintain schemas in other interesting ways. Because the prospect of change arouses anxiety, we look for data and evidence to maintain them, while discarding or revising contradictory evidence. We simply don't believe the conflicting information.

Sam managed to hang onto his *Inadequate⁻* schema in spite of the fact that his co-workers often sought his advice. They recognized his abilities better than he or his boss did. Sam figured that they came to him to avoid the embarrassment of asking someone else a simple question. He thought that by asking him, they were not risking much. Of course, the questions were only simple to Sam because he really knew his business. Many times, no one else had the answer. Sam also discounted praise by thinking it was undeserved or only given to make him feel better. And when Sam was occasionally criticized, he magnified its meaning and importance, often dwelling on it for days. These actions illustrate ways in which we all maintain our schemas, sometimes in spite of mounds of contradictory evidence.

Numbness

We also maintain schemas through the numbing process. People using this strategy will often report having no feelings at all, even in situations that would upset most of us. In order to avoid the horrible negative feelings associated with their maladaptive schemas, they may dissociate from reality by feeling "out of it," unreal, or as though things were happening to someone else. Confusion is a similar way to maintain schemas. Such confusion makes it hard to identify the issues behind a maladaptive schema, which helps maintain the schema. When we point out to clients that a particular schema appears to be controlling them, they often report feeling numb, "out of it," or confused. Sam became disoriented at work whenever he received praise for his performance. At those times, he found himself so out of it that he started making trivial, easily avoidable mistakes. The praise threatened his *Inadequate⁻* schema, so he maintained the schema by inadvertently goofing up.

Hopelessness

Hopelessness is an especially common schema maintenance technique. You can avoid the anxiety associated with changing schemas simply by convincing yourself that you are more hopeless and more incapable of change than others. It may surprise you to learn that most people who work at changing schemas feel hopeless about the process at some point. At first, they think they are the exception to the rule, the one person who can't change successfully. But inevitably, they learn to overcome this obstacle and make changes in their lives.

Others with severe hopelessness about schema maintenance chronically consider suicide. They may make many suicidal attempts, sometimes tragically succeeding. This is most true for those with a wide range of extreme, maladaptive schemas. Their emotional pain runs so deep that almost anything seems worth trying in order to avoid their feelings. They don't realize that there are other ways out of their dilemmas. Fortunately, most people's schemas are not quite that extreme.

Reinforcement by Others

Other people maintain our maladaptive schemas by unwittingly reinforcing and supporting them. If a person is *Domineering⁺* and *Omnipotent⁺*, that person often seeks out those who feel *Acquiescent⁻* and *Powerless⁻*. Unfortunately, those with negative maladaptive schemas frequently believe they deserve the abuse and allow the partner's outrageous behavior to occur. They find themselves unable to set a limit or exert their right to leave an obviously dysfunctional relationship. Over time, however, through therapy or other means, they often do leave these relationships. Their partners with positive maladaptive schemas are often shocked and devastated. When their illusory self-concept has been badly punctured, they sometimes switch to negative maladaptive schemas, if only briefly.

STEP 5: SCHEMA TRIGGERS

If you are going to understand your schemas fully, you must learn to recognize the events or people that activate them. We call these cues *triggers*. Remember how you can have several schemas on a continuum? For example, you may usually feel quite *Adequate*[*], yet after a minor failure, plunge into despair brought on by an underlying *Inadequate⁻* schema. If you understand the events that tend to trigger or elicit your problematic schemas, you can prepare for them. Sometimes such preparation can help you prevent a maladaptive schema from activating.

Spend some time thinking about what types of events arouse negative emotions in you. What maladaptive schemas seem associated with those emotions? If you have a strong *Undesirable⁻* schema, perhaps events such as meeting new people or being the center of attention will create a great deal of anxiety in you, thereby triggering your *Undesirable⁻* schema. If you have a powerful *Vulnerable⁻* schema, you may find it triggered by driving in heavy traffic or by making a doctor's appointment. People with the same problematic schemas may have very different triggers. Thus, it is important to learn what triggers *your* negative and positive maladaptive schemas.

CONCLUSION

This chapter explained how to prepare for schema change. We described adaptive schemas in more detail in order to provide you with some personal goals. We presented the balance between acceptance and change and asked that you not punish yourself when your efforts to change are not proceeding as smoothly as you would like. Self-abuse only slows things down. We told you about the pace and process of change, so you would know to expect slips and slides along the way. Understanding the schema maintenance process should help you realize that what may look like crazy, self-defeating behavior actually has a basis. We maintain schemas by being avoidant, discarding contradictory evidence, numbing our feelings, and feeling hopelessness. Other people sometimes support our schemas both intentionally and unintentionally. You need to remain on the lookout for these schema maintenance processes as you start to make changes. They will make their presence known at some point. When they do, you won't be caught off guard.

Now you are ready to start developing your adaptive schemas. We have found that building these up first makes it easier to knock down your negative and positive maladaptive schemas later. Remember that change happens one phase at a time.

EXERCISES FOR ENHANCING SELF-ACCEPTANCE

1. Schema Triggers and Schema Maintenance Exercise

We recommend that you list your two or three most problematic maladaptive schemas, accompanied by their typical triggers and the things you do to maintain them. This exercise doesn't actually ask you to change anything, just to increase your *awareness* of these issues. Such awareness will help you in your later attempts to change. Knowing your troubling triggers will help you prepare for difficult challenges, and understanding what you do to maintain your maladaptive schemas will help you figure out how to stop sabotaging your own efforts to change.

Sharon, a forty-one-year-old educational diagnostician, filled out the following exercise.

Problematic Maladaptive Schemas	Triggers	Schema Maintenance Strategies
1. *Vulnerable*—I feel my health is very fragile. I don't like to take risks of any kind.	1. Anything in the news about health. 2. Heavy traffic. 3. Any ache or pain in my body.	1. **Avoidance**—I always avoid the freeway, even though it takes me twenty minutes longer to get to work every day. 2. **Discarding contradictory evidence**—Even when my doctor gives me the OK, I think he has missed something important.
1. *Other-Centered*—I always take care of everyone else. I never look out for myself. Sometimes I get resentful, but I can't do anything about it.	1. Anytime someone asks for a favor. 2. Anytime I see that someone could use my help. 3. When my kids get frustrated, I always help them.	1. **Avoidance**—I always avoid doing anything just for myself. 2. **Hopelessness**—Sometimes I fall into despair and think I will never be able to enjoy life for myself. 3. **Discarding contradictory evidence**—I can't hear it when the psychologist says I do too much for my kids and that I am spoiling them to death.

151

Problematic Maladaptive Schemas	Triggers	Schema Maintenance Strategies
_____	_____	_____
_____	_____	_____
_____	_____	_____
_____	_____	_____
_____	_____	_____
_____	_____	_____
_____	_____	_____
_____	_____	_____
_____	_____	_____
_____	_____	_____
_____	_____	_____
_____	_____	_____
_____	_____	_____
_____	_____	_____
_____	_____	_____
_____	_____	_____
_____	_____	_____

2. Accepting Others' Shortcomings

Think of two individuals whom you know personally and admire or love. Write down each person's name, and then below the name, record five of their flaws or foibles.

Name_____   **Name** _____

Foibles_____   **Foibles**_____

a. _____   a. _____

b. _____   b. _____

c. _____   c. _____

d. _____   d. _____

e. _____   e. _____

Now ask yourself why you can't love yourself with your flaws when you can love other people who have shortcomings.

3. Assessing Your Strengths

Below, describe your positive qualities. Don't skip this exercise! It is especially important for people who dwell on their shortcomings, but everyone needs to do this exercise. You need to discover or reaffirm that just because you want to make some changes in yourself does not mean that you are not a worthwhile person already. Remember the basic qualities that are important to us in others: being trustworthy, honest, dependable, helpful, kind, friendly, compassionate, generous, warm, forgiving, loving, funny, and empathic, as well as being a good listener and a hard worker. Include as many of these as you think apply to you. Now list your positive qualities, and do not be modest. In fact, if you are hesitating out of modesty, then you need to list modesty as your first positive attribute.

_____

_____

_____

_____

_____

_____

_____

_____

_____

8

Adaptive Schemas in the Self-Worth Zone

The shortest answer is doing.
—*English proverb, George Herbert,* Jacula Prudentum

If you read the previous seven chapters and completed the exercises, you are already on the road to schema change. If you skimmed some of the chapters and skipped the exercises, you are only at the on-ramp, but at least you are headed in the right direction. Either way, by now you should have a vivid self-schema portrait. You have identified both your adaptive and maladaptive schemas and you understand how you might have developed them. In the last chapter, you learned more about adaptive schemas and how beneficial they are. You also learned how people seek out information that confirms schemas, so that once a schema has been created, it tends to persist. Thus, creating a new, more adaptive schema requires a concentrated effort.

This chapter and the following two chapters will present examples of how people have created adaptive schemas in the Self-Worth, Empowerment, and Relationship Zones. These examples will provide you with blueprints to develop your own adaptive schema in any of the continua. Even though the circumstances of these people may differ from your own, adaptive schemas are essentially similar for everyone. This chapter will focus on the four adaptive schemas in the Self-Worth Zone: *Adequate**, *Accepting**, *Worthy**, and *Desirable**. All of these schemas influence our personal sense of worth. They reflect a sense of our own essence. They also impact schemas in the zones of Empowerment and Relationships.

CREATING A SCHEMA-DEVELOPMENT PLAN

A schema-development plan consists of two parts. The first part is an analysis of your maladaptive schemas to determine which circumstances and triggers activate it and to identify which thoughts and actions reinforce it. In the second part, you will use this information to create an adaptive schema on that continuum. There are seven steps to each part. As we go through both parts, you may be surprised to discover that you already have completed the majority of the steps in earlier chapters. First, we will present the fundamental procedure for schema development. Then we will show you detailed examples of how to apply it.

For now, just read through this chapter. You will find a place to complete a schema-development plan at the end of the chapter. You might find it preferable to finish reading the next two chapters before you complete the exercises at the end of each of the three chapters on creating adaptive schemas (Chapters 8, 9, and 10). Or you might find it easier to read the entire book and then go back and complete the exercises. Do not let yourself get bogged down in an exercise for which you are not ready. The exercises will become clearer as you read on. The point is not *when* you do the exercises but *that* you eventually do them.

Part 1: Maladaptive Schema Analysis

By now, you have selected a troublesome maladaptive schema and recorded several examples in Appendix B. If you haven't recorded your examples, you cannot design a change plan yet. If you try to analyze your maladaptive schema without actual examples, you are only guessing. We don't want you to guess. If you have picked a problematic schema, you easily can collect at least half a dozen examples. As soon as you have that many examples, you can begin your maladaptive schema analysis.

Step 1: Define Your Maladaptive Schema in Your Own Words

You already did this in Appendix B. If you didn't create your own definition, you can use all or parts of our definition. You may be concerned that you won't pick the right maladaptive schema. You cannot goof this up. Repeat: You cannot goof this up. There is no "right" maladaptive schema to choose. If you have several problematic schemas, you can pick one that occurs frequently. You also can make several change plans for different schemas before you decide which one you want to implement first.

**Step 2: Describe Your Thoughts When
Your Maladaptive Schema Is Active**

Think of situations when your maladaptive schema is active and write down the typical thoughts you have in those situations. Again, you already have this information in Appendix B.

**Step 3: Describe How You Feel When
Your Maladaptive Schema Is Active**

By now, you should be very pleased with yourself for completing Appendix B, because this information is also in it. For each example, you were to write down how you felt at the time. If you haven't done that yet, read your examples and record your feelings for each situation. Then review your feelings for all of your examples and record those for this step.

**Step 4: Describe What You Do When
Your Maladaptive Schema Is Active**

Reread your examples in Appendix B. Write down the typical way you react to or handle situations involving that maladaptive schema. Two or three statements are enough for this part.

Step 5: Describe the Origins of Your Maladaptive Schema

You already did this in the Chapter 6 exercises. Review your answers there, and then write the origins for this schema in your plan. Often, people or situations who influenced the development of a schema may still be triggers for it. If this is true for you, write that information as part of step 6.

Step 6: Describe the Triggers for Your Maladaptive Schema

Remember, triggers are the people or situations that seem to set off your schema. You may have a very good idea of the triggers, but if not, review your examples. Do certain people seem to be present? Do the situations have something in common, such as requiring you to perform or be accountable to an authority figure? Does your schema emerge when you are tired? All of those are examples of triggers. You also might ask someone to read your examples to see if they can identify any triggers. You should have answered this question already at the end of Chapter 7. Put that information here.

**Step 7: Describe What You and Others
Do to Maintain Your Maladaptive Schema**

The people and situations involved in the origins of your schema may still be present and may reinforce it, either because you are still being exposed to those

157

situations and people or because your own memories of them are still very powerful. You also do things to maintain your maladaptive schema. Again, you already answered this question at the end of Chapter 7, so put that information in your plan.

Part 2: Adaptive Schema Development

Now, we will describe the seven steps to create an adaptive schema. You will use the information from the maladaptive schema analysis in your development plan. This is why you need to complete the two parts and their steps in sequence.

Step 1: Define the Adaptive Schema You Want to Develop
You can use all or parts of our definition, or you can create your own definition. Make your definition fit the way you want to be.

Step 2: Describe the Thoughts Your Adaptive Schema Would Produce
You need to read your definition and then review your own examples of your maladaptive schema. Now imagine what you might have thought in those same situations if you already had your adaptive schema. Write down those thoughts.

Step 3: Describe the Feelings That Would Accompany the Thoughts of Your Adaptive Schema
Read the thoughts you just wrote down for the last question, and imagine how you would feel if you were having those thoughts. Then write those feelings here.

Step 4: Describe the Steps or Actions You Need to Take That Are Consistent with the Thoughts and Feelings of Your Adaptive Schema
This is the hardest part of the change plan to create, but your answers to the preceding questions will provide you with lots of ideas. We will give you more suggestions for this step in the next chapter.

Step 5: Identify at Least One Person Who Has the Adaptive Schema You Are Creating
Find a role model for your new schema. This person can be real or fictional, such as a television or movie character. Observe how that person handles situations relevant to your schema. Imitation is invaluable, but observing other people also gives us new ideas and stimulates our own creativity. View other people as potential resources. Consider using a role model as a consultant. Don't restrict yourself

to reinventing every wheel ever designed. Use somebody else's wheel and put your energy into personalizing the hubcap.

Step 6: Find a Support Person
You certainly can make schema changes on your own, but the process will be easier if you have someone who can support you when you are discouraged, brainstorm with you when you are stuck, and encourage you when you are afraid. You can role-play situations and review your progress regularly together. Your support person needs to be someone who is trustworthy and has good judgment. Many people use their psychologists for this role, but some use friends or family members as well. You only need one or two support people.

Step 7: Select One or Two Actions to Try
Working on only one or two items at a time is essential. If you do not limit yourself to only one or two action items, you will not be able to stay focused on each action step. Don't set yourself up for failure here. A major source of discouragement in changing ourselves is taking on too large a task and then becoming disheartened when feeling overwhelmed. Start small. Trust us on this. You cannot start too small. Record what happens every time you try your action item. If it doesn't work as hoped, write how you might handle the situation differently in the future, and then try that the next time a similar situation arises. Staying aware of an item and recording your examples are time-consuming activities, as is analyzing how you might revise your item when you obtain unexpected consequences. So limiting yourself to a few action items at a time is essential. Only after an action item has become comfortably routine should you move on to a new one.

CREATING ADAPTIVE SCHEMAS

Let's see how this schema-development plan is implemented. Dana is a twenty-nine-year-old married woman with two children in elementary school. She did not work outside the home for the past five years. Her younger child entered first grade in the fall, so she arranged to sell cosmetics to earn extra income for the family. This sales position allowed her to set her own hours and be home for the kids. After six months of minimal sales, Dana became increasingly depressed and angry with herself. In therapy, she identified her adaptive and maladaptive schemas. She thought her most troublesome schema was *Inadequate⁻*, so she began to keep a schema diary on this maladaptive schema, just like the diary you are keeping. After only a few days, Dana recorded several examples of her *Inadequate⁻* schema. A typical diary entry follows.

Dana: *Inadequate⁻* Schema

Example (include who, what, where, outcome information, your thoughts, and your feelings):

I got out my list of names that the company had provided for my area. I looked at the names and chose one. I picked up the phone but before I dialed, I realized that I didn't know exactly what I would say. I did imagine what the other person would say. I thought she would act annoyed that I had bothered her and try to get me off the phone as fast as possible. Then I felt really nervous, so I hung up the phone. Then I got up and went into the kitchen and ate a cookie. That made me feel better, so I ate three more cookies. After that, I decided to clean up the kitchen before I started calling. I did that and then went back to my desk. I glanced at the list of names and then thought how I could do a load of laundry while I made the calls. So I gathered the laundry, sorted it, and began a load. Then I went back to my desk again. By now it was almost 10:30, so I needed to get cleaned up to go to my 11:30 dental appointment. I felt relieved about avoiding the phone calling then, but later in the afternoon I felt bad about myself for not calling. Then I thought, I am never going to be able to do this. No one is interested in my products. I am no good as a salesperson. I will never make any money at this— just like my husband and parents told me. I can't do anything right. By now I felt upset, on the verge of tears, helpless, sad, and nervous, and the kids were due home at any moment.

After Dana acquired a week of examples of her *Inadequate⁻* schema, she completed a maladaptive schema analysis. Notice how she gets much of the information for these steps from her example above.

All the schema analyses presented in these chapters, including Dana's, were developed in collaboration with psychologists. Don't expect your own analyses to be nearly so detailed or long, and they don't have to be. Our goal in giving you so much detail is to provide lots of different ideas to help you develop your own analyses.

Dana: *Inadequate⁻* Schema

Part 1: Maladaptive Schema Analysis

Step 1: My definition of my *Inadequate⁻* schema: I feel I am inadequate compared to others. I don't feel I am very capable. I am not as talented as other people. Other people seem to be able to figure things out better than me.

Step 2: What do I think when my *Inadequate⁻* schema is active? I am no good as a salesperson. I will never make any money on my own, just like my family said. I can't do anything right. Nobody is interested in my products. I am only bothering people. I can't succeed at anything.

Step 3: How do I feel when my *Inadequate⁻* schema is active? Anxious, fearful of being exposed as inadequate, embarrassed, angry.

Step 4: What do I do when my *Inadequate⁻* schema iss active? I do other things to avoid working on the task. I isolate myself from others. I don't go to the monthly sales meetings for my region. I sleep excessively. I overeat.

Step 5: What are the origins of my *Inadequate⁻* schema? My father was a successful businessman and drove himself relentlessly. He never had time for fun and scorned frivolity in other people, even in my brother and me when we were kids. My mother was the perfect wife and mother. I was expected to meet their standards and was criticized when I did not. I got a lot of criticism because I seldom met their standards, no matter how hard I tried.

Step 6: What are the triggers for my *Inadequate⁻* schema? Being around anyone who has achieved more than me in some area; when I set unrealistically high goals and then realize I cannot meet them; when I am supposed to do something that might result in failure, like making sales calls; when someone criticizes me; when I am around certain people, especially my parents and my husband; when my brother and sister-in-law come over and talk about how their kids love private school and about what expensive vacations they have taken with my brother's bonus checks.

Step 7: What do I and others do to maintain my *Inadequate⁻* schema now? I am very critical of myself. I compare myself to other people who are more successful than me. I think Angie is a better mother, because she never seems upset and is so organized. I think I will never be as good in sales as Sarah, who started in the cosmetics business the same time I did and already has a stream of steady clients. I think how I need to prove to my parents and husband that I can be successful in sales, but when I think like this, I get so nervous that I can't concentrate on my sales activities. I procrastinate at the tasks that would help me. I try to avoid anything I think I can't do, and then feel bad about myself because I think I am such a failure. My parents criticize me for my housekeeping, my supposedly unruly kids, my appearance, my choice of this sales position. My husband is also critical. He always notices what I haven't done or when my plans don't turn out the way I want. He asks me every night if I have made any sales. When I say no, he lectures me on how I am wasting my time on this pursuit and how we need me to earn some dependable income.

Part 2: Adaptive Schema Development

Step 1: My definition of the *Adequate** schema I want to create: I am OK the way I am. I am a competent person, even if I do not achieve as much as some other people do. I am good enough the way I am.

Step 2: What thoughts would my *Adequate** schema produce?
My competence does not depend on any one skill. I am capable of many things. Of course there are things that I am inadequate at doing. That's true of everyone. If there are things I cannot do, I will try to learn how to do them if I think they are important to me. I will remind myself that I am doing the best that I can at any time. I will not beat myself up anymore. Putting myself down only discourages me and does not solve any problems. I will remind myself that I have chosen these activities or tasks because I thought they would be fun or useful, not to prove anything to someone else. I must stop letting fear of disapproval run my life. I am going to try to enjoy each day of my life and take reasonable risks to learn new things. If some people think that I am inadequate, I cannot control that. I can work on not worrying about that.

Step 3: What feelings would accompany the thoughts of my *Adequate** schema? Contentment, pleasure, calmness, joy in trying new things.

Step 4: What steps or actions do I need to take that are consistent with the thoughts and feelings of my *Adequate** schema?

Action Item 1. I will stop comparing myself to other people. Who knows what their histories or current circumstances are, or what motivates them. Comparing myself to people is pointless. Instead, when I notice that someone is more skilled than me in an area where I want to improve, I will ask them for suggestions. I will view people around me as potential resources or teachers, not as threats anymore. I will call Sarah and ask if she would meet with me and teach me some of the techniques she has used so successfully in her sales.

Action Item 2. I will set goals that are under my control. I will set my goal for my morning work session as the number of telephone calls I make, not the number of sales. I can control the number of calls, not the number of sales. If I make enough calls, I should begin to get the sales.

Action Item 3. I will set realistic goals. I will ask my sales director what the average income is that I could realistically expect to make at the end of one year, two years, and three years. Then I will have to decide if that income meets my expectations. If not, I will have to reconsider whether to pursue this career. If the income is enough, then I will see if I meet those income goals over the next eighteen months. If I don't, then I can evaluate whether to continue or seek some other employment, but I don't have to make that decision now.

Action Item 4. I will talk to my husband about how his lectures and criticism are not helpful. I also will tell him what he could do that would be helpful, such as watching the kids two nights a week when I make my sales calls and not complaining about that. He also is very good at organization, so I will also ask him to review my sales routine to see if he has any suggestions for improvements. I will remind him that he agreed with my original plan for this sales position. I will ask him if he has changed his mind, and if so, discuss what options we both think I have to earn money and still be home with the kids most of the time.

Action Item 5. I will talk to my parents about how their criticisms are not helpful, no matter how well intended they might be. I also will ask them for ideas about how they can be supportive of me. And I will tell them which of those ideas would be helpful. I will remind them that I am an adult and that I do not have to live my life by their rules anymore, just as they do not have to live by mine. I also will ask my husband to not join in with my parents when they forget and do criticize me. I will tell him that I feel ganged up on by the three of them and abandoned by him. I have never told him that. Maybe he doesn't realize how I feel.

Action Item 6. I will try to enjoy my brother's success. I don't think he or my sister-in-law talk about those things to make me feel inadequate. I think I do that to myself. Why shouldn't they talk about the details of their lives? He wants me to be proud of him and his family. He has worked hard for what he has achieved, and I am proud of him. Maybe I am afraid that he is not proud of me, but he has never said anything to give me that impression. I will remind myself that my brother's success does not make me inadequate. No more comparisons.

Action Item 7. I am going to try to stop thinking in all-or-none terms. No more "I am no good" statements. I am going to make a list of different ways that I do feel competent. Then I will make a list of how I want to be more competent. From that list, I will choose one or two items that I want to work on now, like how to be more effective in my sales. Then, whenever I think that I am inadequate, I will review my two lists and remind myself that I am competent at lots of things and working to be competent at others.

Action Item 8. When I am procrastinating, I will try to figure out what I am afraid of. I will remind myself that my psychologist told me that procrastination is usually produced by fear, not by laziness. When I figure out the fear, then I will develop a plan to conquer it.

Action Item 9. I will begin keeping a journal and record each evening what I did that day. In the past, I only kept a list of what I did not do.

Action Item 10. I also will make a list each Sunday night of what I want to accomplish that week, and I will estimate a realistic amount of time for each task. I will stop setting up idealistic schedules that inevitably leave me disappointed in myself.

Action Item 11. I will pay attention to my feelings. If I am feeling stressed, I have probably slipped back into my old Inadequate⁻ schema. I will review this list of actions and see which of them would be helpful to counteract my thoughts of inadequacy.

Step 5: Who could be a role model for my *Adequate** **schema?** I can use Sarah and my sales director as role models.

Step 6: Who can support my efforts to create an *Adequate** **schema?** I will ask my best friend, Maria, to meet with me once a week to review my progress and to offer me support.

Step 7: Select one or two action items to try. I will start with action items 1 and 9.

Dana considered how her diary example might have been different with an *Adequate** schema. The following is her description of what could have happened in that situation.

Dana: *Adequate** Schema

After my husband and the kids had left, I would have sat down at the desk and called people for at least an hour before I stopped. Even if no one scheduled, I would have felt proud of myself for sticking with the task. I would have felt good that I became more confident and comfortable calling as the hour passed. I would have felt pleased that I had eliminated the names of people not interested in my products. I also think I would have scheduled at least one appointment. I would have viewed my time as well spent and as helping me better develop my telephone approach, so I would not be so nervous about doing it next time. I would have been in a positive mood when I finished the task and been in a good mood when the kids came home.

The goal of schema change is to help Dana develop the adaptive schema she described for herself and to make the above example a reality. By recording several examples of her *Inadequate⁻* schema and doing the maladaptive schema analysis, Dana found answers that would help her create an *Adequate** schema. You saw how she used that information in the steps of the adaptive schema–development section.

Dana's psychologist helped her create a comprehensive list of actions to develop her *Adequate** schema. But you don't always need a psychologist to come up with good items. You can use the ones in this book as a guide. Notice how specific

*Adequate** Schema

The *Adequate** schema produces the idea that you are doing the best you can at any moment as long as you are trying, thereby allowing you to feel good about yourself regardless of your level of achievement. There is an acceptance that some people will do some tasks better than you and other tasks not as well, but such comparisons are irrelevant to your own sense of adequacy. An *Adequate** schema does not produce the constant biased comparisons to selected others that occur with either the *Inadequate⁻* or *Perfectionistic⁺* schemas. With both of these maladaptive schemas, the person's sense of adequacy depends on the accomplishments of others.

An *Adequate** schema also acknowledges that you may have more talent in one area than another, but that your level of achievement in any area depends on a variety of factors. An *Adequate** schema creates expectations that you can improve your performance in most areas with training or practice, but that all of us have limitations. We may never do some things particularly well. Although we may be inadequate in some areas, that does not make us inadequate as people.

Below, notice how similar Steven's *Adequate** schema is to Dana's, even though their maladaptive schemas were at opposite ends of this continuum. As you already are familiar with Steven, we will skip his schema diary entries as we go through his schema-change steps below.

Steven: *Adequate** Schema

Part 1: Maladaptive Schema Analysis

Step 1: My definition of my *Perfectionistic⁺* schema: Everything I do has to be perfect. I cannot make mistakes.

Step 2: What do I think when my *Perfectionistic⁺* schema is active? I have to do everything just right. I can never do less than my best. I cannot make mistakes. If I am not perfect, people will think I am incompetent. They will doubt me. I need to be perfect. I cannot take time to relax until I have all my work done.

Step 3: How do I feel when my *Perfectionistic⁺* schema is active? Tense, nervous, impatient, irritable, angry.

Step 4: What do I do when my _Perfectionistic+_ schema is active? Push myself relentlessly; cancel other individual or family activities unrelated to my tasks; eliminate any recreational or pleasurable activities; drink to relax, so relaxing will be quick and not time consuming; get angry over minor irritations and anything that interferes with my tight schedule; push others away so they do not take time away from my work.

Step 5: What are the origins of my _Perfectionistic+_ schema? My father was an alcoholic and I was ashamed of him and, thus, of me. I felt I had to be perfect to make up for him. He was inadequate, and I was afraid others would think I was, too. My outstanding academic performance brought me respect from others. I always have felt a need to be perfect to keep that respect.

Step 6: What are the triggers for my _Perfectionistic+_ schema? When anyone questions one of my medical decisions; well, actually, when anyone questions anything I think or do; when I am around other doctors in my specialty area; when I am given or assume any task, even minor things; when I am getting dressed to go out socially.

Step 7: What do I and others do to maintain my _Perfectionistic+_ schema now? I keep accepting more patients and hospital responsibilities to show how competent I am. I am only on call with one other physician, who is not as good as me and won't criticize my work. I work all the time, so the only facet of my personality that I or others know is my professional one. I never tell anyone, not even my wife, about any mistake that I make or if I am feeling overwhelmed. I am not open with others about anything personal unless it is about some success. My family and I like the lifestyle I have created through my perfectionism. I am afraid of disappointing others if I am not perfect. I don't want others to think less of me if I am not perfect. Other people maintain my perfectionism by praising me for being so successful.

Part 2: Adaptive Schema Development

Step 1: My definition of the *Adequate** schema I want to create:
I am OK the way I am. I am not perfect and I never will be, but I do not have to be. I am a competent, capable person just the way I am.

Step 2: What thoughts would my *Adequate** schema create?
I have already spent most of my life trying to be perfect, giving up fun, feeling guilty if I am not working. I can be capable without being perfect. I will be more selective about where I put my greatest effort. I do need to do my best in medical procedures, but even then most mistakes could be corrected. In really important situations, I am not alone; there are other staff involved. Most things do not need to be done perfectly. It is okay and human to make mistakes—I have to remind myself that I am human. I am no more perfect than anyone else. My medical degree means that I am capable as a physician. It doesn't mean I have to be a junior god. It is OK if people see that I am not perfect. If they need me to be perfect, that is their problem, not mine. Life is not just to achieve and impress others. A capable person also knows how to enjoy life, and that is where I am going to put more effort.

Step 3: What feelings would accompany the thoughts of my *Adequate** schema? Contentment, confidence, calmness, excitement in trying new things, cheerfulness instead of fear.

Step 4: What steps or actions do I need to take that are consistent with the thoughts and feelings of my *Adequate** schema?

Action Item 1. Stop being threatened by doctors who seem to be better than me. No matter how good I am, someone will be better. I will learn from doctors who have more knowledge or better skills than I do.

Action Item 2. Set my standards at 80 percent of what they have been on anything other than a life-threatening situation. Tell myself that B's are usually good enough for most life tasks. Remind myself that other people are usually satisfied with my results, even if I am not.

Action Item 3. Create realistic work schedules that leave me time every day and on weekends for myself and my wife, Ann, and my kids. I will not bump those times. If something needs to be bumped, it will be some work task.

Action Item 4. Talk to my office nurse about how to decrease the demands on me in the office and how to create a more reasonable schedule, so that most days we can finish by 6 P.M., even if that means decreasing the number of new appointments we schedule. My nurse has asked to go to office-management seminars in the past. I will agree to that if she agrees to use that information to decrease the pressure on me and to organize the office better. I also will ask her to talk to Ron's nurse, as his office is less chaotic than mine.

Action Item 5. Stop being defensive when other people ask me questions. Remind myself that questions are not criticisms. Remind myself that other people like to have good ideas, too. I will especially remind myself of that with my family and my office staff. I am going to listen more and disagree less. I am going to give in more often on things that really are unimportant.

Action Item 6. I am going to work on being kind and loving to the people around me. It is not OK for me to be irritable or harsh with others because I have put too much pressure on myself. When I am harsh, I will apologize and not make excuses.

Action Item 7. I am going to stop drinking to relax. I used to love to read fiction and historical books. I will buy some books I would like to read and begin reading every night before bedtime. I will also make up a list of things I have found pleasurable and things that I would like to try for fun. I then will make a plan to make those activities occur regularly for me. I am going to make fun a priority. I will talk to Ann about this, so we can come up with ideas for both of us and the kids.

Action Item 8. Ask Ann if we can set aside thirty minutes after dinner without interruptions for us just to talk about my day, so that I can review any problems that I am ruminating about and work on taking a nonperfectionistic perspective. Maybe we can go for a walk while we do that.

Action Item 9. Try to be more open with other people. Stop trying to appear perfect to everyone.

Action Item 10. Pay attention to how I feel. When I am feeling stressed or irritable, it is almost always due to my *Perfectionistic*[+] schema. If it is, I will review this action plan for alternative ideas.

Step 5: Who could be a role model for My *Adequate*[*] schema?
One of my colleagues, Ron, who is well-respected but also well-liked. He doesn't act superior. He is comfortable asking for help or asking for other opinions. He also works well with the nursing staff. He sees them as colleagues and treats them more like equals. He also works more reasonable hours and has turned down professional requests so he can be with his wife and kids. He does make less money, but he seems a lot more relaxed and happier than me. I can look for other examples, too.

Step 6: Who can support my efforts to create an *Adequate*[*] schema? Both Ann and Ron would be supportive if I explained to them what I am trying to do and what I need from them.

Step 7: Select one or two actions to try. I will start with action items 4 and 8.

Reread Steven's and Dana's definitions of an *Adequate*[*] schema. You can see how similar the definitions are, even though their maladaptive schemas were at opposite ends of the Adequacy Schema Continuum and even though Dana and Steven have very different lives. They are both aiming for the middle. An adaptive schema is always a balance between the two poles or ends of any continuum. The way we maintain a maladaptive schema may differ, just as the steps to create an adaptive schema may differ for individuals, but adaptive schemas on any given continuum will always be similar. If you look at Steven's and Dana's plans for change, you will even see some similarity in their action items. This is why you can use the schema-development plans described in this book as models for your own change plans.

IMPROVING SELF-WORTH:
SCHEMA PORTRAITS IN TRANSITION

Now you have two examples of plans to develop an *Adequate** schema. Let's look at the schema-development plans of Steven, Lynn, and Sylvia for the other three continua in the Self-Worth Zone.

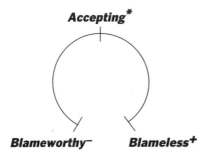

*Accepting**

Blameworthy⁻　　　*Blameless⁺*

*Accepting** Schema

An *Accepting** schema produces the expectation that you will occasionally make mistakes, and that you will not flagellate yourself as a result. Unlike with the *Blameworthy⁻* and *Blameless⁺* maladaptive schemas, a person with an *Accepting** schema does not feel an urgent need to establish blame or to extract a confession of guilt from oneself or others. When mistakes are made, someone with the *Accepting** schema focuses on how to rectify the situation or make amends with the injured party. With the *Accepting** schema, a person feels willing to apologize and to take responsibility for accidents without experiencing an overwhelming sense of guilt.

As you recall, Steven has positive maladaptive schemas that reinforce each other on two of the Self-Worth Zone continua. He has a *Blameless⁺* schema on the Acceptance Schema Continuum and a more powerful *Perfectionistic⁺* schema on the Adequacy Schema Continuum. His need to be perfect has reinforced his need to be blameless. Steven's *Blameless⁺* schema will be activated less often as he feels more *Adequate**. However, Steven created the following schema-change plan for his *Blameless⁺* schema, so he could work on both maladaptive schemas simultaneously, as they were so closely connected.

Steven: *Accepting** Schema

Part 1: Maladaptive Schema Analysis

Step 1: My definition of my *Blameless⁺* schema: I always need to be right. It is hard for me to admit a mistake or to apologize.

Step 2: What do I think when my *Blameless⁺* schema is active? I am not wrong. I can't be wrong. I don't make mistakes. I am too thorough and cautious to err. If I did make a mistake, someone or something else must have caused it.

Step 3: How do I feel when my *Blameless⁺* schema is active? Defensive, tense, superior.

Step 4: What do I do when my *Blameless⁺* schema is active? Argue until the other person admits wrongdoing; criticize others for any mistakes or accidents; try to blame others when anything goes wrong; rationalize how errors or accidents are not my fault.

Step 5: What are the origins of my *Blameless⁺* schema? My maternal grandparents were very critical of my parents. My mom was somewhat critical, but mostly I think my need to be perfect meant I could not be wrong.

Step 6: What are the triggers for my *Blameless⁺* schema? When something goes wrong or not as expected; any mistake that could possibly be associated with me; when I lose in games or sports.

Step 7: What do I and others do to maintain my *Blameless⁺* schema now? Mostly, my own *Perfectionistic⁺* schema convinces me that I am blameless. I try to be perfect. I am compulsive about not making mistakes. I blame other people. I make excuses when I lose at something.

Part 2: Adaptive Schema Development

Step 1: My definition of the *Accepting** schema I want to create:

I make mistakes occasionally, just like everyone else. Mistakes are not a big deal. If I do something that hurts or inconveniences someone, I need to apologize. I also need to be more forgiving of others' mistakes.

Step 2: What thoughts would my *Accepting** schema produce?
Mistakes happen. Accidents occur. People do not mess up on purpose. Criticism and blame are destructive to self-esteem. Just solve the problem as well as possible . . . and do it calmly, not angrily or with disgust. People's feelings are more important than events.

Step 3: What feelings would accompany the thoughts of my *Accepting** schema?
Empathy, calmness, kindness.

Step 4: What steps or actions do I need to take that are consistent with the thoughts and feelings of my *Accepting** schema?

Action Item 1. I will try to be less judgmental and critical of other people and myself. I will try to be more aware of those thoughts and will counteract them with reminders to myself that people do not make mistakes on purpose, that everyone is trying to do the best they can. I will remind myself of how bad I felt as a boy when people criticized my family.

Action Item 2. When things do not go as planned, I will stop finding fault and focus on solving the problem. Finding fault does not fix anything. I will stop trying to extract confessions from others, especially my kids.

Action Item 3. I will take responsibility for the mistakes I make. I will simply admit the mistake, apologize, and see if there is anything I can do to fix it. I will also try to change if I am doing something that is problematic or hurtful to another. I will not beat myself up for my mistakes either.

Action Item 4. I will try to be a better sport in games when I lose. I will remind myself that other people like to win, too.

Action Item 5. I will try to be more accepting and kinder, as Ann is.

Step 5: Who could be a role model for my *Accepting** schema? I can use Ann as a role model for this schema. Fred could be another role model, as he looks for solutions instead of blame.

Step 6: Who can support my efforts to create an *Accepting** schema? I will ask Ann to be my support person for this. She would love to see me change this.

Step 7: Select one or two action items to try. I will start with action item 3.

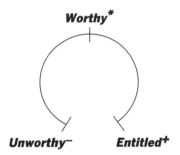

Worthy*
Unworthy⁻   *Entitled*⁺

*Worthy** Schema

The *Worthy** schema produces a sense of self-worth that makes one feel equal to others, regardless of ethnic, racial, or economic background. The *Worthy** schema creates a perspective that all people are inherently valuable. One person's needs are not more or less important than the comparable needs of another. The *Worthy** schema differs from the unbalanced views of the *Unworthy*⁻ and *Entitled*⁺ maladaptive schemas, which either greatly underestimate or overestimate the importance of one's own needs.

Lynn, the thirty-two-year-old marketing analyst, identified a strong *Entitled*⁺ schema in the Self-Worth Zone. She now realizes how destructive this is in both her personal and professional relationships. With her psychologist, she developed the following schema-change plan.

175

Lynn: *Worthy** Schema

Part 1: Maladaptive Schema Analysis

Step 1: My definition of my *Entitled+* schema: I expect the best. I am superior to most other people. I am special. I need to be treated as if I am special.

Step 2: What do I think when my *Entitled+* schema is active? I should get what I want. I shouldn't have to wait for things or even wait in line. My needs are more important than anyone else's. Few other people are as good as I am.

Step 3: How do I feel when my *Entitled+* schema is active? Superior, smug.

Step 4: What do I do when my *Entitled+* schema is active? I act as if I think I am better than other people. I treat people somewhat condescendingly. I act indignant when I don't get my way. Really, I act like a spoiled brat.

Step 5: What are the origins of my *Entitled+* schema? Except for a brief period between my mother's marriages, I always got what I wanted. My father spent money like it was water, before he went bankrupt and left us. My stepfather was wealthy, and we had an expensive lifestyle with private schools and expensive vacations. I always had the best, so I came to expect it. I learned that material things are the source of happiness. My mother always has had an *Entitled+* schema and was absolutely outraged when she had to work briefly before meeting my stepfather. She isn't even particularly nice to him anymore except when she wants something. She told me she married him because he could afford her, not because of love.

Step 6: What are the triggers for my *Entitled+* schema? When I see something I want; when someone else has something I envy; when I am around my wealthy childhood friends.

Step 7: What do I and others do to maintain my *Entitled+* schema now? I let my boyfriends know I like expensive gifts, and I pout until I get what I want. I use sex as a reward for letting me have my way. I buy whatever I want, which keeps my credit cards maxed out all the time. I act as if I should be treated differently, as if the rules do not apply to me. Most of my boyfriends initially buy me expensive presents. My mother has an *Entitled+* schema and acts like she is royalty. People give in to my requests for special treatment.

Part 2: Adaptive Schema Development

Step 1: My definition of the *Worthy** schema I want to create: I am as worthy as anyone else, but no more so. Everyone is special, but people are not superior to each other. Wealth does not make anyone more special or worthwhile. I am worthwhile and special just for being a good and decent human being.

Step 2: What thoughts would my *Worthy** schema produce? Acting superior hurts other people's feelings and alienates people I would like to have as friends. Basing my relationships on money will produce an emotionally empty marriage like my mother has.

Step 3: What feelings would accompany the thoughts of my *Worthy** schema? Empathy, kindness, compassion.

Step 4: What steps or actions do I need to take that are consistent with the thoughts and feelings of my *Worthy** schema?

Action Item 1. I need to be more thoughtful of other people. I am going to try not to be the center of attention. I will listen more, talk less about myself, and show more interest in the people I work with by asking questions about their lives and remembering what they tell me.

Action Item 2. I will meet with a financial adviser in my company's credit union and set up a realistic budget and a plan to close my charge accounts.

177

Action Item 3. I will tell my mother I do not want her to criticize me for not shopping at her expensive department stores. I also will tell her that I do not want to go window-shopping anymore with her, because I buy things I cannot afford. We will have to find other things to do together.

Action Item 4. I will stop buying things to make myself feel better.

Action Item 5. I will stop asking for special treatment or exceptions to the rules.

Action Item 6. I am going to look through my psychologist's book on volunteer activities and select an organization where I can spend a few hours a week volunteering. I am going to select something that will help make me more sensitive to the plight of others.

Step 5: Who could be a role model for my *Worthy** schema? One of my co-workers, Pam, lives a middle-class life and has good relationships with her husband and kids. I could use her as a role model, as I envy those relationships. She seems to have a strong *Worthy** schema unrelated to her financial status.

Step 6: Who can support my efforts to create a *Worthy** schema? I could ask my supervisor to support me in these changes, as she has commented on the hostile relationships I seem to create with others. She has encouraged me to change.

Step 7: Select one or two action items to try. I will start with action item 1 this week.

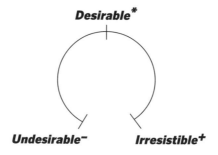

*Desirable** Schema

With the *Desirable** schema, one accepts one's own social and physical attributes. One does not deny that there may be ways to improve social skills or appearance, but one is not obsessed with those aspects. Nor is a person with the *Desirable** schema preoccupied with personal shortcomings in the same way as someone with the *Undesirable⁻* schema. In contrast, a person with the *Irresistible⁺* schema adores his or her social desirability to the exclusion of other valued social traits, such as kindness, thoughtfulness, and compassion. The *Irresistible⁺* schema is not necessarily characteristic of the devastatingly attractive person, who may just as easily have the self-schemas of *Desirability** or *Undesirability⁻*. Remember, schemas are not an exact reflection of reality.

Remember how Sylvia struggled with an *Undesirable⁻* schema most of her life? She has come to realize that this is a maladaptive schema that has to change if the quality of her life is to improve. So she created the schema-change plan below.

Sylvia: *Desirable** Schema

Part 1: Maladaptive Schema Analysis

Step 1: My definition of my *Undesirable⁻* schema: I am physically unattractive, even repulsive to some people.

Step 2: What do I think when my *Undesirable⁻* schema is active? I am too fat. I don't look good in anything. People notice how fat I am immediately. I will never be as attractive as my sister. My family is embarrassed at my weight. Waiters think I eat too much. They must be shocked when I order dessert.

Step 3: How do I feel when my *Undesirable⁻* schema is active? Sad, depressed, ashamed, embarrassed, angry.

Step 4: What do I do when my *Undesirable⁻* schema is active? I am moody, irritable, and sulky with my family. I make life unpleasant for all of us. I spoil happy occasions when we go out by first getting upset about how I am not thin enough and don't look good.

Step 5: What are the origins of my *Undesirable⁻* schema? My mother's and sister's obsessions with thinness and appearance, which were their primary criteria for evaluating women; their criticisms of my weight and eating habits since childhood; the monopoly of anorectic women in magazines and movies.

Step 6: What are the triggers for my *Undesirable⁻* schema? Being around my mother or sister; movies and television programs populated with pencil-thin women with gargantuan breast implants; anytime my scale registers an increase of a pound or two; going out socially.

Step 7: What do I and others do to maintain my *Undesirable⁻* schema now? I ruminate about my weight all day long. I have been obsessing about losing 10 pounds for five years. I weigh myself every morning as soon as I get out of bed. I punish myself if I gain even an ounce. I make jokes about my body. I berate my husband for being interested in me sexually. My mother and sister continue to be consumed by this issue and still suggest diets and exercise gimmicks to me, advice I never solicit. Television, movies, and magazines show only beautiful anorectic women.

Part 2: Adaptive Schema Development

Step 1: My definition of the *Desirable** schema I want to create: I am comfortable with my body. I take good care of myself physically and dress neatly and attractively. I usually look as nice as most everyone else. I have good social skills. I make others feel comfortable. I have a good sense of humor.

Step 2: What thoughts would my *Desirable** schema produce? I look good enough. Besides, people like me because of the way I treat them, not because of how I look.

Step 3: What feelings would accompany the thoughts of my *Desirable** schema? Contentment, pleasure, acceptance.

Step 4: What steps or actions do I need to take that are consistent with the thoughts and feelings of my *Desirable** schema?

Action Item 1. I will stop making fun of my body. I will stop making critical comments about my appearance. I will remind myself that my daughters are beginning to imitate me.

Action Item 2. I will accept compliments by saying "Thank you" and not turning them into jokes.

Action Item 3. I will remind myself that my mother's and sister's lives revolve around their weight. They are not role models of how I want to be. I cannot change them, but I can learn not to react to them. I can change the topic when I am with them. I can tell them I am not trying to lose weight and am not interested in their diet or exercise suggestions. I can either choose to ignore their criticisms of my appearance or tell them that I don't find their comments helpful and I would like them to stop making them.

Action Item 4. I will weigh myself only on Wednesdays. No matter what my weight is, I will try not to let it change my mood, and I will not let myself dwell on it all day. I will remind myself that my weight does not justify making my family miserable. I want them to remember me for making our home life happy, regardless of my appearance.

Action Item 5. I will continue to exercise four times a week and eat moderately, which I have been doing for a long time. I will remind myself that I do take good care of myself and that I am fortunate to be healthy.

Action Item 6. I will remind myself that Jack does find me attractive and enjoys sex with me. It is mean for me to spoil that, especially since I enjoy sex with him, too, when I am not too busy criticizing my body. When he initiates sex, I will not make any negative comments about myself. Instead, I will focus on how to make that pleasurable for both of us. I also will initiate sex once a week with Jack, so he knows I think he is physically desirable, too.

181

Step 5: Who could be a role model for my *Desirable** schema?
For role models, I will begin to keep a list of women—people I know and movie stars—who are not ridiculously thin and who I think are attractive. I will ask Jack for suggestions for this list, too.

Step 6: Who can support my efforts to create a *Desirable** schema? I will talk to Jack about my plan to work on this schema and ask him if we can review my plan together once a week. I will record examples of both of my *Desirable** and *Undesirable⁻* schemas in my schema diary, but I will not let myself talk about this other than when Jack and I have our weekly meeting. That will help me obsess less about my appearance.

Step 7: Select one or two action items to try. I will start with action items 1 and 5.

DESIGNING YOUR SCHEMA-CHANGE PLAN

Now you have models for developing adaptive schemas in each of the four Self-Worth Schema Continua. You also understand the steps to analyze your maladaptive schema and to create your new adaptive schema. Remember that we helped our clients create all the schema-development plans in these chapters. Don't expect your own plans to be nearly as elaborate. They don't need to be. Now select an adaptive schema in the Self-Worth Zone to create. By answering the questions listed in the following worksheet, you can design your own change plan. However, you still need to read the remaining chapters before implementing your strategies.

These next chapters will discuss ways to implement your steps more effectively and to deal with obstacles. We will describe how to prepare for typical triggers and for people who have been maintaining your maladaptive schemas. You will learn to modify troublesome thoughts and to turn unexpected outcomes into learning opportunities. So do not skip the other chapters, even if you do not have troublesome maladaptive schemas in those zones. Otherwise, you may become prematurely discouraged. We want you to be well prepared when you implement your schema-development strategies.

WORKSHEET TO CREATE AN ADAPTIVE SCHEMA IN THE SELF-WORTH ZONE

Part 1: Maladaptive Schema Analysis

Step 1: Define your maladaptive schema in your own words.

_____

_____

_____

Step 2: Describe your thoughts when your maladaptive schema is active.

_____

_____

_____

Step 3: Describe how you feel when your maladaptive schema is active.

_____

_____

_____

Step 4: Describe what you do when your maladaptive schema is active.

_____

_____

_____

Step 5: Describe the origins of your maladaptive schema.

_____

_____

_____

Step 6: Describe the triggers for your maladaptive schema.

_____

_____

_____

Step 7: Describe what you and others do to maintain your maladaptive schema.

_____

_____

_____

Part 2: Adaptive Schema Development

Step 1: Define the adaptive schema you want to develop.

_____

_____

_____

Step 2: Describe the thoughts your adaptive schema would produce.

_____

_____

_____

Step 3: Describe the feelings that would accompany the thoughts of your adaptive schema.

_____

_____

_____

each action step is. Vague steps would leave Dana uncertain about how to proceed. Dana made a plan to implement the two action items she chose. Next, she started recording her schema-change efforts. Each night, she reviewed the action items she had selected and recorded what efforts she had made. Some actions required only one instance of implementation, but with most of them, it took repeated efforts to make them stick. Eventually, Dana spoke to her husband and parents, but she had to remind them of her requests when they slipped up. She recorded both the initial conversations and the times she reminded them. She also kept a daily log of instances where her *Inadequate⁻* schema reemerged. After each *Inadequate⁻* entry, she wrote down how she could handle that situation differently in the future. Instead of viewing those instances as failures, Dana learned to view them as opportunities to expand her *Adequate** schema.

Schema development takes a concentrated effort. That is why we recommend trying to focus on only one adaptive schema at a time. While you are doing that, other adaptive schemas may also get a boost. As Dana worked on her *Adequate** schema, she also strengthened her *Assertive** schema, as a result of dealing with her family more directly. You can work on two adaptive schemas simultaneously if they are closely connected, as Dana's *Adequate** and *Assertive** schemas were. Usually you will need to limit yourself to focusing on one adaptive schema at a time. Do not become distressed if your schema change takes time. After all, how many decades have your maladaptive schemas gone unchallenged?

WORKING TOWARD THE MIDDLE

People often have maladaptive schemas at both ends of the same continuum. If Dana also had a *Perfectionistic⁺* schema, she could have aimed to acquire the same *Adequate** schema that she defined in assessing her *Inadequate⁻* schema. Both continuum ends lead to the same adaptive schema in the middle. Moreover, adaptive schemas on any given continuum are similar for different people. We can illustrate both of these points with Steven, the physician who had a *Perfectionistic⁺* schema. First, let's take a closer look at the *Adequate** schema.

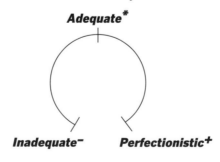

Step 4: Describe the steps or actions you need to take that are consistent with the thoughts and feelings of your adaptive schema.

_____

_____

_____

_____

_____

_____

Step 5: Identify at least one person who has the adaptive schema you are creating.

_____

_____

Step 6: Find a support person.

_____

_____

Step 7: Select one or two actions to try.

_____

_____

_____

9

Adaptive Schemas in the Empowerment Zone

I hope our wisdom will grow
with our power, and teach us,
that the less we use our power
the greater it will be.
—*Thomas Jefferson*, Letter

The adaptive schemas in the Empowerment Zone will be the focus of attention in this chapter: *Assertiveness**, *Capability**, *Empowerment**, and *Resilience**. These schemas influence how you deal with the world around you and the unexpected but inevitable setbacks and disappointments in life. People who have adaptive schemas in the Empowerment Zone deal effectively with their lives, whatever fate may conspire to deliver, and do so without denying reality or overpowering those around them. This chapter will present ways to create these important adaptive schemas.

HEY! I'VE DONE THIS BEFORE!

Before we continue with the specifics of developing new adaptive schemas, we want to demonstrate that what you are learning is not entirely new to you. When Gretchen graduated from high school, she had a strong *Acquiescent*⁻ schema. She wanted to live on her own in an apartment, so she needed to find a full-time job to support herself. After a few weeks of job hunting, Gretchen obtained an entry-level position in a customer service department of a large home appliance store. At first, the job was very stressful for her because she received many calls from angry, demanding customers. She could not appease them, because sometimes their requests were unreasonable. Many times she felt as if she would burst into tears. And many nights at home, she did. Her stomach seemed tied in a permanent knot. She would replay telephone conversations in her head and discover better responses that she wished she had made.

Over time, Gretchen realized that she did not feel as much stress in her work. The calls seemed easier to handle, even though the number of angry callers had not decreased. Angry customers did not intimidate Gretchen anymore. She was able to talk to them in a calm, understanding manner and resolve the problems. They were not always happy with the results, but she felt that she resolved each call as well as she could have. After about six months in her new position, her friends noticed that Gretchen seemed more confident. She expressed her preferences and opinions. She was not uncomfortable when others disagreed with her. She felt more sure of herself. She was more willing to try new things. She even took up skiing, which she had always feared. A year later, Gretchen thought the *Assertive*[*] schema was more descriptive of her than the *Acquiescent*[-] schema. What happened?

What happened is that Gretchen was put in a situation that allowed and encouraged her to change her *Acquiescent*[-] schema. In her new job she had initially received training in how to deal with angry people. Her supervisor modeled negotiation skills for her. She learned that she could not just give in to solve customer complaints. She learned new problem-solving skills, and her supervisor praised her for using them. Gretchen needed the job to survive, so she couldn't quit—although many times in the beginning she wished she could. Essentially, Gretchen learned how to change and was motivated to change. She turned her *Acquiescent*[-] schema into an *Assertive*[*] schema. She did that on her own, before she ever had heard the word *schema* and without consciously attempting to make a schema change.

It is not unusual for people to convert maladaptive schemas into adaptive ones without even knowing what a schema is. Like Gretchen, you have probably done this without realizing what you were doing. Let's find out. Read the list of schemas in Appendix A and see if you can find any maladaptive schemas that you had in the past but that you replaced with adaptive schemas. Think about how you developed those new schemas. What factors contributed to the change? Imagine how much easier it will be to create an adaptive schema now that you know what schemas are and how to develop a specific plan for change.

DESIGNING ACTION ITEMS FOR AN ADAPTIVE SCHEMA

In Chapter 8, we described how creating action items was an important part of developing adaptive schemas. Many people initially find it quite difficult to design action items. Here are some suggestions to create more helpful action items.

Be Specific

Your action items need to be specific enough that you will know exactly what to do to implement them. Vague, abstract action items cannot be implemented. How would you implement an action item for a *Capable** schema such as "Be more responsible"? That is the beginning of an action item, but the item needs to include specific steps or actions, such as "Try to figure out problems at my work first by reviewing the situation by myself. Ask for help only after I have made an initial attempt to identify what to do differently. Try to figure out at least one possible solution." Now you will know what to do to "be more responsible."

Be Positive

You can include actions you intend to stop, but you should also include actions you plan to take. If you are developing an *Assertive** schema to replace a *Domineering*[+] schema, the item "Stop getting angry at the kids" is not very helpful. What can you do differently in those situations? A positive and more specific item would be, "Start trying to give the kids firm limits rather than yelling and screaming. Instead, first get their attention by calmly stating their names and asking them to look at me. Then state what I do not want them to do, and tell them what I want them to do instead. I also will tell them that I am working on not yelling, because I know that is hurtful. Each time I yell at them, I will mark that on a chart on the refrigerator, and for every five marks, I will rent them a video for the weekend." People cannot stop doing something without having an alternative reaction. You need to figure out what you want your replacement action to be, such as setting firm limits.

Take Responsibility

Create action items that you control. Remember Lynn's action steps to create a *Worthy** schema? She could have told her mother not to let her buy things when they went shopping together, but that would place the responsibility on her mother, not on Lynn. Instead, Lynn realizes that she needs to avoid shopping with her mother, because she has a hard time not buying what she sees. Here, Lynn has the responsibility, not her mother. Dana's action item to make a certain number of telephone calls each day is within her control, but the number of sales she makes is not. Similarly, Sylvia cannot stop her sister and mother from giving her diet and exercise advice, but she can tell them she is not interested whenever they do that. Again, Sylvia has control of her action item. For each action item you create, ask yourself if you have control over whether it happens or not. If not, rework the item until you are in control.

React Differently

Review your triggers and your analysis of what and who maintain your maladaptive schema. How would you like to react differently in those situations or with those people? Write an action item for each trigger or maintenance factor. This means describing what actions or thoughts you would like to produce in reaction to your typical triggers. Your thoughts and actions need to be consistent with your new adaptive schema. Be specific. Describe what you would do, say, and tell yourself. Try to make it simple and short. Longer, more complicated reactions will be harder for you to remember in the trigger situation. Both Dana and Steven have action items to change the way they react to people they perceive as being more competent. Their action items include what they could say to themselves and reminders to try to use those other people as resources to learn new skills. Essentially, this is the Scout principle of schema development: Be Prepared. Once you know what your triggers are, you can develop action items to be ready for them.

Face Your Fears

Review your examples to see what you are avoiding. Remember how Dana avoided making phone calls to her potential customers? What fear did she have? What was she afraid would happen? Dana was afraid the other person would be angry that she called and would hang up in a huff. She also was afraid that people would not be interested. Both of those fears were realistic. Some people probably would hang up, and lots of people would not be interested. That is the nature of sales. Those reactions are not personally directed at Dana but at the product or at the interruption. Without quickly weeding out those responses, Dana would never reach the smaller percentage of people who were interested.

Here was where role-playing was critical for Dana. After she and her sales director role-played several different versions of this situation, she realized that turndowns were not that bad. She didn't burst into tears or fall apart or begin rambling incoherently. She just said "Thank you" and hung up. Role-playing this situation and actually experiencing her anticipated dreaded outcomes allowed Dana to face her fears and move beyond them. Now Dana routinely uses role-play when she finds herself procrastinating out of fear. Until you face your fears, your maladaptive schema will have a stranglehold on you. But if you carefully think out a plan to face that fear, practice your new plan, and try it, you can break free.

Think Supportive Thoughts

Identify thoughts that support each action item. Then, when you implement that item, review those thoughts. For example, Steven planned to reduce his standards to 80 percent of his usual criteria and intended to remind himself occasionally that other people were usually satisfied with his results. To be less defensive while being asked questions, he planned to remind himself that questions are not criticisms. Developing supportive thoughts is essential. Remind yourself of why you need to do each action item. Anticipate obstacles to action items, and figure out how to encourage yourself in those circumstances. Your supportive thoughts need to be things you can say to yourself to coach you through your action plan. They should not be Pollyannaish statements but the same kind of verbal support you would offer a friend in a similar situation.

Practice

If you are anticipating a problematic situation, review your relevant action item ahead of time. Practicing what you would do is even more effective. Practicing, or role-playing, is a simple but powerful tool for change. You can role-play by yourself what you would do in a given situation. Some people find it helpful to record their practice sessions and then to replay them until they feel comfortable with their response. If possible, role-play with another person your anticipated situation. Your partner can use different tones, and you can try various responses to these scenarios. Also, you can switch roles at times to give you an idea of how the other person might perceive different possible responses. Remember, you do not have to have your new reaction down perfectly, but you will be more effective if you have practiced it at least a few times. Again, keep it simple.

These tips will help you write more effective action items and implement those actions effectively. As we look at the change plans for the Empowerment Zone, pay attention to the action steps in each example. The more examples you have of action steps, the easier it will be for you to create your own.

DEVELOPING EMPOWERMENT: SCHEMA PORTRAITS IN TRANSITION

Next we look at Sylvia's, Lynn's, and Steven's plans to develop adaptive schemas in the Empowerment Zone. We also will examine their action items more closely. You will see how they applied the action item characteristics we described in the last section.

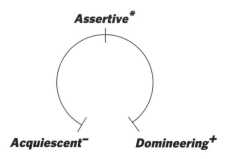

*Assertive** Schema

The *Assertive** schema enables you to express your thoughts and feelings without being disrespectful or nasty to others. You don't expect everyone to agree with you, just as you don't agree with everyone else, yet you listen to others' opinions and expect them to listen to you. Assertive people often appear to be more interesting than submissive people, because they express their thoughts. The submissive person may have those same thoughts, but no one knows, because their ideas never see daylight.

An *Assertive** schema recognizes that being assertive will sometimes create conflict, but conflict is not viewed negatively. Conflicts produce compromise, tolerance, and innovative thinking—all worthwhile processes. Sylvia hates conflict, so she has learned to give in to the demands of others, regardless of how unreasonable they are. Her acquiescence to her friends and acquaintances has often made her family resentful, because they were frequently inconvenienced so that Sylvia could accommodate others. Sylvia's acquiescence simply moved the conflicts to a different arena.

With an *Assertive** schema you accept that sometimes people will dislike you for your opinions, but you also realize that to deny your own beliefs and feelings is to betray yourself. An assertive person is sometimes disliked but rarely disrespected. Neither an *Acquiescent⁻* nor a *Domineering⁺* schema engenders respect or genuine affection. Sylvia knows that she is often submissive because she does not want anyone to be angry with her, yet she realizes that some of these people view her with contempt. Sylvia's fear of their anger arouses a lot of unexpressed anger at them and at herself. She knows that she has let people's real or anticipated anger control her, and she has come to think less of herself because of it. Here is her plan to change.

Sylvia: *Assertive** Schema

Part 1: Maladaptive Schema Analysis

Step 1: My definition of my *Acquiescent⁻* schema: I give in to avoid conflict. I routinely let other people have their way. I don't want anyone to be mad at me.

Step 2: What do I think when my *Acquiescent⁻* schema is active? Don't make anyone mad. Give in. Let others have their way. It doesn't matter. Don't disagree. People may not like me then. Keep the peace, no matter what the cost.

Step 3: How do I feel when my *Acquiescent⁻* schema is active? Nervous, fearful, tense, guilty, resentful.

Step 4: What do I do when my *Acquiescent⁻* schema is active? I agree to do things I don't want to do. I don't object to requests that will inconvenience my family and me. I volunteer when no one else will. I don't stand up for myself. I apologize for things that are not my fault. When I do try to say no, I offer twenty reasons to justify my refusal.

Step 5: What are the origins of my *Acquiescent⁻* schema? My older sister was very demanding and entitled, and a source of much distress to my parents. I worked very hard at being agreeable, so no one would be upset. My mom reinforced that by telling me and others how wonderful it was that I was so agreeable. When I did try to stand up to my sister, she would resort to physical force or say mean, hurtful things to me. Both my mom and sister are domineering, so it was easier to go along with them.

Step 6: What are the triggers for my *Acquiescent⁻* schema? Being around domineering, forceful people; being around my mom and sister; meetings that request volunteers.

Step 7: What do I and others do to maintain my *Acquiescent⁻* schema? I try to avoid making anyone mad at me by giving in.

I don't like to be the center of attention, so I won't stand up for myself in public, for fear of creating a disturbance. I want everyone to like me, even people I don't like. My mom and sister and other people tell me they appreciate what I do for them, which makes me feel good. I let anger in other people intimidate me.

Part 2: Adaptive Schema Development

Step 1: My definition of the *Assertive** schema I want to create: I have the right to stand up for myself and express my own opinions and have my own preferences. My thoughts are as important as anyone else's.

Step 2: What thoughts would my *Assertive** schema produce? I can't blame other people for taking advantage of me. If others take advantage of me, it is because I am letting them. If people do not like me because I no longer let them take advantage of me, then they were not my friends anyway. I am the one who needs to make the change. By not standing up for myself, I teach others not to respect my feelings or opinions. If people get mad at me for disagreeing or not accommodating them, that is their problem, not mine. I will remember that old saying, "A person with no enemies has no character." My goal is to build more character.

Step 3: What feelings would accompany the thoughts of my *Assertive** schema? Self-respect, confidence, calmness.

Step 4: What steps or actions do I need to take that are consistent with the thoughts and feelings of my *Assertive** schema?

Action Item 1. When people ask me to do favors, if I do not want to do them, I will just say no. I will stop offering a ten-minute monologue on how come I can't do something. I will not give any excuses. If the person presses me, I simply will say I can't do that this time. Period. If the person persists, I will say in a curious tone, "Why are you not listening to me? I said I could not do it." And then I will wait for their reply. I will stop talking so much in those situations, because inevitably I give them an excuse that they then try to get around. I will remind myself that I do not need excuses. If I do not want to do something, that is enough of a reason. I will still do favors when I want to, but I will no longer do them out of irrational guilt.

Action Item 2. I am going to start carrying a weekly planner with me. I will cross out times that I am saving to spend with Jack and the kids and just for myself. When volunteers are sought, I will check my weekly planner before I volunteer. I will limit my volunteer activities to two events per week.

Action Item 3. I will remind myself that other people will seem to resist my making changes in this schema, because they are used to having their way with me. I can expect them to try to talk me out of my position, because they have usually been able to do so in the past. I will not get mad at them, but I will be prepared to stick to my position. I can do that just by repeating myself, not by offering additional excuses.

Action Item 4. I am going to ask the other mothers to make other arrangements to have their kids picked up after school, so that I am not tied down anymore. I will give them one week to do that. I also will tell them that I am willing to take their kids to school if they have them here by 8:00, but that I am not going to pick them up anymore. I will role-play with Jack how I will say this. I will remind myself that in the past, people have used anger to get me to do favors for them. My giving in didn't make them like me. If they really care about me, they also will care about my feelings and needs. I will remind myself that people cannot use me if I don't let them.

Action Item 5. When my parents visit in the fall, I will talk to my mother alone about how she criticizes the kids and me about our appearances and our eating habits. I will tell her that I know she is trying to be helpful but that it is not helpful and I want her to stop. I will remind her of this if she forgets. I also will tell her that Jack and I are responsible for disciplining the kids, not her, and that we do not want her to try to set new rules for them. I will role-play this conversation with Jack several times before she arrives.

Step 5: Who could be a role model for my *Assertive*[*] schema? I will use Paula, the other teacher's aide, as my role model for this schema. Paula is very good at setting limits and taking care of herself without being rude or abrasive. People like and respect her. Well, some people don't like her, because they can't boss her around, but they do respect her.

Step 6: Who can support my efforts to create an *Assertive** schema? I can use Paula and Jack as my support people for this schema. They will both encourage me to make these changes, and they also are good at problem solving. Some of the assertive changes I need to make are with Jack, so Paula can be my support person on those situations.

Step 7: Select one or two action items to try. I will start with actions items 1 and 3.

Go back to chapter 4 and reread Sylvia's cost-benefit analysis for her *Acquiescent*⁻ schema. You can see how her analysis has given her specific ideas for her action items. Her examples can also do that. The more detailed your own cost-benefit analyses and examples are, the easier it will be for you to create specific action items. Often, your action item simply will be the opposite of what you are doing now.

Let's review Sylvia's seven action items in step 4 of her schema-development plan. See how they follow the suggestions laid out in the beginning of this chapter. All of the items include positive actions Sylvia plans to take. All of the items are also specific enough that even a stranger would know exactly what to do in each situation. Items 1, 2, and 3 describe how Sylvia plans to react differently in trigger situations. By reviewing her triggers, she can develop alternative actions.

Sylvia has planned to practice her proposed actions for items 4 and 5, but she can also role-play her actions for items 1 and 3. Actions 1 through 5 are all aimed at helping Sylvia face her fear of having people be angry with her for her choices. She has decided that she has sacrificed too much by avoiding the anger of those who want to control or use her. She also believes that most people would not be angry with her for being assertive and that she can handle the anger of those who are. She also plans to use Jack and Paula to role-play those potential situations and to support her assertive actions.

You can see that Sylvia has taken control of all of her action items or, at least, all of the actions that she could perform independently. In items 1, 3, and 4, Sylvia describes compatible thoughts that she can think when she is in those particular situations.

When you make up your own action items, review them just as we have here to see if they include the characteristics of effective action items.

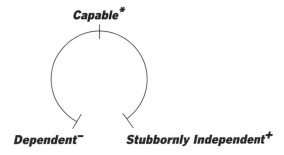

*Capable** Schema

The *Capable** schema produces expectations that you can handle most situations, but that when you cannot, seeking assistance is appropriate. A *Capable** schema is accompanied by the self-confidence that allows you to try to figure out most situations before seeking aid. Unlike one with the *Stubbornly Independent+* schema, a person with a *Capable** schema does not view asking for help as a sign of weakness and does not stubbornly persist in situations in which she is hopelessly inept.

In contrast to the *Dependent−* schema, the *Capable** schema does not construe every situation as a looming disaster, regardless of how minor the event might be. Our marketing analyst, Lynn, has a strong *Dependent−* schema. She had been so overprotected by her family that she only developed self-confidence in academics and later in her profession. She has not had the opportunity to discover that she is able to handle most situations, or that when she is not, the situation is seldom dire. So any minor disruption has the potential to evoke terror in Lynn, further decreasing her coping ability. Let's look at the change plan for Lynn.

Lynn: *Capable** Schema

Part 1: Maladaptive Schema Analysis

Step 1: My definition of my *Dependent−* schema: I need to depend on other people to take care of me. I cannot handle most things on my own. I cannot take care of myself in the long run. I need a man to take care of me.

Step 2: What do I think when my *Dependent−* schema is active? I can't handle this. I need help. Someone has to help me. I can't figure this out by myself. If I don't get help, something awful will happen.

Step 3: How do I feel when my *Dependent⁻* schema is active?
Frightened, desperate, embarrassed, ashamed.

Step 4: What do I do when my *Dependent⁻* schema is active?
I act helpless. I cry. I sometimes hyperventilate. I panic. I seek help from whoever is available, even people I don't care for. I don't think the situation through on my own before asking for help. I get irritated or angry when other people won't help me. In many respects, I act like I am twelve. Even my voice changes into a pathetic little-girl whine.

Step 5: What are the origins of my *Dependent⁻* schema? My
world turned upside down when my dad left. My mother reacted so helplessly that I began to believe that women can't survive without a man. Plus, my mother has told me that for the last twenty-seven years. She probably wrote it in my baby book. My stepdad was domineering and overprotective, so he solved all of my crises, big or little, and even intervened in my friendships. Outside of academics, I did not develop much self-confidence in my ability to handle life.

Step 6: What are the triggers for my *Dependent⁻* schema?
Any financial problem; anything that goes wrong at my condo; any car problems I have; whenever I feel a situation is out of control.

Step 7: What do I and others do to maintain my *Dependent⁻* schema? I keep asking for help. I don't try to think the situation through on my own first. I dwell on catastrophic outcomes, thereby becoming panicked and increasing my feelings of desperation. My mom still reminds me every time I see her that it is time for me to get married, so that someone can take care of me. My stepdad still rescues me whenever I ask.

Part 2: Adaptive Schema Development

Step 1: My definition of the *Capable** schema I want to create: Life is not beyond my ability to handle. I am able to take care of most situations. If I need help, I ask for it without acting desperate or helpless. However, I do not inconvenience others

with my requests for help. When I do seek assistance, I also try to learn how to handle that situation in the future, so I do not have to ask for help on that again.

Step 2: What thoughts would my *Capable** schema produce?
I can solve most problems if I calm down and think the situation through logically. I am a very logical thinker. Few situations are truly crises, so there is no point in working myself into a state of panic. Even in a crisis, staying calm will allow me to think more clearly. It is normal for things to go wrong at times in life. Learning how to handle those situations just increases my capabilities. I need to look at problems as learning opportunities, not potential disasters.

Step 3: What feelings would accompany the thoughts of my *Capable** schema? Calmness, confidence.

Step 4: What steps or actions do I need to take that are consistent with the thoughts and feelings of my *Capable** schema?

Action Item 1. When things go wrong, I will remind myself to breathe more slowly and talk calmly to myself. I will remind myself that I have solved major problems in my work, so I can handle other problems as well.

Action Item 2. When something goes wrong with my condo, car, or finances, first I will try to imagine what my stepdad would do in this situation. I will then try to take whatever actions I can by myself to fix the problem. I will not ask someone else to take steps that I can take myself, such as calling the garage to pick up my car.

Action Item 3. When I do need to ask for help, I will calm down before I ask for assistance. I will try to eliminate my desperate, little-girl behavior. I will speak in my normal tone of voice. If the other person cannot help me, I will not get angry, but rather I will ask them if they have any suggestions for me.

Action Item 4. When people do assist me, I will record the steps they took, either then or later, so that I know how to handle similar situations in the future.

Action Item 5. When I do receive help from someone else, I will find a way to repay that person, such as offering to help with some task.

Action Item 6. I will try to be more helpful to others. I will begin to look for ways that I can assist other people, even if they do not ask me. If I can reciprocate more, other people will not feel that I only ask for help and never give any.

Action Item 7. I will tell my mother that I do not find her comments about my needing a husband to be helpful and that I would like her to stop making them. I will tell her that those remarks make me think she sees me as incapable and that I do not want to see myself as incapable.

Action Item 8. In relationships, I will stop asking my boyfriends to start doing things for me that I have been taking care of in the past. I will remind myself that being in a relationship does not mean that the man has to assume responsibility for both of us. In a relationship, I need to take care of myself in the same way as when I am not in a relationship. I will remind myself that my dependence becomes a burden to the other person, which has happened in several relationships in the past and caused people to resent me.

Step 5: Who could be a good role model for my *Capable** schema? I can use Abby, my friend since college, as my role model for a *Capable** schema.

Step 6: Who can support my efforts to create a *Capable** schema? I also think Abby would be willing to be my support person. We have lunch every Thursday, and she has frequently encouraged me when I have tried to depend less on others.

Step 7: Select one or two action items to try. I will start with action items 1 and 2.

This time, you critique Lynn's action items. Are her items specific enough that you would know what to do? Do the items describe the actions Lynn needs to take? Can Lynn control these planned actions, or must she rely on someone else to do something? Does she identify how she could react differently to the triggers for her *Dependent*⁻ schema? Which items address Lynn's fear of disaster? Does Lynn describe thoughts she could use to support her new actions? Does she have any items that she can practice before she tries to implement them? You can ask these same questions when you critique your own action items.

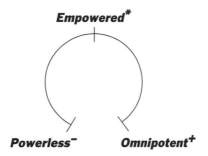

Empowered*

Powerless⁻   **Omnipotent⁺**

Empowered* Schema

The *Empowered** schema creates a sense of influence over the events in one's life. The amount of influence varies with the situation, but some degree of power is almost always present. Being empowered also means recognizing the limits of one's power and accepting that some situations or people are beyond one's influence. There is a recognition that sometimes you are being influenced and sometimes you are influencing others, but most of the time some reciprocal process of influence occurs. There is no question that people born into different socioeconomic and ethnic groups experience different degrees of power. Yet among any socioeconomic class or ethnic group, individuals vary greatly in their Empowerment schemas.

Unlike having a *Powerless⁻* schema, being empowered means refusing to see yourself as a victim. You may have been victimized, as in a rape or by abusive parents, but you still have a choice in how you deal with the aftermath and whether you let that event continue to control and victimize you in the future. Being empowered means not giving up after even the most dire experience. The *Empowered** schema recognizes that you may be powerless in some situations but also recognizes that those situations may need to be accepted and tolerated. All of us are powerless to some degree, yet we are able to wield some influence over most circumstances in our lives.

Being empowered means taking responsibility for the choices you make. Our marketing analyst, Lynn, has had a great deal of power in her relationships with men, contrary to what she believes. In earlier relationships, Lynn chose not to use her power, because she was afraid the man would leave. She could have told her previous boyfriend that he could not live with her unless he paid half of the rent, the utilities, and the groceries. She chose not to, yet she has not wanted to accept that she was responsible for that choice. She prefers to view herself as powerless.

Choice implies power. When there are no choices involved, there is no power. But very few situations involve absolutely no choices. Rather, people often do not want to deal with the consequences of the choices they could make. A person who stays in a high-stress job may do so because less stressful employment would pay a lower salary. Some couples stay in miserable relationships because neither person wants to sacrifice the image of being happily married or the material benefits they derive as a couple. In developing a plan for an *Empowered** schema, you need to identify what choices you have, regardless of how limited they are. They still can provide a beginning for change.

In contrast to the *Omnipotent*[+] schema, being empowered does not mean being able to control others. Accepting this idea has been a struggle for Lynn. She has felt powerless because her boyfriends would not let her control them. She picked men not for who they were, but for who she imagined they could be; ignoring their negative characteristics, she assumed she could change them once they were in a relationship. This assumption came from her moderate *Omnipotent*[+] schema. When she has been unable to change them, her *Powerless*[−] schema has been triggered. Being empowered means recognizing a balance in the control we have over ourselves and others. When we control others, we make them powerless. This is *not* being empowered. Being empowered means recognizing the difference between seeking power over others and trying to decrease unnecessary power of others over you. Let's look at how Lynn has developed her plan to become empowered.

Lynn: *Empowered** Schema

Part 1: Maladaptive Schema Analysis

Step 1: My definition of my *Powerless*[−] schema: I am powerless in making relationships turn out the way I want. I keep picking losers and users.

Step 2: What do I think when my *Powerless*[−] schema is active? I can't control this. I'm helpless. I have to put up with my boyfriend's behavior. I can't make my boyfriend do what I want.

Step 3: How do I feel when my *Powerless*[−] schema is active? Depressed, hopeless, frustrated, angry.

Step 4: What do I do when my *Powerless⁻* schema is active?
I plead with my boyfriends to treat me better. When they don't, I get angry and make empty threats. I put up with the way they take advantage of me. I am afraid to confront them too strongly for fear they will leave me.

Step 5: What are the origins of my *Powerless⁻* schema? I could not make my dad stay with my mom and me. I could never win any dispute with my stepdad. My mom believes women are powerless.

Step 6: What are the triggers for my *Powerless⁻* schema?
Anytime a boyfriend neglects or mistreats me or does not meet my expectations; whenever I am in a conflict with an older male authority figure.

Step 7: What do I and others do to maintain my *Powerless⁻* schema? In my interactions with my boyfriends, I am afraid to exert my power, because I am afraid they will leave me. The more powerless I act, the more they control me.

Part 2: Adaptive Schema Development

Step 1: My definition of the *Empowered** schema I want to create: I can influence most situations to some extent. I realize that some circumstances are beyond my control and I try to accept that. I also realize that I do have the power to stop boyfriends from taking advantage of me, but that means I need to accept that the relationship may end. I can accept that I cannot make people be what I want.

Step 2: What thoughts would my *Empowered** schema produce? I do have power to make choices in most situations. I can either choose to tolerate that my boyfriend does not contribute financially, or I can end our relationship if he doesn't contribute. Whichever I choose, it is my decision. I can choose to enter a relationship with someone who is missing qualities important to me, or I can choose not to, but I should not delude myself that I can create those qualities in another person.

Step 3: What feelings would accompany the thoughts of my *Empowered** schema? Peacefulness, calmness, confidence, sometimes disappointment.

Step 4: What steps or actions do I need to take that are consistent with the thoughts and feelings of my *Empowered** schema?

Action Item 1. In situations where I feel I have no control, I need to ask myself what choices I do have, no matter how small. After listing those choices and the possible consequences of each decision, I will pick one. I will remind myself that I made the decision and that I can handle the consequences.

Action Item 2. My current boyfriend, Jeff, never makes an official date with me. So I wait around all weekend to see if he will call, which leaves me feeling frustrated and powerless. On Wednesday nights, I will plan what I want to do for the weekend. I will make myself do those activities. If I am home when Jeff calls, I can decide if I want to do something with him or if I want to continue with my original plan. The choice is up to me. However, I will not bump plans that I have made with other friends for him, as I have done in the past.

Action Item 3. I will stop lending Jeff money because I have in the past and he has not repaid me, even when I have needed it. When he asks or hints about needing money in the future, I will not offer to help. I also will ask him how he plans to repay me what he now owes me. I will do this pleasantly, not critically or accusingly, because when I offered him the loans, I did not describe any specific plan for repayment.

Action Item 4. When Jeff asks me out to places that cost money, I will ask him how he plans to pay for the activity. I will tell him that I do not want to pay his way or buy his drinks anymore.

Action Item 5. I am going to stop keeping a supply of beer, because I drink very little and Jeff drinks all my beer every week but never replaces it. I will tell him that if he wants beer, he will have to buy it.

Action Item 6. Jeff has been asking about moving in with me, because his lease is up in six weeks. I will tell him no. I will tell him that I have decided I do not want to live with anyone again until I think the relationship is the kind where I would want marriage to be the outcome. There are too many problems in our relationship for me to see a future in it.

Action Item 7. I realize that my relationship with Jeff is never going to evolve into what I want, but I can practice being more empowered by implementing the above actions. When I am ready, I can end the relationship. If he ends it before then because of my new positions, I can accept that.

Step 5: Who could be a role model for my *Empowered** schema? I can use Abby as my role model. She is just as empowered as she is capable.

Step 6: Who can support my efforts to create an *Empowered** schema? I will ask Abby to be my support person for this schema, too.

Step 7: Select one or two action items to try. The easiest actions to start on are items 4 and 5.

Try to see if Lynn's action items include the characteristics for successful change. All the action items need to be detailed enough that she will know what to do. They need to explain how she can react differently in her typical problematic situations. They should also describe specific thoughts she can use to encourage herself when she is taking those actions. Some action items need to tell her how she can handle her predictable fears. Others should also include instructions to practice them before acting.

*Resilient** Schema

A *Resilient** schema produces realistic expectations about the potential dangers that exist in life. There is not a denial of danger, as with the *Invulnerable*+ schema. Nor is there a paralysis from fear, as with the *Vulnerable*− schema. A *Resilient**

schema allows you to take reasonable precautions without preventing you from enjoying life. When misfortune does occur, a *Resilient** schema does not prevent reactions of disappointment or grief. But a *Resilient** schema does generate expectations that eventually you can recover from the experience and create a meaningful existence. A *Resilient** schema does not deny painful realities but rather helps us accept that unhappy events are a natural part of life that can be endured and surmounted.

Actor Christopher Reeve, who was injured in a riding accident, exemplifies the power of adaptive schemas. A paralyzing injury between the first and second cervical vertebrae has restricted the dynamic, athletic 6-foot 4-inch Reeve to an electric wheelchair equipped with a respirator. Despite this drastic change in circumstances, Reeve has already made a major impact on the public's awareness and understanding of spinal cord injuries through his tireless efforts to educate us and inspire greater research in this area. Yet Reeve admits to bouts of depression and despair as he struggles to develop a new existence. He is not in denial. He is not a Pollyanna. He feels the emotional pain of his experience and his subsequent adjustment. Yet Reeve struggles to move on, to reassert his right to a rich, meaningful life. This kind of behavior is suggestive not only of a *Resilient** schema but of all the adaptive schemas in the Empowerment Zone.

This illustrates a critical point: *None of the adaptive schemas will prevent you from feeling sad or anxious or angry at times.* These are normal human emotions that we all experience periodically. You might be able to decrease those emotions by never loving anyone, never having any goals, never taking on any challenges, and never trying anything new. But you also will miss out on the exhilaration of being alive. Adaptive schemas allow you to rebound from the rejections, disappointments, and unfortunate experiences that we all encounter. Adaptive schemas keep you from getting stuck in a mire of distress.

Steven has a strong *Vulnerable⁻* schema. He has taken few risks, seldom has fun, and worries incessantly. His expectations that danger lurks everywhere have overwhelmed him with anxiety and tension. His plan to develop a *Resilient** schema follows.

Steven: *Resilient** Schema

Part 1: Maladaptive Schema Analysis

Step 1: My definition of my *Vulnerable⁻* schema: I always expect the worst. I worry endlessly about money, health, accidents, and criminal acts against myself and my family. I see the world as a dangerous place.

Step 2: What do I think when my *Vulnerable⁻* schema is active? Bad things are inevitable. If things go too well, watch out. My family needs to be careful, or one of us will be hurt. Eventually, some erratic driver will run into me or my family. Sooner or later, some patient will sue and bankrupt me. I can't take more than a few days off. Otherwise, something bad will happen with my practice. Life is dangerous.

Step 3: How do I feel when my *Vulnerable⁻* schema is active? Agitated, tense, fearful, guilty.

Step 4: What do I do when my *Vulnerable⁻* schema is active? All day long, I ruminate about disastrous outcomes that are possible in any situation. As soon as I lie down to go to sleep, I have an automatic worry button that gets pressed so I can review all the bad things that could happen the next day, the next year, the next decade. This happens no matter how exhausted I am. It is as if someone gave me a jolt of caffeine. I am so overprotective with my kids that I have seen them begin to exhibit my worrisome approach to life. I feel guilty whenever I do anything frivolous or nonproductive, for fear that such irresponsible behavior will be punished.

Step 5: What are the origins of my *Vulnerable⁻* schema? When I was growing up, there really did seem to be disaster around every corner. We never had enough money for anything. My dad was repeatedly fired because of his drinking. Several times, we were evicted from our apartment. When we were sick, we had to depend on Medicaid, which was often a humiliating experience, especially when my dad was dying of cirrhosis. If ever there seemed to be a little extra money, something would eat it up, like car repairs or someone needing glasses. There were so many needs for the little money we had that spending money on fun seemed irresponsible.

Step 6: What are the triggers for my *Vulnerable⁻* schema? Whenever I or one of my family members gets sick; when my practice appears to slow down even a little; when I hear how other doctors have been financially affected by managed care or decimated by a malpractice suit; when I see people who have been injured in car accidents, especially when they were hit by a drunk driver.

Step 7: What do I and others do to maintain my _Vulnerable⁻_ schema? I am really susceptible to Chicken Little stories about the sky falling. Several doctors I know reinforce this kind of thinking in themselves and in me. I ruminate about disaster. I never have any fun. I only work. I won't let myself go on any real vacations. I don't want to be away from my practice for fear that something dreadful will happen.

Part 2: Adaptive Schema Development

Step 1: My definition of the _Resilient*_ schema I want to create: I know that bad things can happen to people, but I believe I am capable of rebounding from those experiences. If I take reasonable precautions, I can enjoy life like other people I see. I save some money for the future and for emergencies, but I am entitled to enjoy some of the money I earn now.

Step 2: What thoughts would my _Resilient*_ schema produce? I have survived a childhood of one disaster after another. I have survived many difficult situations as an adult. I know I can handle whatever life brings my way. I am going to enjoy my good health and good fortune while I have it.

Step 3: What feelings would accompany the thoughts of my _Resilient*_ schema? Calmness, confidence, optimism, happiness.

Step 4: What steps or actions do I need to take that are consistent with the thoughts and feelings of my _Resilient*_ schema?

Action Item 1. I need to begin decreasing how much time I devote to work. I will arrange to take one week off every quarter and will plan real vacations with Ann for those times. I will also work out who will cover for me as soon as we figure out the dates of our vacations over the next twelve months.

Action Item 2. I will discuss with Ann how much money it is realistic for us to spend per year on vacations and then plan our vacations accordingly. I will put that money in a separate vacation account, and I will promise Ann that I won't fret about every penny we spend when we are on vacation. I will remind myself that we already have saved the money for this and that I do not need to worry about needing it for something else.

Action 3. I will set up with Ann a regular allowance for us each month for recreational expenses. We also can create a list of fun ways we can use that.

Action 4. I will talk with Ann about creating a separate account for her to use for household items and clothing for the kids and her. I won't monitor it. I will remind myself that Ann always has been responsible with money and that she doesn't need me to act like her father.

Action Item 5. I will try to decrease the number of overprotective statements I make to the kids. I won't remind them to dress warmly or to be careful. They are both responsible. When I do want to say some-thing, first I will ask myself if they don't already know this. I will also tell them how I am trying to change. I will ask them to remind me when I slip up, and I will promise not to get angry.

Action Item 6. I will begin to use the thought-replacement techniques that my psychologist taught me when worrisome thoughts come into my mind during the day. I will make myself stop the thoughts and actively focus on something else, especially pleasurable things that I am looking forward to doing that evening or weekend or sometime in the future.

Action Item 7. Every evening, I will not work after 8:00, excluding emergency calls I get when I am on call. After that, the evening belongs to my family and me. I will do something that is relaxing for at least a half hour before bedtime, such as reading nonprofessional material. I will go to bed at 10:30 every night and will use those thought-replacement techniques then, too.

Step 5: Who could be a role model for my *Resilient** schema?
To address my fear that I cannot survive some disaster, I will start keeping a list of people that I know or read about that experienced traumas and subsequently developed meaningful lives. I will use them as role models of how resilient people can be. I will remind myself that I can be like that also. I have many people in my practice who have experienced the death of a child or spouse and over time worked through their grief and loss and developed satisfying lives. I also have patients who have been severely injured but adjusted to their restrictions and created meaningful existences.

Step 6: Who can support my efforts to create a *Resilient** schema? I will ask Ann to be my support person for this schema-change plan.

Step 7: Select one or two action items to try. I will start with action items 4 and 5.

One more time, review the action items in step 4 of this change plan. Do they have the characteristics you probably have memorized by now—be specific, be positive, take responsibility, react differently, face your fears, think supportive thoughts, practice? In a moment, you will have an opportunity to create some more of your own action items.

DESIGNING YOUR SCHEMA-CHANGE PLAN

Now you have examples of schema-change plans for all the adaptive schemas on the Empowerment Schema Continuum. Each plan followed the schema-change procedures we have described. You are also familiar now with the characteristics of effective action items. You might want to use this new information to go back to Chapter 8 and revise your action items for the change plan you developed in the Self-Worth Zone. Then select an adaptive schema in the Empowerment Zone that you would like to create, and develop a change plan for it.

WORKSHEET TO CREATE AN ADAPTIVE SCHEMA IN THE EMPOWERMENT ZONE

Part 1: Maladaptive Schema Analysis

Step 1: Define your maladaptive schema in your own words.

_____

_____

_____

Step 2: Describe your thoughts when your maladaptive schema is active.

_____

_____

_____

Step 3: Describe how you feel when your maladaptive schema is active.

_____

_____

_____

Step 4: Describe what you do when your maladaptive schema is active.

_____

_____

_____

Step 5: Describe the origins of your maladaptive schema.

_____

_____

_____

Step 6: Describe the triggers for your maladaptive schema.

_____

_____

_____

Step 7: Describe what you and others do to maintain your maladaptive schema.

_____

_____

_____

Part 2: Adaptive Schema Development

Step 1: Define the adaptive schema you want to develop.

_____

_____

_____

Step 2: Describe the thoughts your adaptive schema would produce.

_____

_____

_____

Step 3: Describe the feelings that would accompany the thoughts of your adaptive schema.

_____

_____

_____

Step 4: Describe the steps or actions you need to take that are consistent with the thoughts and feelings of your adaptive schema.

_____

_____

_____

_____

_____

_____

Step 5: Identify at least one person who has the adaptive schema you are creating.

_____

_____

Step 6: Find a support person.

_____

_____

Step 7: Select one or two actions to try.

_____

_____

_____

10

Adaptive Schemas in the Relationship Zone

"The formula for achieving a successful relationship is simple:
you should treat all disasters as if they were trivialities
but never treat a triviality as if it were a disaster."
—*Quentin Crisp*, Manners from Heaven

All schemas can influence our relationships, but some seem to have a more direct impact. The adaptive schemas most relevant to issues in the Relationship Zone are: *Centered**, *Intimate**, *Self-Defined**, and *Trusting**. As we present schema-change plans for each of them, you will see how these schemas directly influence the way we behave in and perceive relationships. If you have relationship problems, these will be the adaptive schemas you will want to develop.

IMPROVING RELATIONSHIPS: SCHEMA PORTRAITS IN TRANSITION

Creating adaptive schemas in the Relationship Zone can meet with mixed reactions from others, because sometimes partners have maladaptive schemas in the same continuum. Any change in one person's schemas can throw off the balance of a partner with maladaptive schemas in the same continuum. You need to think carefully about consequences changes you make might have for others so you can handle any objections or resistance when you implement these changes. In the following examples, notice how Sylvia, Lynn, and Steven consider the possible interpersonal consequences of their plans to develop adaptive schemas in the Relationship Zone.

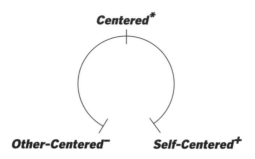

Centered* Schema

The *Centered** schema recognizes that our obligations to others will vary and that we have different commitments to different people at different times. The care you give to an infant or a parent with Alzheimer's should vary greatly from the care you provide to a teenage son or healthy parent in early retirement. The *Centered** schema helps you balance meeting others' needs and meeting your own needs. Sometimes you may feel exhausted caring for others, such as a sick baby, but you realize that this is a temporary state. If you feel trapped in an unremitting caregiving situation, you need to talk to someone about your circumstances. By exhausting yourself, you cannot care for anyone—yourself or others. Many organizations provide respite for people in continuous caregiving circumstances. You are not being selfish by seeking such relief. With a strong *Centered** schema, you would recognize your need for aid. Regular respite can allow people to continue in difficult caregiving situations. Nurses do not work twenty-four hours a day, seven days a week. Exhaustion is dangerous to them and to their patients. An *Other-Centered⁻* schema prevents people from reaching out for help when they need it, often creating unintentional martyrs.

With the *Centered** schema, one conveys to others a confidence that they are competent. By contrast, someone with the *Other-Centered⁻* schema assumes responsibility for others, taking over their obligations and solving their problems. Overprotectiveness is almost inevitable with an *Other-Centered⁻* schema, thereby making others apprehensive and doubtful about their own competence. People with the *Other-Centered⁻* schema mean well. In fact, guilt often drives them to meet the needs of everyone in the universe before even considering their own. But as you can see, this behavior does not produce confident, self-sufficient behavior in others.

With the *Centered** schema, you feel responsible for your own happiness, whereas with the *Self-Centered⁺* schema, you place that burden on others. People with the *Self-Centered⁺* schema assume that other people, particularly their partners, have some moral obligation to make them happy, and the *Other-Centered⁻* schema takes on that burden readily. People with the *Centered** schema recognize that when others try to please them, such actions are a gift, not an obligation, just as their pleasing others is a gift.

You can easily see the impact that schemas on this continuum have on relationships. The *Centered** schema helps maintain balanced relationships, so both members feel their needs are met regularly but not always. Oddly enough, a couple may initially get along quite well if one has the *Other-Centered⁻* schema and the partner has the *Self-Centered⁺* schema. Problems typically arise when the one with the *Other-Centered⁻* schema begins to grow weary of a servile status and starts to develop a more *Centered** schema. The partner with the *Self-Centered⁺* schema usually resists those changes, because the previous arrangement was much more pleasurable. If you have an *Other-Centered⁻* schema, you need to realize that people may fight your efforts to change to the *Centered** schema. You need to identify in your schema-development plan those who may resist your changes and how you intend to deal with their obstruction.

Our full-time homemaker, Sylvia, struggles with the *Other-Centered⁻* schema. You saw in her cost-benefit analysis how she has felt excessively obligated to take care of everyone. She has little time for herself and resents others for that. When she recognized her *Other-Centered⁻* schema, she realized that she had taught others to let her take care of them. She also knew that none of them were likely to change spontaneously. Her strategy for change is described below.

Sylvia: *Centered** Schema

Part 1: Maladaptive Schema Analysis

Step 1: My definition of my *Other-Centered⁻* schema: I need to make sure everyone is happy. If someone is upset, I need to fix that. It is my responsibility to take care of everyone around me, whether they ask or not. My needs are not as important as those of others.

Step 2: What do I think when my *Other-Centered⁻* schema is active? I need to take care of everything. It is my job to keep everyone happy. I have to listen to my friends' problems. It's shameful to put my own needs before other people's. Other people will appreciate how much I do for them. It would be awful to inconvenience anyone else.

Step 3: How do I feel when my *Other-Centered⁻* schema is active? Needed, important, responsible, overwhelmed, exhausted, frustrated, resentful.

Step 4: What do I do when my *Other-Centered⁻* schema is active? I offer to help. I try to solve other people's problems. I take responsibility for other people. I try to keep everyone happy. I try to meet everyone's needs, so no one else is inconvenienced except me. I don't ask the kids or Jack to help until I am absolutely exhausted and resentful.

Step 5: What are the origins of my *Other-Centered⁻* schema? Growing up, I was praised for helping my mom and for doing my sister's chores when she refused; my mom waited on my dad; helping my mother was one of the few ways she paid attention to me that wasn't negative; in my religion and culture women are supposed to be all-giving and self-sacrificing.

Step 6: What are the triggers for my *Other-Centered⁻* schema? When someone has a problem or needs help; when anyone indicates that they need my assistance; when anyone is upset; when the kids or Jack act as if they can't or don't want to do something.

Step 7: What do I and others do to maintain my *Other-Centered⁻* schema? I keep offering to help, even when I don't want to. I listen to my friends' miseries, ad nauseam. I try never to inconvenience anyone. I take on the problems of the people around me. Taking care of everything gives me a lot of control. Being thanked by Jack and the kids or anyone, for that matter, reinforces this schema. Not wanting anyone to be unhappy with me also keeps it going.

Part 2: Adaptive Schema Development

Step 1: My definition of the *Centered** schema I want to create: I take responsibility for meeting my own needs. I don't expect others to read my mind to meet my needs. I can assist others without taking over their responsibilities. I can feel empathy for others without feeling that I have to find remedies for them. When I give help or do a favor, I don't harbor the expectation of being rewarded or recognized later. I give help because I enjoy helping.

Step 2: What thoughts would my *Centered** schema produce?
I can treat myself and not feel guilty. I don't need to feel guilty if I refuse to take responsibility for other people's problems. God wants me to enjoy my life just as much as everyone else. I have not been divinely appointed to be a martyr. If I am not enjoying helping someone else, then maybe I need to reexamine why I am helping.

Step 3: What feelings would accompany the thought of my *Centered** schema? Satisfaction, contentment, guiltlessness.

Step 4: What steps or actions do I need to take that are consistent with the thoughts and feelings of my *Centered** schema?

Action Item 1. When my family or friends come to me with their problems, I can listen to them and show empathy, but not feel that I have to solve them. I will ask myself if the situation is my responsibility. If it isn't, then I will remind myself that I do not have to fix it. I can listen and tell them I am confident they will be able to work things out.

Action Item 2. I really don't want to take care of my family to the extent that I do. It leaves me feeling exhausted and irritable and too tired for fun activities. I will make a list of daily chores for everyone and a list of weekend chores. For the first several weeks, I will monitor the chores and give reminders that they need to be done before dinner during the week and before playtime on the weekends. First, I will run my plan by Jack, and then we can present it to the kids together. There will be some new chores for Jack on this also. I will point out to Jack and the kids that I want to do more fun activities with them, but to do that means they all need to help more with the chores. I also will not redo their efforts at a chore when I can tell they did try, because I know that annoys Jack. He says that is one reason he doesn't help in the kitchen. I also will try to stop doing things for Jack and the kids that they can and need to do for themselves. I will remind myself that sticking to this will give me more time to spend with my family instead of just picking up after them.

Action Item 3. I am going to do something pleasurable for myself everyday. I can make a list of these possibilities, and I will include both brief and more extensive activities. I will remind myself that it is my responsibility to make myself happy, not someone else's.

Action Item 4. I am going to stop being the crying towel for my friends. I will listen to their problems, but not when it inconveniences my family or me. When my friends repeat the same set of woes to me, I can say, "You have talked to me about this several times now. I agree it is a difficult situation. So what are you going to do about it?" I will repeat this as often as necessary. For those really tough situations, I will say, "I agree this is a painful situation. I can't help you, but I am sure a counselor could. Are you in enough pain to see one?" At these times, I will remind myself that this is not my responsibility to fix and to breathe slowly and calm myself down.

Action Item 5. I am going to tell Jack that I want to begin taking paralegal classes in the evening this fall semester. I will remind him that we agreed I could do that when the kids finished kindergarten. I will tell him that I need his support, both emotionally and physically. I will tell him he will need to watch the kids in the evenings two nights a week, which will not be a problem, as he is home then anyway. I will not let him or the girls make me feel guilty for doing this. I can remind all of them that I don't whine and pout when they go to their various activities or friends' houses.

Action Item 6. I know that Jack and the kids will resist some of these changes. I will not get angry. I will remind myself that I have trained them to let me wait on them. I will repeat the request and tell them that I appreciate what they are doing for themselves or the family. The key to success is my being persistent and consistent.

Action Item 7. I know changing this schema will be scary for me, because I have believed I need to take care of others . . . and it allows me to orchestrate our lives. I will remind myself that I am changing the extent of my helping behavior, not eliminating it. I also can tell myself that I am working to decrease their dependence on me and to increase my energy and improve my disposition, which will benefit us all.

Step 5: Who could be a role model for my *Centered** schema? My neighbor Louise can be a role model. Her husband and kids always have helped around the house. She might even have some suggestions I could try.

Step 6: Who can support my efforts to create a *Centered** schema? Louise also can be my support person on this.

Step 7: Select one or two action items to try. I will do items 1 and 4 first.

Over time, the *Self-Centered*+ schema engenders much resentment in others, whereas the *Other-Centered*− schema produces much internal resentment toward others. Neither consequence produces healthy relationships. Both of the maladaptive schemas on this continuum are difficult to change. The *Other-Centered*− schema will be difficult to change because others around you have gotten comfortable with your taking care of them. The *Self-Centered*+ schema is hard to change, because always having your needs met is quite pleasurable (we're told). The key to remember about changing either one of these is that you are simply moving to the middle. The *Centered*+ schema will allow you to be more balanced in meeting everyone's needs, including your own.

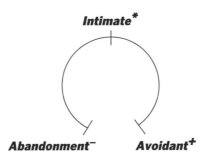

*Intimate** Schema

The *Intimate** schema is elusive for many people, yet it is essential for warm, emotionally close relationships. This schema allows you to be open and sincere with other people, honestly acknowledging fears and disappointments as well as hopes and dreams. With this schema, you can accept others as they are without being unduly judgmental and can expect that others will be equally as accepting of you. This expectation also includes the realization that some degree of conflict is inevitable in any relationship, and that disagreement or constructive criticism does not equal dislike or rejection.

When you have the *Intimate** schema, you can acknowledge the need for human beings to be emotionally close to each other, but you can also recognize that the level of closeness will vary among people. All relationships will not be alike. Everyone will not be your best friend and intimate confidant. An *Intimate** schema allows you to be selective about how you invest yourself emotionally and physically.

With the *Intimate** schema, you can give others freedom to leave and to be independent without fearing that they will not remain connected. School-phobic children often have parents who support clinging and immature social behavior. Such parents often have an *Abandonment⁻* schema. They try to maintain the babylike status of their children as long as possible, delaying any signs of independence from themselves.

The *Intimate** schema includes the belief in our own lovableness. With this adaptive schema, we will feel lovable, no matter whether certain others love us. We are all lovable, but feedback from our relationships may tell us how we sometimes do not act lovably. The *Intimate** schema also allows us to see when a relationship is damaging and enables us to withdraw from hurtful and destructive experiences.

With the *Intimate** schema, we recognize that being emotionally close to others carries the risk of loss and subsequent pain if that relationship ends. We have an accompanying awareness that some relationships will inevitably end. Yet we view the benefits from an emotionally close relationship as outweighing the pain of loss that may occur one day. We see relationships as inherently valuable and enriching, even those that end badly. We do not see them as successes or failures but rather as experiences that expand our understanding of ourselves and others.

If you recall, Lynn flips between her *Abandonment⁻* schema and her *Avoidant⁺* schema. Even when another person is being loving and supportive, Lynn frequently seeks reassurance about the relationship. But when she feels angry or rejected, she pulls away and ignores the other person. Lynn can go for days without speaking. Lynn said that some of her boyfriends and friends have described her as a kind of Dr. Jekyll and Mr. Hyde—unpredictably flipping from being warm and loving to cold and distant.

Because Lynn's *Abandonment⁻* schema is stronger than her *Avoidant⁺* schema, we will present her analysis of her *Abandonment⁻* schema. However, Lynn also reviewed examples of her *Avoidant*⁺ schema as she created a plan to develop an *Intimate** schema. If you find that you flip between maladaptive schemas on a continuum as Lynn does, you can follow this same procedure. Develop a plan for an adaptive schema using your stronger maladaptive schema, but first review all your examples of the opposite maladaptive schema.

Lynn: *Intimate** Schema

Part I: Maladaptive Schema Analysis

Step 1: My definition of my *Abandonment*⁻ schema: I am afraid people will leave me. I am afraid that I will be left alone. I need to have constant feedback that I won't be left or discarded. I do things for others so they will depend on me and not leave.

Step 2: What do I think when my *Abandonment*⁻ schema is active? My partner will eventually cheat on me. My partner will leave me if I am too assertive. I can't be alone. It is awful to be alone. There must be something wrong with me if people always leave.

Step 3: How do I feel when my *Abandonment*⁻ schema is active? Tense, nervous, panicky, desperate at times, stomachaches, headaches.

Step 4: What do I do when my *Abandonment*⁻ schema is active? I repeatedly ask for reassurance that I am loved. I question my partners about whether they are interested in other women or whether they find certain women more attractive than me. I literally badger them until they admit that they find someone else attractive, and then I feel threatened and become withdrawn and cold. I interrogate my partners if they talk or joke with other women. I make unfounded accusations. Sometimes I check on where my partners have been.

Step 5: What are the origins of my *Abandonment*⁻ schema? My dad left my mom and me completely by surprise when I was five. I had no idea he was unhappy. For a long time I thought I had done something to make him leave. I always had been closer to my dad than my mom, but even after he left I didn't become closer to her. She was so focused on herself and so distraught that I just felt lost and alone and confused. Since that time, my mom has stressed how a woman cannot survive without a man, but at the same time she is convinced no man can be trusted. So I have grown up believing that I have to have a man to take care of me, but at the same time I never trust that one will.

Step 6: What are the triggers for my *Abandonment⁻* schema?
Any suggestion of indifference toward me. Others not wanting to be involved with me; when friends do not call for a while; when my mother does not seem concerned about me; whenever men are not interested in me; whenever a boyfriend acts friendly to another female, even a waitress.

Step 7: What do I and others do to maintain my *Abandonment⁻* schema now? I tend to pick men who are cocky and act like they don't need anyone. Once they are interested in me, then I get distressed at how they don't seem to need me or to care about my feelings. I pick men who usually have not been trustworthy in past relationships, and I assume they won't be trustworthy with me. Several of them haven't been. In fact, several of my relationships have started with men who at the time were in relationships with someone else. Some men have left me, including my previous partner. My mother emphasizes that a woman has to have a man but should not trust him.

Part 2: Adaptive Schema Development

Step 1: My definition of the *Intimate** schema I want to create:
I am comfortable sharing my personal thoughts and feelings with some people. I can be emotionally vulnerable with some people and feel they will not betray me. I can believe that others will be available to me when I really need them if they possibly can be. I believe that I can take care of myself if someone leaves me, even though I might be hurt and disappointed. I understand that relationships will vary in their closeness and intensity.

Step 2: What thoughts would my _Intimate_* schema produce?
I am a lovable person, but I need to act more lovingly toward others. I can be more selective in my partners. I can avoid men who have a history of being unfaithful and self-centered. I can have friendships with varying levels of closeness. Some friends are to have fun with. Some are to rely on. Some are to share my most important thoughts and feelings. A few friends might do all of those, but most will only do some of them. I realize that other people cannot always be what I need because of who they are, not because I am unlovable. I can accept people for who they are and what they are able to offer me without being judgmental.

Step 3: What feelings would accompany the thoughts of my _Intimate_* schema? Calmness, contentment, acceptance.

Step 4: What steps or actions do I need to take that are consistent with the thoughts and feelings of my _Intimate_* schema?

Action Item 1. Change my selection criteria for men. I would like to find a long-term partner. I will stop going to the bars on weekends. I will find other social activities as ways to meet men. I will identify a list of red flags in men for me: heavy drinkers, womanizers, frequent job changers, unemployed men, blamers—their problems are always someone else's fault—divorced fathers who are irresponsible in their commitments to their children. I will remind myself that these red flags signal disaster for me in the future. I will remind myself that I am drawn to irresponsible, fun-loving types and then feel frustrated by those same behaviors later when they are irresponsible and unfaithful to me. I will remind myself that I do not want to waste any more time going through that same painful cycle again. I also will remind myself that I cannot change the way a person is. I also will not let my mind create a distorted image of my partner.

Action Item 2. I will change the way I present myself to others. I will stop trying to get every man I meet to pursue me or to think I am sexy. I will stop trying to draw attention to myself by dressing so sexily. I think I am conveying a message that really is not me. I think the way I dress suggests that I am easy and may turn off the men I am more interested in.

225

Action Item 3. I will take the initiative in maintaining relationships. I will initiate contact with others to see how they are doing and not just call them when I need to talk or want to do something.

Action Item 4. I will pay attention to the times when I withdraw from others. I will use that as a signal that I have been hurt and that I need to deal directly with the situation, not withdraw.

Action Item 5. I will try to accept that others are not always available when I want them to be. I will also try to accept without acting irritated the fact that others might not want to do what I want. If people do not call me back, I will tell myself that they are busy and I will call someone else or call them later. I will not be nasty and accuse them of not caring about me. I will remind myself that I do not have to be the center of other people's lives for them to care about me.

Action Item 6. I will find ways to entertain myself, so that I can enjoy being alone at times. I will make a list of things that I can do to nurture myself, and I will do one of them every day.

Action Item 7. I will try to be more open with some of my colleagues and listen to what they tell me, so I can show my interest in their lives.

Action Item 8. I will work on changing those positive maladaptive schemas that seem to alienate or offend others, such as my Entitled, Blameless, and Aggressive schemas.

Action Item 9. I am going to find a way to feel more connected to others. I am also going to volunteer as a math tutor at the high school near my home. I could do that a couple of nights a week. When I feel lonely, I will remind myself that I can feel more connected to other people if I get involved in some helping activity.

Step 5: Who could be a role model for my *Intimate** schema? One of my colleagues, Mona, seems to have this schema. I will try to pay more attention to her.

Step 6: Who can support my efforts to create an *Intimate** schema? I also can use Mona again as a support person.

Step 7: Select one or two action items to try. I will start with action items 4 and 5.

People with the *Abandonment⁻* schema often have not learned how to nurture themselves. They do not know how to comfort themselves or make themselves feel safe. This inability makes them desperate to have someone else in their lives, even though those people can be quite inadequate, as Lynn has experienced. Hence, developing the *Intimate** schema means first learning how to nurture yourself. Treat yourself kindly when you are having a bad day. Do something that will comfort you, such as spending the evening curled up on the couch reading a book or watching a favorite television show. People often find that having a pet allows them to develop their own nurturing abilities. Dogs will love you unconditionally, but be forewarned that cats can be judgmental! Until you can appreciate your own lovableness, you are not going to feel safe being vulnerable with other people.

People who lack an *Intimate** schema often feel disconnected from other people. Consequently, finding ways to be connected can be helpful. Select a volunteer activity that appeals to you and try it for three months. Some people also seek a spiritual connection either through religion or nature. Reading books on spirituality or the meaning of life can help. But the most simple step in developing this adaptive schema is to reach out to others, either the people around you now or those you meet through some activity. Reach out without expecting to be rewarded or recognized, because, honestly, you are doing this for yourself.

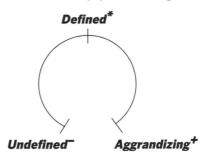

*Defined** Schema

You may be wondering why the Self-Definition Schema Continuum is in the Relationship Zone. After all, the Self-Definition schemas seem to involve individual identity. This is partly true, but our identities evolve through our interactions with others. We acquire a sense of self from our reactions to others and their reactions to us. A *Defined** schema allows us to be our own separate self in relationships. With an *Aggrandizing*⁺ schema, we attempt to swallow up the identities of other people. With an *Undefined*⁻ schema, we seem to have no separate identity and must borrow one from someone else. So the schemas on the Self-Definition Continuum also describe how we are in relationships.

The *Defined** schema produces a clear sense of who one is. People with a *Defined** schema know what they like and dislike, what they value, and what their goals are. They are able to create their own sense of purpose. Yet a *Defined** schema does not compel an individual to impose those same preferences on others. Nor does a *Defined** schema allow an individual to feel intimidated or awestruck by other confident people.

A *Defined** schema allows one to appreciate others' individuality. For example, parents with a *Defined** schema encourage their children to pursue career paths based on the child's interests, not the parents' interests. An *Aggrandizing*⁺ person wants other people to adopt her own values and interests. A parent with an *Aggrandizing*⁺ schema tries to control the extracurricular activities and career choices of his children.

An *Undefined*⁻ schema creates a sense of emptiness, an identity vacuum. Unless undefined people are around other strong people, they feel lost. Their values and interests depend on whoever is present in their lives at that moment. They lack a sense of purpose or direction in their lives, except that which others impose. They often describe their strongest identity as depending on someone else, for example, Jimmy's parent or Jan's partner. Some virtually develop an identity du jour. A *Defined** schema creates a strong sense of self that does not vacillate, no matter who is present.

Sylvia, Steven, and Lynn all have relatively strong *Defined** schemas, but Jason does not. Jason, age forty-one, is the department manager for an accounting department in a government agency. He has not married and has never been in a serious relationship with a woman. He lives alone with two dogs and a cat and seldom dates, although he has a few close women friends and occasionally goes out with them.

Jason initially sought therapy for what he describes as a chronic sense of unhappiness. He feels adrift with no sense of where he wants to anchor. He describes more severe depressions in his early twenties, but has never received psychotherapy or antidepressants. Jason grew up in a small town in the Pacific Northwest and then attended a four-year college not far from home. He has a married sister who is twelve years younger. His mother died several years earlier, which was a significant loss for him, as he was always much closer to her than to his father. His father and sister still live in his hometown, where he visits once or twice a year.

228

According to Jason, "I went to college to get away from home. I was good at math, so becoming an accountant seemed an easy path to take. It's always been easy for me to get a job somewhere. I've had several different jobs before this one. I've had this one now for seven years, the longest I've ever been in one place. When I would get really down in the past, I would just move and find a new job. This time I really don't want to move. My job is OK and the pay and benefits are good, but I am feeling that old sense of dread beginning again."

Jason: *Defined** Schema

Part 1: Maladaptive Schema Analysis

Step 1: My definition of my *Undefined⁻* schema: I have no sense of identity. I do not know who I am or who I am supposed to be. I have never had a sense of purpose. I feel like I don't count. I have no really strong opinions except that I could probably be described as an environmentalist, but I don't do anything about that.

Step 2: What do I think when my *Undefined⁻* schema is active? I don't know what I'm doing. I'm just drifting. I don't know what I want to do or be. I'm lost. I have no purpose.

Step 3: How do I feel when my *Undefined⁻* schema is active? Depressed, sad, empty.

Step 4: What do I do when my *Undefined⁻* schema is active? Nothing. I putz around the house, but I don't get much done. When I am around others who seem powerful, I feel awestruck and I act deferential to them.

Step 5: What are the origins of my *Undefined⁻* schema? When I was growing up, my dad always seemed disappointed or even disgusted with me. He wanted me to be in athletics. But I was just never interested in that. He said I didn't try hard, that I wasn't tough enough. Some of that was true. I didn't try very hard and I didn't like being bounced around by other boys, but I really wasn't very athletic. Dad was my coach most of the time when I was in elementary school, and his coaching never stopped. I loved to hang around with my uncle, my mom's older brother, who taught art at the high school. He would let me paint at his studio, which I loved, but my dad said that was a waste of time for a man. My uncle died of cancer when I was eleven. After that, I never showed much interest in anything. I got average grades in school without trying, which aggravated my dad because I didn't try harder. He was always on my case. Nothing I did was good enough for him.

Step 6: What are the triggers for my *Undefined⁻* schema? When I see other people enthusiastic about something; when I go home to Washington.

Step 7: What or who maintains my *Undefined⁻* schema now? My dad still puts me down when I visit him. He does not think being an accountant is very macho. I know I'm not doing anything meaningful, but I don't know what I should do.

Part 2: Adaptive Schema Development

Step 1: My definition of the *Defined schema I want to create:** I know who I am. I have definite values and interests and I pursue them. I have a meaningful purpose to my life. There are people who care about me, because I am worthwhile. My life matters to them. My life matters to me.

Step 2: What thoughts would my *Defined schema produce?** I am somebody. I am OK. My life matters.

Step 3: What feelings would accompany the thoughts of my *Defined schema?** Calmness, joy, peacefulness.

Step 4: What steps or actions do I need to take that are consistent with the thoughts and feelings of my *Defined schema?**

Action Item 1. I will begin actively exploring activities that I think I *might* enjoy. I can make a list of ideas I have had. I also will look in the weekend paper's section on activities and find something every week that I can attend. I will record how I felt about each activity, what I did and did not like about it. I will also make a list of activities I have done in the past and record how I felt about those experiences. Over time, I will see if I can identify themes about myself.

Action Item 2. I have not pursued painting since my uncle died. I would like to try that again. The community college near my home offers courses in that. I can register for one of them for the next semester. I have thought about doing this for a long time.

Action Item 3. I will try to find ways to make my life seem meaningful to me. I can investigate different environmental organizations and see if I can volunteer in some way. My accounting skills should be benefi cial to some group.

Action Item 4. When I visit my dad next time, I will tell him what I am doing. If he criticizes me, I will tell him that I think what I am doing is worthwhile and that I am disappointed that he cannot accept that I have interests different from his.

Action Item 5. I will take antidepressant medication for a realistic period of time to see if that makes a difference in my depression. I will stop putting myself down for needing medicine to handle life. I will remind myself that if it helps me feel better and become more my "real self," I need to take it—just like some diabetics need insulin.

Step 5: Who could be a role model for my *Defined** schema?
My assistant supervisor is an enthusiastic person who often talks about his different activities. He seems to have a strong sense of purpose, even though he is not doing anything spectacular. I could use him as a role model but not as someone to copy.

Step 6: Who can support my efforts to create a *Defined** schema?
I can use my psychologist for a support person. I also can use Jennifer, a friend who always has been supportive of me.

Step 7: Select one or two action items to try.
I will try items 2 and 5 now.

Moving from an *Undefined⁻* schema to a *Defined** schema essentially means creating an identity, which is no minor task. You will need to explore your values and interests. It will be equally as important to identify your dislikes as your likes. You need to accept that your activities and values are as important as those of other people. Ultimately, you need to feel that your existence in the universe does matter, at least to you, if to no one else. Changing this schema takes time. It will not happen in a few weeks or even a few months. Remember that we spend our childhood and adolescence forging our identities. Changing a schema so critical to identity will require strong support, because progress will be slow. The focus should be on the experience you have while developing an identity, not on what you will become. Our identities evolve throughout our lives as we have experiences—both good and bad—and as we integrate those experiences into our sense of self.

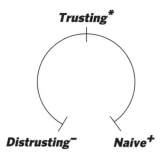

*Trusting** Schema

The ability to trust is essential for an emotionally intimate relationship. The *Trusting** schema produces that ability. The *Trusting** schema creates faith that people usually try to be honorable and ethical and that disloyalty and betrayal are universally acknowledged as undesirable qualities. Societies survive through cooperation, which cannot exist in a world devoid of trust. Trust in humankind must therefore extend far beyond our closest confidants. The *Trusting** schema creates that type of perspective.

At the same time, the *Trusting** schema recognizes that some people simply cannot be trusted. A trusting person enters new relationships optimistically yet cautiously. As someone acquires more evidence of another's trustworthiness, the level of caution subsides but can quickly be reactivated when apparent inconsistencies or deceptions appear. The *Trusting** schema does not produce gullibility but rather healthy skepticism with the hope that in most relationships, skepticism will prove unfounded.

The *Trusting** schema also enables us to forgive. Few people have never told a lie, broken a promise, or breached their personal integrity. The *Trusting** schema realizes that people are human and that occasional lapses of integrity occur. When others show genuine remorse and a commitment to do better, the *Trusting** schema allows us to forgive and trust again. Never is this more painful than in the betrayal of a love relationship. When one's partner is emotionally or physically unfaithful, even someone with a strong *Trusting** schema will need time and evidence to believe in that person again. Many couples are able to reestablish that trust after much effort, but certainly not all of them.

You can readily discern how both the *Distrusting⁻* schema and the *Naive⁺* schema impede relationships, whether casual or intimate. The *Distrusting⁻* schema always expects deception and readily sees deception in ambiguous situations, even when none is there. This repeatedly leads to unjustified and offensive accusations of others, whether verbalized or not. Their partners always have to prove their loyalty, deny malevolent intentions, and justify their actions. Yet any trust earned is temporary for someone with the *Distrusting⁻* schema.

Whereas the *Distrusting⁻* schema makes relationships a struggle for a person's partner, the *Naive⁺* schema often causes anguish for the individual. The naive person seems to lack any reasonable caution, appearing unable to learn even from painful experiences of betrayal. The *Naive⁺* schema seems to foster a commitment not to be discerning and to discount any red flags, no matter how flagrant. People with the *Naive⁺* schema experience repeated betrayals and emotional distress.

Steven, the physician, is wary around other people and has been for as long as he can remember. This mistrust prevents him from developing close relationships or even revealing casual aspects of his life to others. Steven's mistrust also enhances his *Avoidant⁺* schema, which he is trying to change. Below is his plan for the *Trusting** schema.

Steven: *Trusting** Schema

Part 1: Maladaptive Schema Analysis

Step 1: My definition of my *Distrusting⁻* schema: Few people are truly trustworthy. People seldom are capable of unfailing loyalty. Most people are judgmental and intolerant. People are out for themselves. People only act nice to people with money or power.

Step 2: What do I think when my *Distrusting⁻* schema is active? I can't trust other people. I need to be on my guard around others. I should not confide in others, because they won't keep my confidences. I think people are trying to manipulate me. I don't think people are sincere.

Step 3: How do I feel when my *Distrusting⁻* schema is active? Wary, tense, vulnerable, suspicious, fearful.

Step 4: What do I do when my *Distrusting⁻* schema is active? I withdraw. I become very cautious. I don't share any meaningful information about myself. I isolate myself.

Step 5: What are the origins of my *Distrusting⁻* schema? I learned as a little boy that I couldn't trust my dad to keep his word. He promised to stop drinking, to bring home his paycheck, to pay the rent. But he didn't. Some people would act nice to me but make disparaging comments about my dad behind my back. The parents of one of my high school girlfriends didn't want her to go out with me, but once I was accepted into medical school, they acted like I was the Second Coming. So I learned to discount the sincerity of others. In college and med school, I also learned that doctors are no different. A lot of guys would do anything to get into med school so they could become millionaires. They didn't care whom they hurt by cheating. I know doctors that are still like that. They operate in the gray area with patients and insurance companies, which then hurts everyone else who is honest.

Step 6: What are the triggers for my *Distrusting⁻* schema? When certain people act solicitous of me, I wonder what they want. When I make a mistake or my family does something that is not admirable, I assume others will think or say hurtful things.

Step 7: What do I and others do to maintain my *Distrusting⁻* schema now? I don't let myself be open with people. I never confide anything negative about myself or family. I overhear staff gossiping in the hospital and then see them act friendly to the people they were bad-mouthing ten minutes earlier. I hear how some other doctors take advantage of patients or insurance companies. My schema is strengthened whenever someone close to me does not tell me the whole truth, whether through distortion or omission. I *dwell* on all of these events.

Part 2: Adaptive Schema Creation

Step 1: My definition of the *Trusting** schema I want to create: Most people can be trusted. Most people do not enjoy your misfortune or put you down. Most people are honest.

Step 2: What thoughts would my *Trusting** schema produce? I can be open with people about casual things. Most people mean well. Most people try to be ethical. Most people try to do the right thing. Most people don't try to be hurtful on purpose.

Step 3: What feelings would accompany the thoughts of my *Trusting** schema? Contentment, calmness.

Step 4: What steps or actions do I need to take that are consistent with the thoughts and feelings of my *Trusting** schema?

Action Item 1. Since I don't trust people, I need to do some experiments. I will begin to offer more personal information in conversations with my office staff and the hospital staff. I can start by telling people some of the things we do on the weekends. I will trust that information will not be used against me.

Action Item 2. When other people tell me about something awful that's happening to them, if it would be helpful, I will disclose a similar experience if I have one.

Action Item 3. I will talk to Ann about inviting some couples we know to our house. We have never done that before. I guess I thought they might be judgmental or jealous. Maybe we could invite one couple at a time so I can get more comfortable with this idea.

Action Item 4. The medical staff at my hospital organizes different vacation packages. I will sign us up for one of those, starting with one of the three-day trips. That would be a big risk for me, because that would be the most time I have ever been with any of these people casually.

Action Item 5. My kids say I interrogate them. I will try to change that. I will remind myself that I can trust their judgment, that they have been responsible kids. I will ask them to signal to me when they feel I am cross-examining them.

Action Item 6. I will try to work on being more tolerant and less judgmental of other people. When someone says something that hurts my feelings, I will consider whether they really intended the remark in that manner. If I think they did, I will try to understand why and work on forgiving them. I will remind myself not to interpret ambiguous remarks as directed against me.

Step 5: Who could be a role model for my *Trusting schema?** George, an older doctor in my field, conveys trust in other people but is realistic. I can use him for my role model.

Step 6: Who can support my efforts to create a *Trusting schema?** Ann could be my support person.

Step 7: Select one or two action items to try. I will begin with items 5 and 6.

People with the *Distrusting⁻* schema need to face their fear of being let down by other people in some way. This means that they need to find opportunities to give people a chance to be honest or trustworthy. You can see from Steven's action items that he is going to try to see if people inevitably hurt him when he trusts them in low-risk situations. Thus far, Steven has maintained his *Distrusting⁻* schema by avoiding such risks.

People with the *Naive*[+] schema are also avoiding a fear. They are afraid of being let down, but they deal with it by ignoring or avoiding any evidence that they have been deceived. When they are deceived, they make excuses for the other person's behavior. To acknowledge that some people cannot be trusted produces too much anxiety for these people, so they wear blinders in their relationships.

HAVING SCHEMAS OVERLAP

By now you probably have noticed considerable overlap among the various schemas. You're right. The schemas we have described do overlap. They are not restricted to mutually exclusive areas. This means that two different schemas may reinforce the same thoughts and actions. For example, Lynn has two schemas that tend to make her cling to other people—her *Abandonment*[-] and her *Dependent*[-]. Steven's schemas, *Blameless*[+] and *Perfectionistic*[+], make him consider mistakes intolerable. Sylvia's schemas, *Acquiescent*[-] and *Other-Centered*[-], make it almost impossible for her not to give in to others' needs. This schema overlap explains why making changes in one schema often produces changes in another schema. If you have several maladaptive schemas that you want to change, you will find that working very hard on modifying one maladaptive schema will produce positive movement in other related schemas.

DESIGNING YOUR SCHEMA-CHANGE PLAN

You now have a schema-development plan for every adaptive schema in the three zones. You have seen how the procedure for schema development is applied in each case. When you create your own plan, refer to the example presented here for the adaptive schema you are trying to create. Your plan may not be as elaborate as the plans we have described. That does not matter, as long as you think your plan could eventually produce the adaptive schema you are seeking. But do include each of the steps. Now select a Relationship Adaptive Schema, and make a plan to create it.

WORKSHEET TO CREATE AN ADAPTIVE SCHEMA IN THE RELATIONSHIP ZONE

Part 1: Maladaptive Schema Analysis

Step 1: Define your maladaptive schema in your own words.

_____

_____

_____

Step 2: Describe your thoughts when your maladaptive schema is active.

_____

_____

_____

Step 3: Describe how you feel when your maladaptive schema is active.

_____

_____

_____

Step 4: Describe what you do when your maladaptive schema is active.

_____

_____

_____

Step 5: Describe the origins of your maladaptive schema.

_____

_____

_____

Step 6: Describe the triggers for your maladaptive schema.

_____

_____

_____

Step 7: Describe what you and others do to maintain your maladaptive schema.

_____

_____

_____

Part 2: Adaptive Schema Development

Step 1: Define the adaptive schema you want to develop.

_____

_____

_____

Step 2: Describe the thoughts your adaptive schema would produce.

_____

_____

_____

Step 3: Describe the feelings that would accompany the thoughts of your adaptive schema.

_____

_____

_____

Step 4: Describe the steps or actions you need to take that are consistent with the thoughts and feelings of your adaptive schema.

_____

_____

_____

_____

_____

_____

Step 5: Identify at least one person who has the adaptive schema you are creating.

_____

_____

Step 6: Find a support person.

_____

_____

Step 7: Select one or two actions to try.

_____

_____

_____

11

Dismantling Maladaptive Schemas

Most of us are about as eager to be changed as we were to be born,
and go through our changes in a similar state of shock.
—James Baldwin, "Every Good-Bye Ain't Gone"

If you have gotten this far in the book and worked through some of our exercises, your maladaptive schemas may already have started to change. That is especially likely if you have been working on developing adaptive schemas as alternatives. As you learn to bolster your adaptive schemas, you will inevitably "put the squeeze" on your maladaptive schemas. And more likely than not, some of your maladaptive schemas have already begun to feel the pressure. Now it's time for a more direct, frontal assault on them. You'll see that as you dismantle your maladaptive schemas, your adaptive schemas will flourish and strengthen. They will no longer be constrained by what previously seemed to be omnipotent maladaptive schemas.

Remember: Don't expect your maladaptive schemas to disappear completely from your psychological terrain. They won't just vanish, particularly the strongest ones. Your maladaptive schemas will remain a possible way of viewing reality and yourself, and during stressful times, they will likely return for a while. The goal is to make their reappearance less frequent, less intense, and shorter lived.

SCHEMA-CHANGE STRATEGIES

Some forms of therapy have neglected the importance of taking action; instead, they focus almost exclusively on providing support and insight. Yet accumulating evidence tells us that active intervention creates more change than insight alone. This chapter and the next will describe a number of important schema-change strategies.

Two-Chair Technique

Psychologists have successfully used the two-chair technique on all kinds of issues. We hope you will use it effectively to attack your maladaptive schemas. First, arrange two chairs to face each other. Label one of the chairs with one of your negative maladaptive schemas, and tag the other chair with the adaptive schema you would like to acquire. Then, although it may feel a little silly, sit in the negative maladaptive schema chair and talk to your other, adaptive schema. Tell that imaginary self why you believe your negative maladaptive schema is true and should be trusted. Argue as forcefully as you can. Then change chairs and argue from the adaptive schema perspective. Tell your maladaptive schema why your adaptive schema is more valid and should therefore be trusted. Again, argue with vigor. Then, switch chairs and start the process over again with the same two schemas. Throughout the process, notice how you feel in each chair.

Puzzled by how this really works? We'll illustrate this technique using Bernie, a fifty-six-year-old carpenter. Bernie had the negative maladaptive schemas of *Blameworthiness⁻* and *Inadequacy⁻* in the Self-Worth Zone and used the two-chair technique to counteract his *Inadequate⁻* schema, as shown below:

Inadequate⁻ **Schema Chair (speaking to his *Adequate** schema):** It's over. You've gotten to the point where you can no longer haul heavy lumber around like you used to. You've never made the kind of living you should have, and you've always made more than your share of mistakes. It's amazing you even have a job anymore. I don't know why you don't just quit.

Adequate* **Schema Chair (in response):** OK, so I can't do the work that I used to. And sure, I make mistakes sometimes, but who doesn't? Not many people have the same strength at fifty-six that they did at twenty-two. That doesn't mean I can't do good work.

Inadequate⁻ **Chair:** If you can't do now what you could do then, you might as well hang it up. You're incompetent as a carpenter.

Adequate* **Chair:** Oh, come on! I'm one of the most important people on the work team. Did you forget that raise I got only two weeks ago? I don't need to punish myself like this. Just because I'm getting older and have a little arthritis doesn't mean I should quit. My experience counts for a lot. Look at

242

the number of times people have asked me for advice. Some of those green journeymen lately can't tell a nail from a screwdriver. They need people like me to teach them and to prevent costly mistakes.

Inadequate⁻ **Chair:** OK. You have some valid points and I'm out of good arguments. But this discussion isn't over. The fact I'm feeling so inadequate must mean something.

*Adequate** **Chair:** Sure, it means something. It means my lousy *Inadequate⁻* schema is fighting to defend itself. Well, it didn't win this time!

Are you getting the idea? You may struggle with this strategy at first. Remember to notice how you *feel* when you sit in each chair. With practice and repetition, your adaptive schema will likely feel stronger and more like the "real" you, as it did for Bernie. It helps to repeat this exercise many times because each time you carry it out, it will solidify your new adaptive schema.

A Fictitious Persona

We want you to get a feeling for what it would be like to act "as if" your negative maladaptive schemas no longer existed and your adaptive schemas had always resided in their place. Basically, we are asking you to dredge up the actor or actress inside of you for this exercise.

Here's how it works. List a few of your problematic negative maladaptive schemas and the traits associated with each. Then make up a character who is like you, but who maintains relatively more balanced adaptive schemas in those problematic areas. Give this fictitious person a name. Write out imagined, improved reactions to stressful situations, better ways of dealing with schema-related problems, and so forth. Include occasional lapses of judgment and a few character flaws. Endow this character with a cultural background similar to yours. Imagine what this person looks like. Think about the details—posture, appearance, clothes, personality, and so on. Then try to imagine that you are this person. Act "as if" you have this persona: the same posture, expressions, and reactions. Practice the role at home first; then play the role full-time for three weeks. You are not trying to adopt these characteristics permanently yet—this is just an experiment.

But what would my friends think? you ask. Would they think I've gone crazy? Hopefully not! If you have done this right, the role you are practicing isn't radically different from you, just a little closer to the adaptive balance. Changes from the usual won't be noticed unless they are blatant; even then, the change is likely to be perceived positively rather than negatively.

Try acting "as if." It can be interesting and fun, and you don't have to commit to anything. If the new role feels uncomfortable after three weeks, drop it. In fact, this experiment may feel difficult, uncomfortable, or odd at first. Have patience with the discomfort. It should get easier with practice. You might find it helpful to put the entire role on a flash card and read it through several times every day.

Tom was a thirty-five-year-old engineer who was plagued by a negative maladaptive schema of *Undesirable⁻*. After his divorce, Tom began to believe that any woman who saw him would respond with disinterest. He assumed that she would think he was too fat or simply unappealing. His family, friends, and even his therapist told him these things weren't true, but he didn't believe them. If he went to a party, he quickly shrank from most encounters. If a woman talked to him, he would escape at the first possible sign of disinterest on her part. And he was quite clever at concocting such signs of rejection out of thin air. If the woman turned to talk to someone else even for a moment, he ran. Or if she paused and didn't speak for a few seconds, he assumed she was looking for a way out. Can you see how Tom was doomed with this mind-set? We suggested that Tom develop a role to "try on" for a while. The role went something like this.

> *Chris is a thirty-seven-year-old divorced architect. Sometimes he questions whether women find him appealing, but he also reminds himself about the positive feedback he has gotten from women over the years. For years, Chris avoided available women in order to avoid rejection. Then, slowly but surely, he came to realize he was indeed a desirable person. Now, if a woman shows only an average amount of interest in Chris during a conversation, he knows it's probably because of a reason unrelated to his looks or personality—reasons such as different interests, another relationship, a recent breakup, a different sexual orientation, a depressed mood, or just different taste in men. At any rate, most of these things have little to do with him. This means he can go to a party with reasonable self-confidence. He can encounter a woman and engage her in an interesting conversation. In fact, he has learned that he needs to evaluate whether she is right for him. If she is not, it does not mean anything is wrong with her.*
>
> *Chris stands a little taller than Tom because his shoulders don't stoop. He makes eye contact and maintains it comfortably. He knows deep down that most women will find him interesting, possibly intriguing. Of course, some won't, but he can blow it off when it happens, knowing that it doesn't have a lot to do with him. And when rejection becomes difficult to shake off, causing him to question himself, he reviews the evidence. He knows he has "what it takes." He believes in himself and knows that his confidence will quietly emanate from within. It's something others are bound to sense. There is no need to put on an act or a show—that would only mask his inner strength.*

Tom wrote this role out and read it many times a day. He imagined "Chris" in his mind and tried to adopt his posture and inner feelings. Sometimes, Tom would forget and slip into his old *Undesirable⁻* schema. But slowly, almost imperceptibly, he changed his concept of himself. Over several weeks, he actually began to feel like Chris. In fact, Tom began to feel that this new role was what his true self had always wanted to be. This meant it was a successful experiment. And even when role-playing "Chris" didn't feel right at all to Tom, this too was a success. Why? Because he learned what didn't fit. Let's say Tom had picked a character who was cocky, always sure of himself, and felt superior to others. This role would probably feel awkward and uncomfortable, because this wasn't the type of person Tom wanted to be. Yet this role would teach him something about who he did want to be.

Interestingly, this is a technique at which you really can't fail. It's totally experimental, something to consider. When the role feels good, it teaches you something. When it doesn't, it teaches you something else. Whenever you play these roles, tune into your feelings closely. After a week or two, do you feel anxious, confident, secure, angry, or sad? Does your body generate a variety of sensations—calmness, increased energy, flutters in your stomach, tensed shoulders, whatever? All of this information can teach you what is right about this role and what isn't. Then you can modify the role and try it again.

The overall goal of acting "as if" is simply to find a role that challenges your maladaptive schemas as you move closer to the adaptive balance that feels right for you. This process may take a bit of experimentation. Each new role should be tried on for a long enough period of time to see if it fits. Any new role is going to feel odd at first. But after a few weeks, you'll know if you're heading in the right direction.

Find ways to support your efforts. Use validating self-statements such as "I'm OK as I am, but it can be fun to try new things." Pat yourself on the back for successes, and be forgiving of slips. You can also get feedback from a friend. Ask if your friend notices a difference in your behavior and, if so, in what way.

Flash Cards

For this strategy, you will need a few 4- by 6-inch index cards for recording both important information and reminders. How could carrying index cards help someone change? You may think that you hardly need reminders and that you already know all the information we will be asking you to put on these flash cards. So what's the point?

Frankly, experience has taught us that this technique helps far more than one might think. We'll show you the information you should record on each of these cards and how to record it. We'll also discuss our theory about why these cards work so surprisingly well. Finally, we'll provide you with a number of sample cards.

By the way, these cards should be fairly easy to fill out. You have already prepared most of the information for them in Chapters 8, 9, and 10. Now, you'll just need to summarize the earlier information briefly and to add a little more on the topic of self-acceptance.

Schema Flash Card Instructions

My Maladaptive Schema: Record the definition of the schema you have already developed. Remember, your definition may have started with the one we gave you, but you have probably tailored it to fit yourself better.

Feelings and Bodily Sensations: Describe any sensations you feel in your body when this schema is active.

Childhood Origins: Record one of the memories you previously noted about how the schema originated in childhood.

Current Triggers: Describe what triggers your maladaptive schemas in today's life. You should already have the information for this section, too.

My New Adaptive Schema Goal: Record the definition of the adaptive schema you would like in the future.

Steps Toward Achieving the New Schema: Describe a few of the steps you will take to build your new adaptive schema.

Self-Accepting Statements: Sometimes you will find yourself unable to take the steps you laid out for yourself. When that happens, it is important to remember the "acceptance-change" balance and to write something to help you accept your temporary setback. This is the only new information we are asking of you for this exercise.

Why would carrying around information like this help you? We can think of two reasons. First, we have found that when a maladaptive schema activates, any information stored in an adaptive schema on that same continuum becomes virtually inaccessible. It's almost as though there is no other reality. That is how schemas work. The active schema, positive or negative, will dominate the scene completely. If you think about it, you can probably remember moments when the same thing happened to you. Isn't it almost impossible to think about your good points when negative maladaptive schemas such as *Undesirable⁻*, *Unworthy⁻*, *Inadequate⁻*, and *Blameworthy⁻* are active? And when positive maladaptive schemas such as *Blameless⁺*, *Irresistible⁺*, *Perfectionistic⁺*, and *Entitled⁺* are activated, you're probably feeling unconquerable. Schema flash cards can serve to remind you that other, more adaptive realities exist when their existence doesn't seem plausible.

Schema flash cards can also help you with what psychologists call *over-generalization*, which occurs when you respond similarly to two different situations, even though they call for different responses. For example, soldiers in the Vietnam War appropriately learned to "hit the deck" at the sound of incoming shells. Loud or unexpected noises at home caused some to react identically, even though the context for the noise was completely different. "Hitting the deck" at home represented a case of overgeneralization—a learned response that has generalized past the original, useful limits.

The same holds true for schemas. Lynn, a twenty-nine-year-old information specialist, appropriately learned her *Abandonment⁻* schema from childhood. Today, her overriding concern that all men will eventually abandon her represents a case of overgeneralization. Understandable, but overgeneralized. And, as you know by now, the power of her maladaptive schema will continue to ensure that Lynn experiences further incidents of abandonment. Lynn wrote the following schema flash card as a way of learning to discriminate today's world from her past.

Intimacy Continuum: Lynn

My Maladaptive Schema: *Abandonment⁻:* I always worry that any new man will leave me. I cling to him as hard as I can and worry about everything he does, thinking it is a prelude to his departure.

Feelings and Bodily Sensations: My heart races, sometimes I get dizzy, and my throat gets a horrible lump that won't go away.

Childhood Origins: My father left me when I was young, and my mother emotionally abandoned me after he was gone.

Current Triggers: Anytime my boyfriend is gone for a little longer than I thought he would be or whenever he gets a call from a woman. Also, whenever I see another woman speaking with him or even looking at him in a certain way.

My New Adaptive Schema Goal: *Intimate*[*]: I want to learn to trust that he will stay with me unless our relationship starts getting into serious trouble. In that case, I probably will have a lot of warning at least. And I want to learn to realize that even if it does end, I can be OK either way.

Steps Toward Achieving the New Schema:
1. Work like crazy to stop questioning his every single move.
2. Rather than clinging so tightly, I will start giving him and myself a little space. I will even encourage him to go out with friends occasionally.
3. Work to develop a few interests of my own, independent of him.
4. Try to do caring things, rather than attacking him, so he can see that I really do care. He will be more motivated to stay then.

Self-Accepting Statements: Of course, I will screw up sometimes and get jealous. That is just something that will happen. Change doesn't happen overnight. I simply need to keep working at this goal; it won't happen all at once. I just want to credit myself for my successes and learn from the mistakes. What more can anyone do?

The front of the schema flash card helped Lynn discriminate between the childhood origins of her schema and the events triggering it today. She could see that her feelings and bodily sensations are almost identical to what she felt in childhood but that the triggering events are quite different. In other words, her boyfriend today is not her father, and she is not her mother. Her boyfriend is responsible, shows much caring, and does not give any signs that he is likely to leave.

The back of the flash card helped Lynn to see that a different reality is possible if she starts to take productive steps toward getting there. She had the card laminated and carries it with her at all times. At first, she read it three or four times a day; these days, she only occasionally looks at it as a reminder of how much she has changed.

Now we will provide you with one sample flash card from each schema continuum. Some of them were written by people already familiar to you; we also took a few of them from composites of various other clients. Sometimes the flash card will depict a negative maladaptive schema and sometimes a positive maladaptive schema. A few will show you how to design a flash card if you flip between both a negative maladaptive schema and a positive maladaptive schema on the same continuum.

These flash cards are only samples. You will need to design your own, because everyone's schema problems exhibit slightly different origins, contexts, triggers, sensations, and strategies for change. However, these samples will give you a good idea of how to prepare your own.

SAMPLE SCHEMA FLASH CARDS: SELF-WORTH ZONE

Acceptance Continuum

My Maladaptive Schema: *Blameless*[+]*:* Everyone says I can't take criticism of any kind, and they are right. I never admit to a mistake, and I rarely say I am sorry.

Feelings and Bodily Sensations: When someone blames me for something, I feel a knot in my stomach.

Childhood Origins: My father used to yell at me for everything and anything. I decided that the worst thing in the world would be to admit that he was right.

Current Triggers: Anytime someone criticizes me or I make a mistake of any kind.

My New Adaptive Schema Goal: *Accepting*[*]*:* I want to own up to my mistakes and start accepting my humanness. I also want to learn how to apologize without feeling like I have just admitted to murder.

Steps Toward Achieving the New Schema:
1. Find something to apologize about at least once a week.
2. Intentionally make one or two mistakes a day for a week and then tell people about them. I can start with things like parking over the line, going in the "out" door, and saying "Good morning" in the afternoon.

Self-Accepting Statements: Failing sometimes is what this is all about. I will make mistakes in attempting to accept my mistakes! That's OK and even a good thing.

Desirability Continuum: Sylvia

My Maladaptive Schema: *Undesirable⁻:* I am physically unattractive, to some people even repulsive.

Feelings and Bodily Sensations: Sad, depressed, ashamed, embarrassed, angry, my jaw tightens.

Childhood Origins: My mother's and sister's obsessions with thinness and appearance, which were their primary criteria for evaluating women; their criticisms of my weight and eating habits since childhood; the monopoly of anorectic women in magazines and movies.

Current Triggers: Being around my mother or sister; movies and television programs populated with pencil-thin women with gargantuan breast implants; any time my scale registers a pound or two increase; going out socially.

My New Adaptive Schema Goal: *Desirable*: I am comfortable with my body. I take good care of myself physically and dress neatly and attractively. I usually look as nice as most people. I have good social skills. I make others feel comfortable. I have a good sense of humor.

Steps Toward Achieving the New Schema:
1. Stop making fun of my body.
2. Accept compliments by saying thank you and not turning them into jokes.
3. Remind myself that Jack does find me attractive and enjoys sex with me. Initiate sex at least once a week.
4. Weigh myself only on Wednesdays. No matter what my weight is, I will not let myself dwell on it all day. I will remind myself that my weight does not justify making my family miserable.

Self-Accepting Statements: I know that change always involves setbacks. Berating myself over a lack of progress only keeps me stuck. Who needs to have negative thoughts about their negative thoughts?

Worthiness Continuum: Lynn

My Maladaptive Schema: *Entitled+:* I expect the best. I am superior to most other people. I am special and need to be treated that way.

Feelings and Bodily Sensations: I feel superior and smug but also tense when I am not treated as special.

Childhood Origins: Except for a brief period between my mother's marriages, I always got what I wanted. My father spent money like it was water before he went bankrupt and left us. My stepfather was wealthy, and we had an expensive lifestyle, including private schools and expensive vacations. I learned that material things are the source of happiness.

Current Triggers: When I see something I want. When someone else has something I envy. When I am around my wealthy childhood friends.

My New Adaptive Schema Goal: *Worthy*:* I am as worthy as anyone else but no more so. Everyone is special, but people are not superior to each other. Wealth does not make anyone more special or more worthwhile.

Steps Toward Achieving the New Schema:
1. I will listen to others and consciously ask them questions about themselves on a regular basis.
2. I will remind myself to stick with my new budget plan. I will use post-it notes to remind me.
3. When I feel bad, I will avoid shopping like the plague, because I do that just to make myself feel better. I will find other ways to feel better.
4. I will use my friend Pam as a role model. She feels quite worthy without feeling a need to be special or to have lots of wonderful things.

Self-Accepting Statements: Of course, I will make mistakes along the way. I do not need to berate myself for a misstep. When I do make mistakes, I want to use those times to remind myself of the importance of this goal.

Adequacy Continuum

My Maladaptive Schema: *Inadequate⁻:* I just can't do many things right, especially anything mechanical or physical. Other guys just make me feel totally incompetent.

Feelings and Bodily Sensations: I start to sweat and feel about 2-feet tall whenever I take something on that I can't do.

Childhood Origins: I was terrible in baseball as a kid. And since I gained all my height by the seventh grade, I was gangly and uncoordinated. Others often made fun of me.

Current Triggers: Whenever I try to do something physical or mechanical. Even simple things like changing the oil in my car.

My New Adaptive Schema Goal: *Adequate*:* I want to believe I am OK whether I have great mechanical skills or not. I have plenty of other positive attributes. Appreciate what I can do, not what I can't.

Steps Toward Achieving the New Schema:
1. Start hiring someone to do some of these things. After all, I have plenty of money to do that. Besides, I don't even like doing those things.
2. Start noticing that everyone has things they are good at and things they aren't. No one is good at everything.

Self-Accepting Statements: When I mess up and start to berate myself, I will ask what I would tell my best friend if he made the same backward step. I really want to learn to forgive myself, not only for my mistakes but also when I fail to make the changes I am attempting.

SAMPLE SCHEMA FLASH CARDS: EMPOWERMENT ZONE

Assertiveness Continuum: Sylvia

My Maladaptive Schema: *Acquiescent⁻:* I give in to avoid conflict. I routinely let other people have their way. I don't want anyone to be mad at me.

Feelings and Bodily Sensations: I feel nervous, fearful, tense, guilty, resentful. My breathing also gets tight.

Childhood Origins: My older sister was very demanding and entitled and a source of much distress to my parents. I worked very hard at being agreeable so no one would be upset with me. Both my mom and sister are domineering, so it was easier to go along with them.

Current Triggers: Being around domineering, forceful people. Being around my mom and sister. Meetings that request volunteers.

My New Adaptive Schema Goal: *Assertive*⃰*:* I have a right to stand up for myself and express my opinions and preferences. My thoughts and wants are as important as anyone else's.

Steps Toward Achieving the New Schema:
1. I will listen to my feelings if I don't want to do something for someone. I will simply say I can't do it.
2. I will read the book *Your Perfect Right* by Alberti and Emmons.
3. I will consult my planner and not take on more than two volunteer events in a week. Later, I may cut it down even more.
4. I will use my friend Paula as a role model and ask her how she manages to be so effectively assertive. Maybe we can even role-play some situations with each other.

Self-Accepting Statements: Sometimes I am bound to give in and acquiesce. I will simply try to review what I could do the next time instead of pound on myself like my sister used to do to me.

253

Capability Continuum: Lynn

My Maladaptive Schema: *Dependent⁻:* I need to depend on other people to take care of me. I can't handle things on my own. I need a man to take care of me.

Feelings and Bodily Sensations: I feel frightened, ashamed, embarrassed, and desperate. I feel small, like a child. My stomach ties up in knots.

Childhood Origins: My mother's helplessness and my stepfather's overprotectiveness.

Current Triggers: Whenever anything goes wrong in life or there is a new problem to be solved, I fall apart.

My New Adaptive Schema Goal: *Capable*:* Life is not beyond my ability to handle. I am able to take care of most situations. If I need help, I ask for it without acting desperate or helpless. However, I do not inconvenience others with my requests for help. When I do seek assistance, I also try to learn how to handle that situation in the future, so I do not have to ask for help on that again.

Steps Toward Achieving the New Schema:
1. When things go wrong, I will take deep, slow breaths until I calm down. Then I can go back to it.
2. I will get rid of that little girl voice when I ask for help.
3. I will resist asking my boyfriend for help whenever possible. I can find a way to get things solved one way or another.
4. I will use my friend Abby as a role model. And I will ask how she has learned to be so self-sufficient.

Self-Accepting Statements: I have a habit that has thirty-two years of development. I just need to focus on each successful experience.

Empowerment Continuum

Note that this next flash card depicts a problem with flipping between two opposite maladaptive schemas (*Powerless⁻* and *Omnipotent⁺*).

My Maladaptive Schemas: *Powerless⁻/Omnipotent⁺:* I usually feel like I can do absolutely anything. I think I should and can control any outcome. When I can't sometimes, I feel the opposite way and become overwhelmed. I feel trapped and helpless at those times. I quit trying. What's wrong with me?

Feelings and Bodily Sensations: Sometimes powerful and puffed up, and at other times weak and helpless.

Childhood Origins: My father always said I could control my own destiny in any way that I wanted. He said that we Stuarts control the world. When that didn't happen, I felt ashamed and helpless, and father told me I was nothing.

Current Triggers: Whenever there is a challenge or problem, I approach it with blind enthusiasm. When my wife complains about our marriage, I just assume I can turn it around. I don't even consider bad outcomes to be possible with my abilities. Then when something doesn't work out, my *Powerless⁻* schema gets triggered.

My New Adaptive Schema Goal: *Empowered*:* I know I can make a difference and affect the outcomes of many things. At the same time, I have limits just like anyone else. I especially can't control other people, and some outcomes lie outside my ability to do anything.

Steps Toward Achieving the New Schema:
1. When there is something to be solved, I need to start appraising it more realistically. I need to think how successful (or not) anyone might be in getting the outcomes they want.
2. Start listening to my wife when she tells me I might be in over my head.
3. Appreciate that when I don't get the outcome I want, it doesn't mean I am totally powerless. At those times, I need to remember that everyone has limits.

Self-Accepting Statements: My father taught me this lesson really well. It will take me time to unlearn it and develop a new habit. When I stumble, self-abuse will not help.

Resilience Continuum: Steven

My Maladaptive Schema: *Vulnerable⁻:* I always expect the worst. I worry endlessly about money, health, accidents, and criminal acts against myself and my family. I see the world as a dangerous place.

Feelings and Bodily Sensations: I feel agitated, tense, fearful, guilty. My shoulders tighten up. I feel weak and small.

Childhood Origins: There was never any money growing up. My father's death from cirrhosis was horrible, and depending on Medicaid for his treatment was humiliating to me.

Current Triggers: When someone in my family gets sick, I panic, even though I should know better. When my practice slows a little, I go berserk. If a patient gets unhappy with me, I am convinced I will get sued.

My New Adaptive Schema Goal: *Resilient*[*]: I know bad things can happen to people, but I believe that I am capable of rebounding from those experiences. If I take reasonable precautions, I can enjoy life like other people I see. I save some money for the future and for emergencies, but I am entitled to enjoy some of the money I earn now.

Steps Toward Achieving the New Schema:
1. Make my savings plan more realistic, in consultation with Ann. I need to trust that she isn't out to ruin our finances any more than I am.
2. I vow to decrease my work hours and take more time off.
3. I will quit being so overprotective with the kids.
4. I will think about others who have survived calamity to remind myself that I can, too.

Self-Accepting Statements: I had good reasons for developing this schema. It scares me to death to change it. I don't have to do it overnight. One step at a time is fine.

SAMPLE SCHEMA FLASH CARDS: RELATIONSHIP ZONE

Centeredness Continuum: Sylvia

My Maladaptive Schema: *Other-Centered⁻:* I need to make sure every-one is happy. If someone is upset, I need to fix that. It is my responsibility to take care of everyone around me. My needs are not as important as those of other people.

Feelings and Bodily Sensations: I feel needed and important. I also feel exhausted, and my back aches. Sometimes I feel frustrated and resentful.

Childhood Origins: One of the main ways I got praise was for helping mom. My mom waited on my dad hand and foot. My religion and culture also encouraged women to be all-giving and self-sacrificing.

Current Triggers: When someone has a problem or needs help. When anyone indicates they need my assistance. When anyone is upset. When the kids or Jack act as if they can't or don't want to do something.

My New Adaptive Schema Goal: *Centered*:* I will take responsibility for meeting my own needs. I can help others sometimes without treating them like they are incapable. I will give help when and if I enjoy doing it, not all the time.

Steps Toward Achieving the New Schema:
1. I will remind myself that if someone brings me a problem, I don't have to solve it unless it's really my problem.
2. I will stop doing things for Jack and the kids that they can do for themselves.
3. I will do at least one pleasurable thing for myself every day.
4. I will persist in meeting my needs when Jack and the kids resist my changes. I trained them, after all.
5. I will use my neighbor Linda as a role model and as a support person.

Self-Accepting Statements: This will be very hard for me. I need to pat myself on the back for my successes and not worry about the setbacks. No one changes overnight.

257

Intimacy Continuum: Lynn

My Maladaptive Schema: *Abandonment⁻:* I am afraid people will leave me. I am afraid I will be left alone. I need to have constant feedback that I won't be left or discarded. I do things for others so they will depend on me and not leave me.

Feelings and Bodily Sensations: I feel tense, nervous, panicky, and desperate. My stomach aches, and I get headaches.

Childhood Origins: My dad left my mom and me when I was five. I was very close to him and had no idea why he left. All my mother did was focus on herself, leaving me completely lost and confused. My mother always said a woman has to have a man, yet she says men can't be trusted.

Current Triggers: Even the slightest indication of indifference from a boyfriend. If a friend doesn't call for a while. If a boyfriend is nice to another female, even if he isn't really flirting with her.

My New Adaptive Schema Goal: *Intimate**: I am comfortable sharing my personal thoughts and feelings with others. I can believe that a variety of others can be available to me when I need them, but everyone doesn't always have to be available. I can be OK as a single woman, and I would love to find a man to be close to and to trust. If it doesn't work out, I will be OK.

Steps Toward Achieving the New Schema:
1. I will look for men in different places, not at the bars anymore.
2. I will quit trying to dress so sexily and will learn to base a relationship on other qualities.
3. I will take more initiative in calling my friends.
4. I will work on enjoying some time alone and develop things to do at those times.
5. I will try to show more interest in other people's lives and not just focus on whether they are showing enough interest in me.

Self-Accepting Statements: I didn't get this schema yesterday. I was blown away as a child. This will take time. I will be terrified sometimes and give in to my old habits. When I do, I will just work on getting back on my plan.

Self-Definition Continuum

Note that this next flash card depicts a problem with flipping between two opposite mal-adaptive schemas (being *Undefined⁻* and being *Aggrandizing⁺*).

My Maladaptive Schemas: *Undefined⁻:* I often don't know who I am or what my purpose is in life. Sometimes I don't even know what my own values are. Being *Aggrandizing⁺:* I seek out people to be with who have less of a sense of who they are than I do. And I try to find people who will look up to me. I strive to be completely adored by the women I date. I pretend to have a very strong sense of identity.

Feelings and Bodily Sensations: When my *Undefined⁻* schema activates, I feel empty, hollow, and phony. When my *Aggrandizing⁺* schema activates, I feel special and warm, yet oddly insecure.

Childhood Origins: My father was always away on business trips. I often got passed around from one relative to another because my mother was overly busy, too. I never really had a strong role model.

Current Triggers: Whenever I ask someone out, I try to get her to look up to me. When other people talk about their values and priorities, I want to leave because it feels uncomfortable.

My New Adaptive Schema Goal: *Defined⁺:* I have a strong sense of who I am, my values, and what I want out of life. Others do not have to agree, and they certainly do not need to adore me.

Steps Toward Achieving the New Schema:
1. I will start listening to my own feelings about issues and try to decide what I believe, as though no one else in the world existed.
2. I will write out a story of how I would like my life to look in ten years.
3. I will look for women who don't need someone to adore.
4. I will look for various role models, but only adopt the things from each that truly feel right to me.
5. I will enroll in a philosophy class and read books about the meaning of life.

Self-Accepting Statements: I realize now where my problems with identity came from. No wonder I struggle with this. It will take time to create a full sense of myself. I think I skipped that stage of adolescence. Change in this area would have no meaning if it came too quickly. That would be phony.

259

Trust Continuum: Steven

My Maladaptive Schema: *Distrusting⁻:* Few people are truly trustworthy. People are out for themselves. People are only nice to you if you have money or power.

Feelings and Bodily Sensations: I feel wary, tense, vulnerable, suspicious, and fearful. Sometimes my jaws tighten and I grind my teeth at night.

Childhood Origins: I could never trust my dad to keep his word about anything. He always said he would stop drinking and that he would get caught up on the rent, but he never did.

Current Triggers: When people act like they like me, I figure they want something. When someone close to me doesn't give me the complete truth about something, I think there is an ulterior motive. Whenever anyone promises me anything, I don't trust it.

My New Adaptive Schema Goal: *Trusting*:* Most people can be trusted. Most people don't go out of their way to put me down. Most people are honest. Of course, I can maintain reasonable caution in dealing with people, but I don't always have to assume the worst in advance.

Steps Toward Achieving the New Schema:
1. I will disclose a little personal information with the staff and trust that they will not take advantage of it.
2. I will stop interrogating the kids.
3. If I feel that someone has said something hurtful, I will consider whether I feel this way because I have made an unwarranted assumption, rather than because they have actually said something hurtful. If it was truly hurtful, I will simply try to understand it.
4. I will make a note of times when people are more trustworthy than I expected them to be.

Self-Accepting Statements: Another issue I am working on is perfectionism. Setbacks are just another good opportunity to practice imperfection.

EMPATHY DEVELOPMENT

You can use any of the strategies in this book for attacking positive maladaptive schemas. Throughout, we present more information and examples for dealing with negative maladaptive schemas than positive maladaptive schemas, because those with greater numbers of negative maladaptive schemas generally want to change more and tend to buy more self-help books! They feel miserable more often, which creates motivation to change. However, those with positive maladaptive schemas also find themselves vulnerable to negative feelings when life goes badly. And life often does go worse than they expect it will.

People with the positive maladaptive schemas of *Blameless*[+], *Avoidant*[+], *Entitled*[+], *Self-Centered*[+], and *Omnipotent*[+] sometimes find themselves disliked. At times, without even knowing it, they run over others and show little concern for people's well-being. Is it any wonder people with such maladaptive schemas are often criticized? When attacked, they may become overly defensive and even more critical. People mired in a preponderance of positive maladaptive schemas rarely think about changing until their illusory, puffed-up images of themselves begin to crumble in the face of repeated confrontation or loss, such as a spouse's threat to leave or the loss of a job. When these events finally get their attention, they usually realize that they have to change something about themselves.

A major part of the problem with people with overwhelming positive maladaptive schemas is that they lack empathy for others. Review the list of positive maladaptive schemas and you'll see what we mean. Most of these schemas would be very hard to sustain if one felt reasonable empathy for others. Almost every one of the positive maladaptive schemas can lead one either to bully other people or, at the very least, to annoy and irritate them.

If you have only a few positive maladaptive schemas, or the ones you have don't seem especially powerful, these exercises may not apply to you. On the other hand, if you possess a lot of powerful positive maladaptive schemas, developing empathy may help. Try the following steps.

Decentering

This technique asks you to move away from focusing, or centering, on yourself and to put yourself in other people's shoes. Before asking for something, getting angry, or making a critical remark, ask yourself how the other person might feel about what you are going to say. It might help to ask how you would feel if someone made that statement to you. Other people would likely feel the same as you would, but maybe not if they possess different schemas. Consider which schemas another person seems to have in order to help you anticipate their reactions to what you plan to say. For example, if your wife has an *Undesirable⁻* schema, what effect do you think it will have if you say that you don't like her new dress without at least softening your comments? We hope the answer doesn't require too much thought. To carry this step out successfully, you will literally need to imagine looking through other people's eyes. Try to see and feel the world through their schemas. Sometimes, that can be quite a revelation. Keep track of how often you do this and what you discover. Plan to put yourself in someone else's shoes at least two to three times every day. The following table shows what Lynn discovered using this strategy one day.

What I Plan to Say to My Boyfriend	Likely Way He Will Think and Feel
1. Why don't you make as much money as the other people with your job description?	1. He might feel *Inadequate⁻*, since that is one of his schemas. He might also think that I am being *Entitled⁺* again, which would be true.
2. You haven't paid any attention to me all day.	2. He would think it isn't true (and it isn't). He would think I am being demanding and clingy again, which is true. He might get angry. He would feel like backing away from me, the opposite of what I want.
3. Why are you always late getting home from work? It's only a fifteen-minute drive, and it's almost been an hour! Are you cheating on me?	3. Because of my *Abandonment⁻* schema he would think I sound jealous and like I don't trust him. Besides, he said it hurts his feelings and frustrates him when I confront him like that.

She knew from this data that she didn't want to say those things. At the same time, she didn't think that she could keep quiet about all of her concerns. So she filled out empathic possibilities like those below.

What I Planned to Say to My Boyfriend	Empathic Possibilities (Alternative Things I Could Say)
1. Why don't you make as much money as the other people with your job description?	1. I think I can stuff this one and not say anything at all. For one thing, as I think about it, he makes almost the same money as his co-workers, he works very hard, and he hasn't been there as long as others. Just because I would like him to make more doesn't mean he (or we) are entitled to it.

What I Planned to Say to My Boyfriend	Empathic Possibilities (Alternative Things I Could Say)
2. You haven't paid any attention to me all day.	2. Say, I'm feeling a little lonely and deprived for some reason today. Any chance you might consider giving me a little time and attention? (Note: If you think this might work better, you are right!)
3. Why are you always late getting home from work? It's only a fifteen-minute drive, and it's almost been an hour! Are you cheating on me?	3. So, have they been working you overtime again or were you just running some errands? (Note: See the assumption of goodwill here? And she will still find out what he has been doing.)

Try this decentering exercise if you keep getting into conflict with your spouse or other important people in your life. Think about what you want to say, especially if you are feeling annoyed or upset. Rarely will you say something productive when you act on first impulse, so write out some empathic alternatives before that first impulse escapes from your mouth. Then see if the new empathic approach doesn't work better.

Looking for Subtle Facial Expressions

Don't wait for other people to clobber you over the head about what you have done or said. Check it out. Often your first clue is their subtle facial expression of disgust, irritation, hurt, and so on. You may not know how to read these expressions yet. So if you see any change in expression, simply ask the person how they are feeling about what you did or said. You might be in for a surprise. And you will learn how to read expressions better with practice. Once again, write down the results and think about them.

For example, Derrick often found himself on the receiving end of an angry outburst from Belinda. He had no idea what set her off. With some trepidation, he tried this exercise. He started to look for subtle cues. So he asked Belinda immediately what she was thinking and feeling when he saw even the smallest sign that her face was clouding over. Often he discovered that she had completely misunderstood what he was trying to say. By catching her emotions early, he was able to clarify his points before things turned sour. Belinda expressed both surprise and delight in his new interest in her feelings.

Searching for Truth in Other's Views

Remember: There is almost always some truth or validity to another person's view. Look for it. If someone is critical of you, try to ask yourself what part might be true, and acknowledge it before you respond with your own view. Acknowledging your own vulnerabilities, flaws, and weaknesses can have an amazing impact on others. And finding validity in the other person's view can defuse a situation. Remember that your own positive maladaptive schemas can lead you to believe that you are correct more than you are and that others are wrong more than they are. Ask yourself whether the other view is true now, sometimes, or in some way. You can also consider whether the view might at least make sense from another perspective. Track the results of this experiment and use three columns as in the following examples.

Henry

Henry was a forty-nine-year-old dentist with the positive maladaptive schemas of *Blameless*[+], *Omnipotent*[+], *Entitled*[+], *Avoidant*[+], *Self-Centered*[+], and *Aggrandizing*[+]. Six months after his wife left, he sought therapy for depression. He couldn't believe how much his life had collapsed and shattered. He was currently dating Cindy, and she was starting to get annoyed with him. He realized that something might actually have to change in his own behavior. Here's what Henry recorded:

What Cindy Said	What I Wanted to Say on First Impulse	What I Said to Find Some Truth in Her View
1. Sometimes you are so full of yourself that I could scream.	1. If that's how you feel, get lost.	1. I hate to admit it, but sometimes I am. What are you referring to right now?
2. Do you always have to think you are right? You're not, you know, not now (referring to a disagreement over what type of paint would be most durable).	2. Yes, I am. And you get way too angry over nothing, I hate that!	2. I guess I do act like I have to be right a lot of the time. That must be incredibly annoying. I am sorry. I guess I do think that this paint will work best, but because neither of us knows a lot about paint, why don't we just call an expert and find out?

Henry struggled with this exercise, but Cindy hung in with him because she could tell he was trying. They sought couple's counseling, which helped even more. In therapy, they tried one more technique that helped a lot. They role-played each other. Henry had to pretend to be Cindy and Cindy imagined that she was Henry. This experience was eye-opening for both of them, but more so for Henry. Henry claimed that this was an easy exercise to understand in his head but that it was a whole different matter when he had to force himself to do it. Ultimately, he found the exercise worthwhile.

Now let's take a look at what Melissa, a reluctant psychotherapy client, did with this exercise.

Melissa

Melissa was a thirty-two-year-old loan officer with the positive maladaptive schemas of being *Irresistible*[+], *Blameless*[+], *Entitled*[+], *Self-Centered*[+], *Domineering*[+], and *Stubbornly Independent*[+]. She came to therapy at the suggestion of her supervisor, who had concerns about her relationships with her co-workers. Prior to the supervisor's suggestion, Melissa had always thought psychotherapy was for weak people. She never thought the difficulties with her colleagues were her fault. As you might imagine, she initially resisted practicing empathic comments, but over time she learned to do it with excellent results. She couldn't believe how much nicer her co-workers became toward her.

What a Co-Worker Said to Me	What I Wanted to Say on First Impulse	What I Said to Find Some Truth in Their Comments
1. Can't you ask for help when you don't understand something? You set us two weeks behind on this new computer program by entering the data wrong. What's wrong with you?	1. It isn't my fault that no one explained this thing to me well enough. I did the best I could. You guys just expect way too much. And you don't teach this stuff right, either.	1. Well, I do struggle with asking for help sometimes. I always think I should be able to do it myself, and that isn't realistic. It might help me if you give me a little of Randy's time, because I understand him better than Gene, who was training me before.
2. Your earrings don't go well with that outfit.	2. So who do you think you are to criticize what I am wearing? You could make the worst-dressed list of the year.	2. Maybe they don't.

What a Co-Worker Said to Me	What I Wanted to Say on First Impulse	What I Said to Find Some Truth in Their Comments
3. I am moving into that corner office next week.	3. Who in hell gave you permission to do that? I want that office and I deserve it.	3. I can see why you want that office; it is nice. Actually, I have been interested in it, too, and I have been here a year longer than you. Isn't seniority how we usually deal with these things?

CONCLUSION

We hope you are making progress with your maladaptive schemas at this point. If you aren't, don't worry. The next chapter will have more strategies for weakening them. We believe you must keep chipping away at them. No single tool or approach will do. It takes a full armament of ideas and techniques to defeat something that has lived with you as long as most schemas have. Just remember, you can make changes if you keep at it. Persistence is the key. So is the tolerance to achieve part of your goals without insisting on the entire pie.

EXERCISES FOR
SCHEMA-CHANGE STRATEGIES

1. We have described over a dozen different flash cards for various schemas. Below we have created a flash card for you to complete. Refer back to the flash card examples for help in completing your own here. You might want to copy these pages so that you can carry your flash card(s) with you.

Flash Card

My Maladaptive Schema: _____

_____

_____

Feelings and Bodily Sensations: _____

_____

_____

Childhood Origins: _____

_____

_____

Current Triggers: _____

_____

_____

My New Adaptive Schema Goal: _____

_____

_____

Steps Toward Achieving the New Schema:

_____

_____

_____

_____

Self-Accepting Statements: _____

_____

_____

2. This exercise is to help you develop empathy if you have one or more strong positive maladaptive schemas. The procedures were described in the text with examples, so we have given you some empty tables to complete as we demonstrated earlier.

a. Decentering

What I Planned to Say to _____	Likely Way That Person Would Think and Feel
1. _____	1. _____
_____	_____
2. _____	2. _____
_____	_____
3. _____	3. _____
_____	_____

b. Searching for truth in others' views

What _____ Said	What I Wanted to Say on First Impulse	What I Said to Find Some Truth in _____'s View
1._____	1._____	1._____
_____	_____	_____
2._____	2._____	2._____
_____	_____	_____
3._____	3._____	3._____
_____	_____	_____

12

Scrutinizing Thoughts and Schemas

Wisdom lies neither in fixity nor in change,
but in the dialectic between the two.
—Octavio Paz, Times

We will now present additional strategies for challenging your maladaptive schemas. Most of these are based on time-honored cognitive therapy techniques, which have repeatedly proven effective for producing change. Our use of these techniques differs, however, in that we will not focus simply on thoughts, as is often done in cognitive therapy, but also on maladaptive schemas. First, let us explain the relationship between thoughts and schemas and how you can challenge both of them at once.

THE RELATIONSHIP BETWEEN THOUGHTS AND SCHEMAS

Generally, your thoughts do not occur just out of the blue; they are based on a foundation of schemas that have accumulated over a lifetime. Schemas underlie thoughts. Think of schemas as the base of a fountain, and thoughts as myriad streams of water coming up from the base. For example, let's assume that you become intensely anxious when you have to give a speech. You may *think* to yourself that the audience will likely give you a hard time because you are not an accomplished lecturer. You *think* that disaster awaits you as you timorously walk toward the podium to deliver your talk. You may *think* that entering a lion's lair sounds more appealing than what you are about to do. These various thoughts are not without basis; they stem directly from the schemas triggered by your fear of giving a speech. In this case, the *Inadequate⁻* schema from the Self-Worth Zone is responsible for all of your nervous thoughts and feelings. It is your *Inadequate⁻* schema that says you are not up to the challenge and will encounter a cold reception.

TECHNIQUES FOR CHALLENGING
YOUR THOUGHTS AND SCHEMAS

In Chapter 7, we explained that, as you collect information about your schemas, you will learn what events trigger them. Recognizing the triggers isn't enough, though; you will need to subject both your thoughts and schemas to careful scrutiny. Believe it or not, many of your thoughts and schemas cannot be supported by actual evidence. Yet people often believe that something is true simply because it *feels* that way. Dr. David Burns calls this assumption *emotional reasoning*. We all make this common error at times. Thoughts and schemas often seem valid because they concur with the way you have thought your entire life. However, we will show you that a basis often cannot be found to support them. That is why you need to check the evidence.

Checking the Evidence

Start by recording the triggers that precede your most problematic thoughts and schemas. Write down the evidence that either supports or contradicts your maladaptive schemas and related thoughts. You may have spent many years firmly convinced of the unassailability of your schemas and their premises. You may have to look hard for contradictory evidence, not because it can't be found but because your schema-maintenance strategies can block you from seeing the truth.

Charlene, a thirty-six-year-old executive secretary, had two negative maladaptive schemas in the Self-Worth Zone. She fervently believed she was both undesirable and unworthy. When she was a child, her parents paid little attention to her because of their own constant conflicts. Furthermore, her older brother suffered from severe learning disabilities, and caring for him consumed what remained of her parents' time and energy. When Charlene wanted something, her wishes were paid scant heed. Predictably, she learned to believe she was unworthy of their attention and that her needs would fall second to those of her brother. She also believed she was undesirable as compared with her younger sister, Susan. Relatives showered Susan with praise for being adorable and cute but rarely said a complimentary word to Charlene. As a result, Charlene became increasingly withdrawn.

As an adult, Charlene wrestled with her *Unworthy⁻* schema. She occasionally felt she deserved to have her needs met as much as the next person, yet she rarely was able to act on that belief. She described a typical trigger and its resulting schema and thoughts. Then she wrote down any and all experiences that might either support or contradict her schema and her schema-related thoughts. Here are her results:

Trigger	Schema	Thoughts
Tried to flirt with some- one who turned to talk to someone else at a party.	*Undesirable⁻*	I can't even buy a date. I must turn men off before I open my mouth. I don't think I will ever find someone.

Supporting Evidence for Charlene's Schema and Related Thoughts

1. I haven't gone out with anyone in the past few months.

2. My friend Martin told me I don't know the first thing about flirting.

3. My mother always said I was an "ugly duckling."

4. My sister Susan attracts men like flies—now that's desirable.

5. Men like me just as a friend, not as a date.

It was rather easy for Charlene to find supporting evidence for her schemas. Finding evidence to contradict her schemas and the thoughts that stemmed from them was much harder. However, when encouraged by her therapist, she surprised herself by finding evidence to refute her *Undesirable⁻* schema and its associated thoughts.

Contradictory Evidence for Charlene's Schema and Related Thoughts

1. Actually, over the years, I have dated quite a few men. When I think about it, I often didn't find them desirable enough for me in one way or another.

2. Being flirtatious isn't my strong point, as Martin was trying to tell me. But that doesn't mean I am inherently undesirable. I'm not sure I want to be a "flirt" anyway.

3. Yes, Susan attracts more men, and she may actually be more physically attractive than I am. But I don't need the attention of every man I meet. Susan practically throws herself at men. That isn't me, and I don't want it to be.

4. Frankly, my mother was cruel. She said mean things to my younger sister, and I know those things weren't any truer than what she said about me.

5. Men do like me as a friend. And some men must also like me as a date or they wouldn't keep going out with me.

6. I have gone through a bit of a dry spell with dating, but I think it's partly because I have been so down on myself that I have withdrawn from men.

7. I was married for ten years to a man who adored me. I was the one who ended it. I divorced him because he was really irresponsible, but at least he found me very desirable.

8. I have friends who get fewer dates than I do.

9. Men always say I have a great sense of humor and personality once they get to know me. And I really do. Much as a "great personality" gets ridiculed, it does count as part of the overall picture.

Charlene was nonplused when she finished her list, because the evidence clearly indicated that she was *not* the least attractive woman in the world. In fact, she realized that she was a reasonably desirable woman overall. She didn't have to keep buying into her mother's old messages. She realized that increasing her self-confidence would also have a direct impact on her desirability to others. She learned that desirability doesn't simply consist of an inherited set of physical characteristics immutably chiseled in flesh. Far more is involved, including humor, friendliness, personal style, clothing, and a range of other subtleties. On balance, checking the evidence helped Charlene see what she had going for her. Later in this chapter, we'll show you what Charlene did with her *Unworthy*⁻ schema.

Notice the difference between "checking the evidence" and just "thinking positively." Just making all your negative thoughts positive doesn't cut it; rather, you must carefully scrutinize your negative maladaptive schemas and thoughts for their validity or lack thereof. Charlene realized that she had been tense when meeting strangers because of her *Undesirable*⁻ schema, and she wanted to change that habit. By simply telling herself "I am an attractive person," she would be ignoring possibly valuable evidence that she could use to make changes in her schema. For example, the evidence from a friend that she is not good at flirting might or might not be something she would want to change but could be useful for her to know. Don't be afraid of checking the evidence, because it almost always helps find a balance of both supportive and contradictory examples. After a review, you might want to change some negative aspects. Maybe not. *Nobody's perfect*, and that is not your goal anyway. Remember?

Let's look at what Steven, our physician, did when his *Perfectionistic*⁺ schema slid into an *Inadequate*⁻ schema under duress.

Trigger	Schema	Thoughts
My son Kevin goofed off in his last semester in high school and got two B's and three C's. He had been getting almost straight A's before.	*Perfectionistic*[+] & *Inadequate*[−]	My son is a failure. If he gets bad grades in high school, his plans for graduate school are doomed. What will my colleagues think? I will look like a failure in their eyes. And Kevin will be as poor as I was growing up. I will have failed as a parent.

Supporting Evidence for Steven's Schema and Related Thoughts

1. Kevin hasn't picked up a book once in the last two months. If he does that in college, he really will flunk out.

2. Frank, my colleague, loves to shove it in my face when his kid does better than mine at anything. I can just see now what he will say.

3. College dropouts don't make nearly as much money as graduates do.

Contradictory Evidence for Steven's Schema and Related Thoughts

1. Kevin already told me he goofed off intentionally. He said that since he'd already gotten into the college of his choice, he wanted to have a little fun for a change. He also said that fun is something we don't have much of in our household. Just because he wanted to have a little fun for once in his life doesn't mean he won't get back to work. He's always come through before.

2. My other colleagues have had far worse trouble with their kids than Kevin's one lousy semester. I have no idea what they will say to me, but what difference does it make anyway?

3. I have no real reason to believe Kevin won't finish college. If he does drop out, there's a good chance he'll go back later. If not, I'll have to work on accepting it, because getting an education is no guarantee for long-term happiness and success. In fact, I can think of a number of my patients who never graduated from college and who are much happier than I am.

4. Kevin is a great person. He has a wonderful sense of humor, he is well liked, and he has a kind heart. Even if he doesn't make a lot of money, I still can say I succeeded at being a parent in many of the ways that count.

Steven came to realize that his son wasn't likely to drop out of college and that his own *Inadequate⁻* schema was creating a large number of inaccurate, unsupported thoughts that collapsed under the weight of contradictory evidence. You might note that Steven's exercise was actually aimed at his *Inadequate⁻* schema more than his *Perfectionistic⁺* schema. Although Steven was habitually controlled by his *Perfectionistic⁺* schema, his inability to deal with his son's grades triggered his *Inadequate⁻* schema. And, as you can see, Steven's fear of inadequacy actually provided the impetus for his *Perfectionistic⁺* schema; his *Perfectionism⁺* literally existed to help him avoid the horrible thoughts and feelings produced by his underlying *Inadequate⁻* schema.

Sylvia struggled more than Charlene and Steven when she tried the checking the evidence. Sylvia recognized some interesting thoughts and feelings that contradicted her *Undesirable⁻* schema, yet the evidence failed to affect her schema. She absolutely couldn't get herself to believe the information, no matter how logical it seemed. And when she did try to incorporate new information about her desirability into her schema, it lasted only a short while.

For example, when she made a note of her husband's compliments, she quickly discounted them, thinking, "He's my husband, he has to say those things." Even recording the frequency with which people expressed shock when they heard she was thirty-five years old failed to make a difference to Sylvia. In Sylvia's case, it took additional techniques and some therapy to help her. Remember, every schema within each person requires a different amount of effort and sometimes a different technique to effect change. Yet we usually find that if you try enough keys, you will find the one that unlocks the door to change.

Now we want to illustrate how checking the evidence can be applied to positive maladaptive schemas. Dale came to us for help when his wife threatened to leave him. We won't review all of Dale's copious positive maladaptive schemas here. Instead, we will show you how he checked the evidence for his *Blameless⁺* schema from the Self-Worth Zone:

Trigger	Schema	Thoughts
My wife said I rarely listen to her.	*Blameless⁺*	That's total nonsense! I listen to her. She just wants to leave me. Fine! Let her!

Supporting Evidence for Dale's Schema and Related Thoughts

1. I know I hear most of what she has to say.

2. No one should have to listen to others all of the time.

3. Lots of my friends say their wives complain about the same thing.

Contradictory Evidence for Dale's Schema and Related Thoughts

1. According to my psychologist, I must not have been listening if she got to the point of wanting a divorce when I had no clue she was unhappy.

2. As I think about it, I do *pretend* to listen a lot of the time.

3. My complaining friends also have unhappy wives. Maybe we are all doing something wrong. Even if we listen to each other, perhaps we don't do as good a job with our wives.

4. My psychologist said I sometimes don't listen very well to him, either. Maybe I am missing something here.

Dale took a long time to collect this contradictory evidence. He rankled to think he might actually be screwing up his marriage. Every fiber of his being rebelled at the idea that he was in the wrong. Yet he had to conclude that he had indeed bungled critical aspects of his marriage, including listening to his own wife. It took longer, though, for Dale to appreciate why that was so important. As we have said, people who have one or more positive maladaptive schemas are not easily convinced that they truly have a problem.

Narrowing the Focus

Maladaptive schemas and the thoughts they generate usually suffer from a problem we call *overgeneralization*. Though they may contain a grain of truth, maladaptive schemas manage to make you believe that they apply to everything in your entire life. For example, although Sylvia had heard bad things from her family about her appearance as a child, she was overgeneralizing when she believed everyone else thought the same way. By recognizing when she was overgeneralizing, Sylvia learned to *narrow the focus*, which means limiting the range of the statements, not exaggerating, and being more specific.

We have an exercise for narrowing the focus to help you overgeneralize less. With this exercise, we recommend that you record a trigger for any maladaptive schema and its associated thoughts. Then look specifically at the thoughts; study whether or not they might be overgeneralized. If so, you will need to narrow the focus. Decide when the schema and its associated thoughts might truly be valid and when they clearly are not. Let's take a look at what Peter did with this exercise for his *Abandonment⁻* schema. Peter was a successful dentist, but he struggled with relationships.

Trigger	Schema	Thoughts	Exceptions
Kristen said she found another man.	*Abandonment⁻*	Women always eventually leave the men they are with. They get bored or fed up, and then they split.	Jessica and Liza have been with their partners for years. Aunt Phyllis and Uncle Ray have been married for thirty-five years.

After Peter examined his thoughts carefully, he could identify several exceptions, so he realized that he had been overgeneralizing. He had to admit that women didn't always leave their husbands and boyfriends; in fact, he knew several friends whose partners had been fiercely loyal. He also knew that a few of his own partners had been loyal to him and that he had been the one to move on. He forced himself to revise and narrow the focus of his schema and related thoughts.

> Narrowed, focused thoughts: *Some women leave the man they are with. When they do, there is usually a good reason. It doesn't happen randomly. Nor is it always due to simple boredom, though that could sometimes play a role. My task is to find the right match for me; when I do, that woman will be no more likely to leave than the women in the best relationships I know. Kristen truly wasn't the right one for me, so it doesn't make much sense for me to conclude that all women will leave me just because a wrong one did.*

We recommend that you try to narrow the focus of your schemas and related thoughts. You may be surprised at how often overgeneralization permeates your thinking. Narrowing the focus can reduce the negative impact of your schemas on your psyche, because it creates a more realistic view of the situation.

Using the Friend Perspective

Our next two techniques involve backing away from your issues, schemas, and problems in order to gain some objectivity. So often, maladaptive schemas loom so large that they completely block your ability to see any other reality. The first strategy is called the friend perspective. It involves asking yourself what you might tell a good friend about how to deal with a troubling issue rooted in a maladaptive schema.

Charlene, the executive secretary from earlier in this chapter, had an *Unworthy⁻* schema in addition to her *Undesirable⁻* schema. She used the friend perspective to tackle her *Unworthy⁻* schema. Remember that when she was a child, her family rarely took time away from her older brother's problems to focus on anything she might need. She carried this legacy into adulthood through her *Unworthy⁻* schema. This schema managed to convince her that her needs didn't count, she didn't really matter, and she didn't deserve the time of day from the world. When she was treated poorly, Charlene accepted it as a given, squelching any words of discontentment well before they could reach her mouth. It almost seemed that Charlene believed that a mass murderer deserved more from life than she did! And she maintained this belief even though she gave much to other people and to her community. She devoted time to the Red Cross, gave her local community theater both money and time, offered to bail her friends out of any kind of jam, and on and on.

Her therapist presented her with a basic task: the friend perspective. The therapist said, "Charlene, I want you to imagine that a friend named Michelle is sitting over there. Michelle is much like you. She helps out *her* friends at the drop of a hat. She contributes to causes whenever she can. Like you, she lets people walk all over her. She claims that *her* needs are just not that important. Besides, she doesn't feel as worthy as other people. What would you tell her if you could?" Charlene didn't even hesitate in saying, "Michelle, what's wrong with you? Don't let people walk over you. Clearly, you count as much as anyone. What makes someone worthy anyway? Isn't it the type of person they are, how they treat others, their heart? You matter as much as anyone else in this world, maybe even a little more." Charlene was forced to admit that she should be saying some of those things to herself. And she was perplexed that she could say them so easily to someone else. Charlene found it much easier to come up with realistic thoughts based on adaptive schemas when talking to Michelle, even though Michelle was simply a fabricated friend representing herself.

Does the friend perspective seem surprisingly simple? It is, and it's also very effective. We are amazed at how often our clients immediately come up with more realistic thinking based on adaptive schemas when they take the issue away from themselves and talk to a "friend" about it. Try it yourself. The next time you find yourself bogged down in a swamp of distorted thoughts generated by your maladaptive schemas, talk to a mythical friend about it. See if the issue doesn't look a little different when you tell a friend how he or she should think. It probably will change your view, because the strategy allows you to back away from your issues. Then you can be more objective.

Using the Time Perspective

The time perspective technique is equally simple, yet useful. This strategy also allows you to back away from your issues and to gain greater objectivity. We especially recommend this strategy when your thoughts and schemas manage to enrage or distress you. Simply ask yourself how important a given issue will be at some point in the future, rather than at the moment it is affecting you.

Bob found himself becoming upset and enraged repeatedly. He had various positive maladaptive schemas, but *Entitled*⁺ stood out from the rest. He felt entitled to have everything go his way all the time. Things that truly annoy all of us actually enraged Bob. Take this classic, pesky tribulation we all face from time to time. You're standing in the Twelve Items or Less checkout line at the grocery store. The person in front of you has at least eighteen items. Not only that, but she writes a check, even though the sign says *Cash Only*. She rummages through her purse to find the checkbook and upon discovering it, writes the check more slowly than any human before. Most people start feeling annoyed. Bob explodes when these things happen. Later, he ponders why he can't seem to control his temper better.

The time perspective technique asks you to do one simple thing: Ask yourself how important this upsetting event will be to you in a year. Possibly in even a month. When Bob started asking himself that question, he realized he was becoming outraged by things that would seem meaningless even a day later. Slowly but surely, he learned to quit taking things so seriously. They just were not that important. The next time you feel your blood boiling, you might find it useful to ask yourself the same question.

Both the friend perspective and the time perspective give you greater objectivity than your maladaptive schemas would normally allow. Using these techniques is a way of taking a detour around your maladaptive schemas. We think that's only fair, as they have certainly caused you to go on endless, destructive detours throughout life. Next, let's take a look at another technique for challenging your maladaptive schemas and related thoughts.

Determining True Responsibility

The technique of determining true responsibility comes into play whenever your negative maladaptive schemas convince you that you alone are to blame for a bad outcome, thereby sending you into a fevered pitch of self-incrimination. This technique asks you to track down all possible causes for a bad outcome, including any responsibility you may own.

Cecilia found it very helpful to determine true responsibility. She had been lambasting herself because her son Mack had evolved into a rebellious, demanding, inconsiderate teenager. He had started to fail in school and truly appeared to be on a path to self-destruction. Cecilia needed to learn that she did not own the entire responsibility for her son's problems. So her therapist asked her first to list *all* the possible causes for *any* child's miscreant deeds. This is her list:

1. School

2. Peers

3. Television

4. Genes

5. Father's influence

6. Mother's influence

7. Culture

8. Random circumstance

9. The child's own thinking

Her list helped Cecilia see that she was not the sole architect of her son's troublesome situation. She might not even have been the primary culprit, and she unnecessarily added burdensome guilt by blaming herself for all of Mack's problems. By no means do we intend to suggest that she had nothing to do with her son's current quagmire; as she later came to realize, her maladaptive schemas had caused her to parent in an overly harsh and restrictive manner, which had nudged Mack toward an overly rebellious mode. But she wasn't *solely* responsible for her own maladaptive schemas!

Ultimately, learning to reduce self-incrimination helped Cecilia to ease up on herself, thereby giving her more energy to deal with her son's problems. Solving problems is far more helpful than criticizing yourself. The next time you find yourself engaged in harsh self-blame, we suggest that you lighten up a little on yourself and determine true responsibility for the situation.

Facing the Worst Possibility

Now comes our final remedy for dealing with maladaptive schemas. We find it quite useful to face the worst possibility. Often people act as though schemas and their related thoughts will produce such catastrophic outcomes that all of life's pleasure will be sucked out of the universe, or at the least, that they will be totally unable to cope. In cases like that, we recommend that you ask yourself what the worst possible outcome might actually be and to consider whether you could deal with that eventuality or not.

Darlene believed that she would almost die if Lionel left her. She loved him more than any man she had ever known. Yet her *Abandonment⁻* schema told her that her relationship was doomed. She thought she would either die when it ended or be so mired in misery that she would never know happiness again. Facing the worst possibility was just the ticket for her. Here is her analysis.

Schema	Worst Imagined Outcome	How Would I Cope?
Abandonment⁻	I will die if Lionel leaves me. I won't be able to stand it. I will never find someone like him again.	Well, I was OK on my own for almost a year before he came along. I don't like being single, but I know I can deal with it. I would grieve terribly, but I would survive and love again. Of course, I would not find someone like him again, but I could find someone else to love who would be just as good in different ways.

Whenever your schemas create catastrophic scenarios like these, you need to ask yourself two questions. First, "How *likely* is this imagined, horrible outcome?" Usually, you will find that the probability is much lower than your initial, schema-based assumption. Second, "What could I do to cope with this outcome if it *did* occur?" More often than not, you will find that you are far more able to cope than your maladaptive schema would lead you to believe.

CONCLUSION

This chapter has focused on dismantling your maladaptive schemas. We previously told you that maladaptive schemas often fight hard for survival. Be on the lookout for schema-maintenance strategies such as hopelessness, avoidance, emotional numbing, and so on, which we examined in Chapter 7. These signs are not necessarily a bad thing. In fact, sometimes they mean that you are successfully attacking your maladaptive schemas. That will naturally lead to various schema-maintenance strategies, as well as considerable anxiety. It only means you need to continue the assault. But if the anxiety gets too intense, seek professional help.

If you do see progress, but not as much as you wish, we suggest that you reread all the chapters about change (Chapters 8 through 12). Lots of repetition is essential to get where you want with schema-related issues. And remember, none of us will ever reach the point in life that we can always feel smugly secure with our adaptive schemas. Everyone gets snared by maladaptive schemas from time to time.

EXERCISES FOR CHANGING YOUR MALADAPTIVE SCHEMAS

1. Checking the Evidence

It's time for you to try checking the evidence. First, write down the events that trigger your most troubling schemas and thoughts. Then check the evidence that both supports and contradicts your schemas and thoughts. Work particularly hard on the second part of the equation. Don't let schema-maintenance strategies (see Chapter 7) such as avoidance, hopelessness, confusion, or numbing keep you from seeing the contradictory evidence.

Trigger	Schema	Thoughts
_____	_____	_____
_____	_____	_____
_____	_____	_____
_____	_____	_____

Supporting Evidence for Your Schema and Related Thoughts

1. _____

2. _____

3. _____

Contradictory Evidence for Your Schema and Related Thoughts

1. _____

2. _____

3. _____

Repeat this exercise for each maladaptive schema you want to change. Keep track of how often the same schema gets triggered. Even if a schema activates frequently, your thoughts might vary each time, as may the evidence. So pay attention to both parts of this exercise, recording your thoughts and collecting the evidence. A powerful maladaptive schema will crumble after you have chiseled at it many times.

2. Narrowing the Focus

You can now try an exercise for narrowing the focus, which will help you decrease inappropriate overgeneralization. Record a trigger for any maladaptive schema and its associated thoughts. Then look specifically at the thoughts and study whether or not they might be overgeneralized. Recording exceptions to the thoughts and schemas will help you determine whether you are overgeneralizing. If so, you will need to develop a set of narrowed, focused thoughts.

Trigger	Schema	Thoughts	Exceptions
_____	_____	_____	_____
_____	_____	_____	_____
_____	_____	_____	_____
_____	_____	_____	_____

Narrowed, focused thoughts:

_____

_____

_____

_____

3. Facing the Worst Possibility

Now, try our final strategy for dealing with maladaptive schemas as we showed you before. For each maladaptive schema, record an imagined worst outcome and then think about how you could cope if the worst occurred. You might also ask yourself how *likely* the worst outcome actually is.

Schema	Worst Outcome	How Would I Cope?
_____	_____	_____
_____	_____	_____
_____	_____	_____
_____	_____	_____

13

Where Do You Go from Here?
Wrapping It All Up

"What is there more of in the world than anything else? Ends."
—*Carl Sandburg,* The People, Yes

You now have a warehouse full of information about yourself. You also know a lot about what makes people tick. You can use the self-knowledge to understand why you do what you do, to realize the origins of your problems, and to select what you would like to change about yourself and when. Knowledge about others also can serve you well. That knowledge can help you relate to people better. By exploring the schemas of others in your life, you can more effectively avoid pushing their "hot buttons," as well as depersonalize their outbursts toward you. At this point, we would like to provide you with a brief summary of our Schema Polarity Model.

THE SCHEMA POLARITY MODEL

In the Schema Polarity Model, each schema continuum consists of a negative maladaptive schema at one extreme(−), a positive maladaptive schema at the other extreme (+), and an adaptive schema (*) between the two:

Conceiving of the continuum as circular allows the extremes to be placed more closely together and further away from the adaptive schema, thus reflecting their nonlinear relationship. This approach contrasts with the more traditional, linear idea, which would display the continuum on a straight line.

Schema Power

We illustrated the power that schemas wield over your perceptions, emotions, and behavior. We depicted this power in the discussion of the various schematic lenses with which people viewed the exact same events. Being aware of schemas' power can help you feel less "insane" when you find your emotions and behavior inexplicable. With your new knowledge of schemas, you will now find few things people do or say incomprehensible. For example, schemas can readily explain why in reply to a compliment, one person responds as though it is a gift from heaven, another reacts as one would to a pile of manure, and someone else takes it in stride. Each person perceives the compliment from a different schematic lens and sees it as having a different meaning and intent.

The Polarity Paradox

The polarity paradox is based on nonlinear principles and states: *The more opposite two phenomena appear, the more they become the same.* We showed you that opposite dualities form the basis for understanding ourselves and the world. Thus, *light* has little meaning without *heavy*, as is true for *pleasure* and *pain*, *off* and *on*, and *love* and *hate*. At the same time, a thing usually contains the seeds of its own opposite as illustrated by the dots in the figure of yin and yang:

Oddly, the further away from something you try to go, the more likely you are to end up where you started. That's because we live in a nonlinear world,

although our minds often think in straight-line, linear terms. Because of
tendency to think in linear terms, many of life's paradoxes surprise us. For ex
ple, how often do you see someone who seeks the total *opposite* after a relation
failure meets with equivalent, disastrous results? Schemas work the same
Two extremes inflict similar damage. Fulfillment and enlightenment resid
what the Buddhists call the "middle way"—and in what we refer to as adaj
schemas.

Multiple Possibilities

The Schematic Polarity Model also demonstrates that none of us is quite as
sistently stable as we would like to believe. We all possess multiple possibil
that sometimes appear contradictory. You might be introverted in one setting
quite outgoing in another. Some people might describe you as cold and dis
whereas others see you as warm and caring. We do not recommend that
strive for perfect consistency. Some inconsistency is a basic part of human na
and it gives us the flexibility to respond appropriately to different circumsta
We advise aiming for a different goal—learning to flip between extremes
often. By strengthening your adaptive schemas, you will spend less time unde
influence of your extreme maladaptive schemas.

Life Zones

We showed you the three zones of Self-Worth, Empowerment, and Relation:
in Chapters 3, 4 and 5. These three zones encompass more than 95 percent c
complaints that our clients bring us. We hope you increased your self-awar
by exploring both your adaptive and maladaptive schemas in all three zones
had you conduct a cost-benefit analysis of each problematic schema in all
zones. Remember, no one would put out the effort to change a schema unl
had substantial costs.

Schema Origins

Schema information is funneled through four channels: how we are treated,
we manipulate the world, what we hear, and what we see. Multiple factors,
cially your personal history and biological predispositions, contribute t
development of any schema. We hope this knowledge enables you to accep
forgive yourself more, as those are critical precursors to change.

THE PROCESS OF SCHEMA CHANGE

If you have not yet made the changes you want, among other things, we think you should reread Chapter 7 concerning the critical preparation for change. There, we elaborated on the nature of adaptive and maladaptive schemas so you know what you are confronting when you attempt to change them. We told you about the acceptance-change balance; paradoxically, you won't go very far down the path of change unless you first accept where you are now. You don't have to like it, but try to accept the way you are. Self-abuse is only surpassed by child and spouse abuse in destructive potential. Learn to develop self-tolerance and acceptance.

Understanding the pace and process of change may help you accept your less-than-perfect efforts. Change always proceeds in uneven, irregular stages. If you aren't ready to take action yet, spend more time contemplating and preparing.

You can't push the process; you can only nudge it along. Largely, that's because schema-maintenance strategies work hard to obstruct change. Your brain finds it easier to maintain existing schemas than to create new ones. You likely hold onto schemas with the illusion that your existing schemas are self-protective. Only when you recognize these maintenance strategies (such as avoidance, numbing, hopelessness, and procrastination) will you be able to plow through them slowly.

Maladaptive Schema Analysis

In Chapters 8, 9, and 10, we asked you to analyze your maladaptive schemas. We took you through a variety of steps so you would learn how you feel and what you do when your schema is active, understand the triggers for your schemas, explore the origins of your schemas, and think about what you do to maintain them. A thorough understanding of your maladaptive schemas helps you to construct more adaptive schemas as alternatives.

Adaptive Schema Development

As far as we know our Schema Polarity Model is the only approach to therapy that focuses on moving toward whatever you want to become, not just eliminating what you don't like about yourself. That seems ideal to us. Our approach is also effective because if you develop adaptive schemas first, you will find it easier to let go of maladaptive schemas later. Why? Developing adaptive schemas provides you with new possibilities and ways of being. Strengthening adaptive schemas does not remove any options. You can still be as maladaptive as you want to be! You are *not* changing your basic nature—just adding possible alternatives.

However, as your new adaptive schemas strengthen, you will find that your maladaptive schemas activate far less often.

Tools for Dismantling Your Maladaptive Schemas

We gave you a variety of weapons with which you can attack your maladaptive schemas. In Chapter 11, we provided strategies such as the two-chair technique, a fictitious persona, flash cards, and three ways of developing empathy. In Chapter 12, we presented six more techniques: checking the evidence, narrowing the focus, using the friend perspective, using the time perspective, determining true responsibility, and facing the worst possibility.

Sticky Schemas

As you tried these techniques out, things may have become a little dicey. Maybe you found yourself stuck. Almost everyone does at some point or another. Attacking maladaptive schemas is hard work. Schema-maintenance strategies such as procrastination, hopelessness, and avoidance can bog you down. If so, go back at it again when you are ready. Then do it again.

We might as well say it one more time, major changes of ingrained habits don't happen quickly, smoothly, and instantly, at least not very often. Rather, change involves uneven progress with numerous plateaus and dips along the way. Give yourself a break. Eventually, you are likely to extricate yourself successfully. Most smokers try to quit dozens of time before they finally succeed, but most who keep trying eventually do break the habit. Only when you start thinking you are less able to change than others will you find change impossible. (Do you recognize the schema-maintenance strategy of hopelessness in that style of thinking?)

MENTAL HEALTH MYTHOLOGY

Don't let yourself remain stupendously stuck for long. Many readers might get all they want from this book alone. But if you are still struggling, you don't have to go it alone. A cadre of mental health professionals exists expressly to help you get through problems such as those described in this book. Use these professionals! Many people stubbornly refuse to do so. We want you to consider some of the reasons people avoid seeing a psychologist. Then we will tell you how to find the right therapist.

Therapy Doesn't Work

Actually, the data say it does work. Study after study has shown that psychotherapy works for most people most of the time. Although it used imperfect methods, *Consumer Reports* has also surveyed patients to examine this issue and formed this same conclusion. Even when therapy doesn't work, it remains possible that further attempts down the road could. As we have said repeatedly, it is quite common to try many times before finally changing successfully. Almost all studies of therapy investigate a single attempt at change. Even then, therapy usually helps.

Therapy Is Too Expensive

Yes, therapy can run several thousand dollars or even more. However, if you have health insurance, it will usually provide coverage for at least a significant portion of the cost. Also, many therapists are willing to work with you for a relatively short time on some of your problems. Later, when you can afford it, you can return for more work on other issues. It strikes us as odd that many people will readily spend at least as much money on their children's braces while balking at paying to resolve problems that have caused them far greater distress than slightly misaligned teeth. Such persons might be suffering from an *Other-Centered⁻* schema that prevents them from making their own needs a true priority. If cost is truly a problem for you, there are low-cost and no-cost clinics at community mental health centers, medical schools, and psychology departments.

People Who Go to Therapists Are Weak

We think just the opposite is true. It takes courage to face the power of schemas and to deal with the pain that change sometimes creates. We think people who choose to go to therapy are demonstrating courage to engage in this battle. Those who avoid it can't possibly be "stronger." If you have this objection, you likely also have the *Stubbornly Independent⁺* schema. That's one of the targets you can take into therapy!

Only Crazy People Go to Therapists

We hope by now you don't believe this one. Our perspective is that people do what they do because of their history, biology, temperament, and current situations. They originally processed information quite effectively, but that original information may no longer be valid. They have trouble adjusting to the changes in their worlds because their schema-maintenance strategies make change difficult.

Therapists Are Crazier Than Their Patients

Many people seem to believe this idea. Of course, therapists have some problems! We told you before that no one is immune to these issues; they are part of the human condition. Why should therapists be any different? In fact, it is often possible for therapists to help you quite well with an issue that they struggle over themselves. That's because they can look at and deal with your issues far more objectively than their own. Remember the technique called the *friend perspective* in Chapter 12? In a similar way, that technique helps you deal with your issues more objectively by having you imagine that they belong to someone else. If a specific therapist is clearly dysfunctional, you may need to find another one. But a dysfunctional therapist is the exception, not the rule.

Seeking Therapy Is Shameful

What if someone found out you had seen a therapist? First of all, it isn't very likely that they will know this unless you tell them. All licensed mental health professionals abide by strict ethical codes that dictate confidentiality not only over what you say in therapy but also about the fact that you are even a client at all. Of course, anything is possible. For example, you could run into someone you know in a therapist's waiting room. The odds are small, but that could happen. As that would most likely happen because the other person was also seeking therapy, the repercussions would probably be minimal, maybe even positive. Seeking therapy does not have the stigma it did twenty or thirty years ago. In fact, many people today view it in highly positive terms. We know people who are quite reluctant to get into a relationship with someone who has never been in therapy. We think that having been through therapy can indicate emotional health. People who view therapy in negative terms are increasingly rare.

If you have other objections, try to work out similar answers to them. Your objections most likely originate in maladaptive schemas or misinformation. Don't let yourself be fooled by either your schemas or a lack of correct information.

CONSIDERATIONS IN CHOOSING A PROFESSIONAL

Once you have made the decision to see a therapist, how do you go about finding one? Issues include cost, credentials, theoretical orientation, and your own good judgment. We already covered the cost issue above. Try one of the less costly alternatives if that's necessary. If cost doesn't present a major impediment, then consider credentials next. Of all the mental health professionals, clinical psychologists have received the most extensive training in the science of human behavior. Psychiatrists receive more training in medical and biological aspects of mental health and often prescribe medications.

We recommend that you seek therapists licensed to practice in one of the mental health professions, such as psychology, social work, counseling, or psychiatry. Make sure the license is still current. You might call the board that governs that profession to see if the therapist has violated the ethical standards of the profession.

Another good strategy is to ask friends if they have seen a therapist who helped them. And check with other professionals you already trust, such as physicians or clergy. Sometimes a psychology department at a local college will have ideas as to good professionals in the community. Finally, most professions have state associations that sometimes run referral services. In other words, check multiple sources. A good therapist is a valuable resource, and it is worth the effort to find the right one for you.

Most therapists have some preferred way of looking at people and their problems. That's what they call their *theoretical orientation.* Perhaps you have heard of some of these orientations, including psychoanalytic, existential, Gestalt, humanistic, cognitive-behavioral, eclectic, and integrative approaches, among others. Does it make any difference? Arguments abound on this issue.

The data show that cognitive-behavioral approaches work well for certain problems, including anxiety, depression, compulsions, and phobias, and that therapies based on other approaches have also demonstrated effectiveness in some of these areas. Our Schema Polarity Model is based on a cognitive-behavioral perspective. You and your therapist can incorporate the Schema Polarity Model into almost any theoretical model. Most therapists would quite readily agree to help you with the problems you identified in your schema analysis. They might be more comfortable calling your schemas *core issues* or simply *trouble spots,* but that doesn't really matter. What matters is that you and your therapist agree on your goals, even if your therapist is unfamiliar with this model. Your therapist might even want to read this book.

Another important issue, in our estimation, is that your therapist be willing to take a somewhat active stance and help you develop an action plan with specific steps and goals. Studies now support the idea that planning such actions and carrying them out between sessions helps. So ask two questions of any potential therapist. First, do the maladaptive schemas I have identified sound like appropriate issues to address in therapy? And, second, can you help me develop an action plan with various readings, assignments, and tasks for guiding me toward my goals? If the answers to these questions seem reasonable, you may have found the right therapist.

Finally, don't neglect your own good judgment. Just because you want to go to a therapist doesn't mean your judgment is shot. If a therapist doesn't feel like a good match, discuss it with him or her. If the answers sound defensive, critical, cold, judgmental, or simply mismatched with your ideas, consider looking for someone else. If that happens several times in a row, it is possible that your schemas are part of the problem. That would be a good time to seek a second opinion from one more therapist for just a session or two. With this outside consultation, you could decide whether your issues are creating problems or whether you have had an unusually bad run of luck in finding a therapist. Don't get the wrong impression. Most people find effective therapists without much trouble. Yet, as with finding a good doctor, dentist, investment counselor, housekeeper, insurance agent, or accountant, sometimes it takes a little investigation and shopping around. Don't shortchange yourself in this area any more than you would with other service providers. A good fit is probably even more important when you choose a therapist.

Remember to remain realistic about your goals. As we said before, there is no nirvana. No one ever gets it all together. We all struggle at times in life. We all sometimes feel just a bit crazy. None of us is always happy. Occasional short-lived despair, brief mild anxiety, grief over loss—these are the issues every human experiences throughout life. Don't ever expect that they will disappear, never to be seen again. Without these struggles, it would be impossible to appreciate your joys and victories. Once again, a balance in the positive and the negative—the middle way—emerges as the path to enlightenment.

SCHEMA PORTRAITS, FINISHING TOUCHES

After spending so much time with Sylvia, Lynn, and Steven, you may wonder how their schema-change programs evolved. All the case examples in the book are composites of cases both we and our colleagues have had. So although we cannot tell you what happened to our three main characters, we can tell you what has happened to the many clients who made up those cases.

Those who were committed to lasting schema change continued to make progress. They simultaneously experienced more control of their own lives and a decreased need to control others. As their adaptive schemas became stronger, their emotions became less volatile and unpredictable. They spent less time feeling despair and dread. Their anger burned less intensely and less often. They experienced a greater sense of contentment and calmness in their lives.

These clients did not become perfect people, and their lives did not become fairytales. They had disappointments, setbacks, and relationship conflicts. Their old disruptive maladaptive schemas resurfaced occasionally. But their increasingly strong adaptive schemas rebounded. These clients kept pushing themselves forward, while accepting their relapses without needless self-disparagement. They put away the verbal bats they had used on themselves and others in the past. Some found that their partners did not like the changes their adaptive schemas produced. When their growth could not be reconciled with their partners' needs, those relationships ended. But often their own growth spurred complementary changes in the schemas of their partners, enriching both relationships and individuals.

These clients realized that schema change is a lifelong process. Maladaptive schemas do not disappear once an adaptive schema is created. In certain conditions, those maladaptive schemas can still activate. But our clients recognized this as only a temporary state. Their newer adaptive schemas had not disintegrated; they simply needed a more conscious effort to be recalled. No longer was a reawakened maladaptive schema a ticket to an emotional roller coaster. These clients were able to reflect on the setback and recover from it, because their adaptive schemas gave them a more objective perspective on their own reactions.

Schema change is not like whitening your teeth or changing your hair color. Change is gradual and at times jerky, and continued effort is required to perpetuate the change. When obstacles blocked the schema progress of these clients after they concluded therapy, they reviewed their schema-change plans. They examined the triggers, their thoughts, and their reactions. They analyzed their action steps to determine if they needed to repeat some steps or create new ones. They considered how their role models would handle similar dilemmas. They met with their support people to solve problems. These actions were usually sufficient for them to move ahead again.

Sometimes these clients were not able to stop what they saw as a gradual slide backward. At those times they returned to therapy, usually for brief periods. In therapy they were able to determine how to expand or adapt their schema-change plan to address the current obstacles. In some cases, the time had come to modify other interfering maladaptive schemas. These clients had learned how and when to ask for help. And every time they sought assistance, they expanded their repertoire for further schema change.

But not all clients followed this path. Some dropped out after a few sessions because they were not willing to invest the effort that genuine change requires. Sometimes they were simply unwilling to look at what they could change. They dwelled on the flaws and incompetence of those around them. Other clients dropped out of therapy after making initial progress, which seemed sufficient for them at the time. These clients often came back later to continue the journey, sometimes with many stops and starts. But they kept returning, progressing at a pace acceptable to them.

Clients do not all progress through any type of therapy at the same rate. Many come determined to evaluate their circumstances honestly and to expend the effort to improve their lives. Some of these clients do the bulk of their therapeutic work over one period of time, whereas others break therapy into segments. Some never really engage in the process. They may seek therapy from several different therapists but always remain on the periphery, never willing to disclose their inner world fully to themselves, much less to the therapist. Eventually, some of these clients do become earnestly involved in therapy. Others become therapy junkies, participating in several therapies simultaneously, each pushing them in a different direction. Ultimately, the readers of this book will likely fall into one of these client progress patterns.

CONTINUING YOUR SCHEMA PORTRAIT

What pattern will your schema portrait take? Will you work steadily now or only in spurts over time? Or will you never pick up the brushes? Have you identified the adaptive schemas you want to develop and the maladaptive schemas you want to weaken? Have you developed a schema-change plan for each new adaptive schema? Have you recruited a support person for your program? Or have you felt so overwhelmed by all of this that you're heading back to the bookstore for a simpler solution? Feeling somewhat overwhelmed is good reality contact. We have packed more change information into this book than you will typically find in a half-dozen self-help books, because we want you to have enough tools to develop and implement a schema-change program that will endure. But we also want to reinforce a basic theme repeated throughout the book: *Start small, continue small.* Remember, if you keep making small but steady steps to the ocean, one day you will arrive at the beach.

Schema change is the same kind of trip. Do a little bit every day, and after a while you will have completed the schema diary. Then do a little more, and soon you will have finished your maladaptive schema analysis. Set that aside for a short time to relax and pat yourself on the back. Then come back to do some more. Soon, your plan for adaptive schema development will be complete. Then it will be time to try out your different action steps, one or two at a time, never more than that. Record and revise. Record and revise. Over and over. Until there is not much more to revise. Then perhaps select another adaptive schema to adopt. This pattern will become your life.

That is as much our goal as specific schema change is. By learning this schema-change process, you increase your awareness of yourself and the choices you can make. You can select the schemas you want to guide you through life. You are no longer limited to the schemas you had before you read this book.

We don't even know you, and we believe you can change your schemas. Everyone is capable of schema changes. You are not an exception to this rule. We also believe that almost everyone needs substantial support to make their schema changes. You already have traveled a long way with us by reading this book. You have acquired lots of new ideas and a deeper insight into yourself and others. But insight alone does not produce lasting change. Stick with us. Reread this book as often as you need. And buy more brushes. You have new schemas to paint.

Appendix A: Schema Continua in the Life Zones

SELF-WORTH ZONE

Acceptance Schema Continuum

(−) *BLAMEWORTHY*: I feel I often deserve punishment or harsh criticism. I tend to be excessively critical or punitive of myself when I make mistakes.

(*) *ACCEPTING*: I realize that, as a human being, I am going to make mistakes. I can accept responsibility for my mistakes and I can apologize comfortably to others. Although I may choose to try to change, I do not make myself feel overly guilty.

(+) *BLAMELESS*: I feel I have to be right. It is hard for me to admit I am wrong or that I have made a mistake. It is hard for me to say I am sorry.

Desirability Schema Continuum

(−) *UNDESIRABLE*: I feel I am in some way outwardly undesirable to others, either because I am unattractive, poor in social skills, boring, or have other flaws that are visible to people.

(*) *DESIRABLE*: I am comfortable with my looks, social skills, and other visible characteristics.

(+) *IRRESISTIBLE*: I believe I am highly desirable to others in terms of looks, social skills, or other visible characteristics.

Worthiness Schema Continuum

(−) *UNWORTHY:* I feel I do not deserve attention, concern, or consideration from others or deserve to have my needs met. If, on occasion, I believe I deserve it, I still do not expect that my needs will be met. I feel there is something about me or my background that is defective or inferior.

(*) *WORTHY:* I feel I am worthy of having my needs met but not at unnecessary expense to other people. I feel I am as good as anyone else.

(+) *ENTITLED:* I feel I should have whatever I want. Sometimes I don't think about whether my wants are reasonable or what they would cost others. Sometimes others think I walk over them. Nothing less than the best is good enough for me. I feel there is something about me or my background that is superior to others.

Adequacy Schema Continuum

(−) *INADEQUATE:* I feel I have failed or am inadequate compared with my peers in areas of achievement such as school, career, sports, or other activities. I often believe I do not have the intelligence, talent, or abilities to succeed.

(*) *ADEQUATE:* I am adequate and feel good about myself regardless of my accomplishments.

(+) *PERFECTIONISTIC:* I tend to pursue high standards and expectations relentlessly in the areas of achievement, recognition, status, money, or any activity in which I am involved. This pursuit is often at the expense of happiness, health, pleasure, and relationships.

EMPOWERMENT ZONE

Assertiveness Schema Continuum

(−) *ACQUIESCENT:* I tend to give in to others' preferences and decisions. I try to avoid conflict whenever I can.

(*) *ASSERTIVE:* My decisions and preferences are important, and I will express them readily. It is also important for me to listen to the decisions and preferences of others. I will work out compromises whenever possible. I will not let others walk over me and won't take advantage of them.

(+) *DOMINEERING:* I like to be in control. I am often critical of other people's decisions and preferences and can discount them easily. Basically, I like to have my own way.

Capability Schema Continuum

(−) *DEPENDENT:* I often feel incapable of handling everyday decisions and responsibilities. I usually seek help from others.

(*) *CAPABLE:* I believe I am capable of handling most everyday decisions and responsibilities. However, when I do need help, I don't hesitate to ask for it.

(+) *STUBBORNLY INDEPENDENT:* I believe I can handle almost anything. It is hard for me to ask for help. Sometimes I will even refuse appropriate and essential assistance.

Empowerment Schema Continuum

(−) *POWERLESS:* I often feel I can do little to change things. Frequently, I feel overwhelmed by life's events and powerless to do much about them.

(*) *EMPOWERED:* I believe there are many outcomes I can influence to one degree or another. At times, there are things I can't change, and I can accept that.

(+) *OMNIPOTENT:* I believe I can make almost any situation come out the way I want it to.

Resilience Schema Continuum

(−) *VULNERABLE:* I often worry about terrible things happening to me or to those close to me. I worry about issues such as finances, health, crime, or natural calamities.

(*) *RESILIENT:* I recognize that harm and illness will occur at various points in my life, and I take reasonable precautions to prevent them. I also believe that when these things happen, I can bounce back.

(+) *INVULNERABLE:* I believe I am virtually immune to harm or illness. I don't worry about what I eat, exercise, or protect myself. What other people think of as high-risk (hang gliding, parachuting, etc.), I find exhilarating.

RELATIONSHIP ZONE

Centeredness Schema Continuum

(−) *OTHER-CENTERED:* I focus very much on meeting the needs of others, even at the expense of my own needs and preferences. I might, at times, resent those in my care. I am far more likely to take the perspective of other people than to consider my own. When others are upset, I think it is up to me to do something about it.

(*) *CENTERED:* I take responsibility for meeting my own needs. However, I am considerate of the needs of others. I can empathize and care about others without necessarily taking responsibility for or taking care of them.

(+) *SELF-CENTERED:* I believe my own perspective is sufficient for understanding. I don't worry a lot about how other people look at things. People can take care of themselves. I don't have to worry about their needs.

Intimacy Schema Continuum

(−) *ABANDONMENT:* I worry a lot about losing a person or persons close to me. I am afraid they will leave or be taken away from me through death or other circumstances. I need a great deal of emotional reassurance to feel secure. Reassurance never seems to last. I sometimes test the emotional commitment of others in ways that are not necessarily constructive. I am very sensitive to rejection.

(*) *INTIMATE:* I enjoy and feel comfortable getting emotionally close to some people. I realize it would be very painful to lose those people, but I don't spend a lot of time worrying about that possibility, because I know I could cope.

(+) *AVOIDANT:* I don't feel the need to become emotionally involved. I generally keep people at a distance.

Self-Definition Schema Continuum

(−) *UNDEFINED:* I don't have a strong sense of who I am. I define myself in terms of the people who are close to me (that is, my partner or my children). I tend to adopt their beliefs, attitudes, and identities. When I have no one else close to me, I often feel empty.

(*) *DEFINED:* I have a clear sense of who I am. I am aware of my purpose, attitudes, beliefs, and values. However, I don't expect those close to me always to agree with my beliefs. People who love me are free to disagree with me within reasonable limits.

(+) *AGGRANDIZING:* I know who I am. I have such a strong sense of identity and purpose that others often adopt my beliefs, attitudes, and values. Those close to me generally look up to me, sometimes to the point of adoration.

Trust Schema Continuum

(−) *DISTRUSTING:* I do not trust other people's motives. I often believe that other people intentionally hurt, abuse, cheat, lie, manipulate, or take unfair advantage of me.

(*) *TRUSTING:* I generally trust people, unless they give me a reason not to. However, I do show reasonable caution, which has prevented me from being taken advantage of very often.

(+) *NAIVE:* I believe most everyone can be trusted. I don't believe there is a need to question other people's motives. Sometimes I don't even take reasonable precautions to protect myself in relationships.

Appendix B: Schema Diary

This is your schema diary, so you need to personalize it. First, list the maladaptive schema that you would like to change. Then reread the definition for that schema in Appendix A. Next put that definition in your own words. You can use our definition if that fits, but most people modify the definitions to fit themselves better. Then, when that schema occurs, write an example in the diary. When you describe the example, include information about who was there, what happened, the outcome, and what your thoughts were in the situation. Also, describe how you felt both emotionally and physically.

Continue doing this for each maladaptive schema that you want to change. You do not need to rewrite the definition in future examples of the same schema. Also, put the date beside each example. You need to find a time each day that you can record this information in your diary. Many people like to do it in the evening before bedtime, but pick a time that is best for you. Then try to establish this as a daily routine. You can record all the information here in the pages provided, or you can start your own journal in a separate notebook and just follow this format.

Below is an example of what we want you to do.

Schema: *Powerless*⁻

My definition: I don't feel I have any power. I can't change anything important to me.

Example: Thursday night after dinner. Every summer, we use our two-week vacation time to visit my spouse's family. They are nice people, but it is not relaxing for me. They insist that we stay at their house, which is cramped with our family and all of them. Sleeping on a sofa bed for two weeks is not restful for me. Last night, I brought up the possibility of changing our vacation plans this year and going to the ocean with the kids. My husband acted hurt and said his family would not understand.

So I dropped it. I wonder if we have to wait until my husband's family dies before we can have a summer vacation that is not at their house. We will never get to have a family vacation with just the four of us. I like his family, but sometimes I would like to visit other places, especially while the kids are still with us. I never get a vacation that is really a vacation. I'm trapped. I feel frustration, anger, resentment, hopelessness, tension, and I have trouble sleeping.

My Schema Diary

Okay, now it's your turn to write down the maladaptive schemas that you want to change. It may be easier to use a notebook, but follow this format.

Schema: _____

My definition: _____

_____

_____

Example (include who, what, where, outcome information, your thoughts, and your feelings):

_____

_____

_____

_____

_____

_____

_____

_____

Appendix C: Schema Development Worksheet

Part 1: Maladaptive Schema Analysis

Step 1: My definition of my maladaptive schema:

Step 2: What do I think when my maladaptive schema is active?

Step 3: How do I feel when my maladaptive schema is active?

Step 4: What do I do when my maladaptive schema is active?

Step 5: What are the origins of my maladaptive schema?

Step 6: What are the triggers for my maladaptive schema?

Step 7: What do I and others do to maintain my maladaptive schema now?

Part 2: Adaptive Schema Development

Step 1: My definition of the adaptive schema I want to create:

Step 2: What thoughts would my adaptive schema produce?

Step 3: What feelings would accompany the thoughts of my adaptive schema?

Step 4: What steps or actions do I need to take that are consistent with the thoughts and feelings of my adaptive schema?

Step 5: Who could be a role model for my adaptive schema?

Step 6: Who can support my efforts to create an adaptive schema?

Step 7: Select one or two action items to try.

References and Further Readings

Alberti, R., & Emmons, M. (1995). *Your perfect right* (7th ed.). San Luis Obispo, CA: Impact.

Baddeley, A. (1990). *Human memory: Theory and practice.* Needham Heights, MA: Allyn & Bacon.

Bandura, A. (1986). *Social foundations of thought and action: A social cognitive theory.* Upper Saddle River, NJ: Prentice Hall.

Beck, A. T. (1976). *Cognitive therapy and the emotional disorders.* New York International Universities Press. (Paperbound edition published New York: New American Library, 1979)

Beck, A. T. (1988). *Love is never enough.* New York: HarperCollins.

Bransford, J. D., & Johnson, M. K. (1972). Contextual prerequisites for understanding: Some investigations of comprehension and recall. *Journal of Verbal Learning and Verbal Behavior, 11,* 717–726.

Burns, D. D. (1989). *The feeling good handbook.* New York: Morrow.

Capra, F. (1975). *The tao of physics.* Boston: Shambhala.

Chess, S., & Thomas, A. (1986). *Temperament in clinical practice.* New York: Guilford.

Cowen, E. L., & Work, W. C. (1988). Resilient children, psychological wellness, and primary prevention. *American Journal of Community Psychology, 16,* 591–607.

Elliott, C. H., & Lassen, M. K. (1997). A schema polarity model for case conceptualization, intervention, and research. *Clinical Psychology: Science and Practice, 4,* 12–28.

Ellis, A. (1974). *Humanistic psychotherapy.* New York, NY: McGraw-Hill.

Ellis, H. C., & Hunt, R. R. (1993). *Fundamentals of cognitive psychology.* Madison, WI: Brown and Benchmark.

Fiske, S. T., & Taylor, S. E. (1991). *Social cognition* (2nd ed.). New York: McGraw-Hill.

Friedman, H. S., & Booth-Kewley, S. (1987). The "disease-prone" personality: A meta-analytic view of the construct. *American Psychologist, 42,* 539–555.

Gleick, J. (1987). *Chaos: Making a new science.* New York: Viking Press.

Greenberger, D., & Padesky, C. A. (1995). *Mind over mood: A cognitive-therapy treatment manual for clients.* New York, NY: Guilford.

Higgins, G. O. (1994). *Resilient adults: Overcoming a cruel past.* San Francisco: Jossey-Bass.

Kelly, G. A. (1955). *The psychology of personal constructs: The theory of personality* (Vol. 1). New York: Norton.

Loftus, E. F. (1979). *Eyewitness testimony.* Cambridge, MA: Harvard University Press.

Martus, H., & Nurius, P. (1986). Possible selves. *American Psychologist, 41,* 954–969.

Matlin, M. W. (1989). *Cognition* (2nd ed.). Orlando, FL: Holt, Rinehart and Winston.

McCann, I. L., Sakheim, D. K., & Abrahamson, D. J. (1988). Trauma and victimization: A model of psychological adaptation. *The Counseling Psychologist, 16,* 531–594.

Prochaska, J. O., Norcross, J. C., & DiClemente, C. O. (1994). *Changing for good.* New York: Morrow.

Resick, P., & Schnicke, M. K. (1992). Cognitive processing therapy for sexual assault victims. *Journal of Consulting and Clinical Psychology, 60,* 748–756.

Smucker, M. R., Dancu, C., Foa, E. B., & Niederee, J. L. (1995). Imagery rescripting: A new treatment for survivors of childhood sexual abuse suffering from post-traumatic stress. *Journal of Cognitive Psychotherapy: An International Quarterly, 9,* 3–17.

Sommer, R. (1959). The new look on the witness stand. *Canadian Psychologist, 8,* 94–99.

Young, J. E. (1990). *Cognitive therapy for personality disorders: A schema-focused approach.* Sarasota, FL: Professional Resource Exchange.

Young, J. E., & Klosko, J. S. (1993). *Reinventing your life: How to break free from negative life patterns.* New York: Dutton.

About the Authors

CHARLES H. ELLIOTT, PH.D., obtained his doctorate in clinical psychology from the University of Kansas in 1976. Since then, he has served on the faculty in the psychiatry departments of two medical schools. While teaching at the University of Oklahoma Health Sciences Center, he received the Gordon H. Deckert Award for Excellence in Teaching. He also participated in a major National Institute of Mental Health study comparing cognitive therapy to anti-depressant medication and interpersonal therapy. As a cognitive therapist in the study, he trained with many of the founders of cognitive therapy, including Drs. Aaron T. Beck, David Burns, Jeffrey E. Young, Arthur Freeman, Brian Shaw, and Keith Dobson. Dr. Elliott's work as a therapist in the study was often singled out as exemplary. *Psychiatric Annals*, a journal devoted to providing continuing education to psychiatrists, selected him as guest editor for a special issue on cognitive therapy. In addition, he has written numerous articles and book chapters in the area of cognitive-behavior therapies. Currently, he is a faculty member at the Fielding Institute and has a private practice in clinical psychology.

MAUREEN KIRBY LASSEN, PH.D., earned her doctorate in clinical psychology from the University of Arizona in 1974. She did her undergraduate work at the University of Iowa, where she was a summa cum laude and Phi Beta Kappa graduate with honors in psychology. Dr. Lassen has been on the psychology faculties of Baylor University and Arizona State University. At ASU, she was also director of the Clinical Psychology Training Clinic. In 1988, Dr. Lassen joined the faculty of the Fielding Institute. From 1993 to 1996, she was chair of Fielding's psychology faculty. Dr. Lassen has been on the Arizona State Board of Psychologist Examiners since 1994 and has had a private clinical and consulting practice in the Phoenix metropolitan area since 1978. She has written articles on popular topics in psychology for various national publications. Dr. Lassen has been training clinical psychology doctoral students in the theory and application of cognitive-behavioral principles since 1974. Her husband, Gary, claims, however, that she has never used any of these principles successfully with their border collies.

INDEX

Our Schema Polarity Model is a working model of how schemas function in our lives. To date, we have found it to be a very useful conception of how people process and react to information. We are actively investigating the assumptions and implications of this model, so we would greatly appreciate hearing your thoughts and experiences as you use this model in your own lives. You can write to either of us in care of the Fielding Institute, 2112 Santa Barbara Street, Santa Barbara, California 93105.